C000021331

Shot Down in Flames

To

Archie McIndoe

Whose surgeon's fingers

gave me back my pilot's hands

Shot Down in Flames

A World War II Fighter Pilot's Remarkable Tale of Survival

Geoffrey Page

DSO, OBE, DFC and BAR

Grub Street • London

Published by
Grub Street
4 Rainham Close
London
SW11 6SS

Originally published as *Tale of a Guinea Pig*
First published by Grub Street in 1999
This edition first published 2011
Copyright © Grub Street 2011
Copyright text © Geoffrey Page

British Library Cataloguing in Publication Data
Page, Geoffrey.
  Shot down in flames : a World War II fighter pilot's
  remarkable tale of survival. -- New ed.
  1. Page, Geoffrey. 2. Fighter pilots--Great Britain--
  Biography. 3. World War, 1939-1945--Aerial operations,
  British. 4. World War, 1939-1945--Personal narratives,
  British.
  I. Title
  940.5'44'941'092-dc22

ISBN-13: 9781906502966

All rights reserved. No part of this publication may be reproduced, stored in a re-
trieval system, or transmitted in any form or by any means electronic, mechanical,
photocopying, recording or otherwise, without the prior permission of the copyright owner.

Cover design by Sarah Driver
Formatted by Sarah Driver

Printed and bound by MPG Ltd, Bodmin, Cornwall

Grub Street Publishing only uses
FSC (Forest Stewardship Council) paper for its books.

Acknowledgements
Firstly to my darling wife Pauline, whose encouragement and interest were instrumental in producing this book. Also the many hours she and our daughter Shelley
put in typing and re-typing the manuscript are greatly appreciated.
    Also my thanks to Derek Dempster for editing the earlier version and weeding
out the many uninteresting parts, together with constructive work in the presentation.
    Two other good friends, Frank Wootton the artist, and Leonard Moseley the
well-known biographer, must be thanked for their encouragement and practical
help to get the book launched.

One

The dawn broke over Beverly Hills, California as I let myself into a home on North Alpine Drive. Nigel Bruce, my screen actor host, was famous for his jovial and warm-hearted portrayals of Sherlock Holmes's partner, Doctor Watson. I tiptoed into the hall and took off my shoes to climb the stairs to the guest-room. Within no time the four family dachshunds had roused the household and as I reached the landing, Nigel's wife, Bunny, appeared inquiring into the rumpus.

Seeing me, she relaxed – and then her face broke into a broad, impish smile. "Go to bed, Geoffrey," she giggled; "you can tell me about it at lunch."

The source of Bunny's amusement was elementary (My dear Watson). I saw it the moment I got to my room and looked in the mirror. My face was covered in lipstick! Did I grin hugely or did I smile a shy and perhaps slightly raffish smile of deeply experienced joyousness. I had spent a beautiful evening with an indescribably lovely young actress, and best of all we had arranged that this would be but the first of however many evenings we could arrange until my military duties recalled me back to England.

In my bedroom mirror, the sight of red lipstick – merourochrome-antiseptic-red lipstick on my grafted eyelids – drew me slowly back to the reality of my extraordinary good fortune.

Here I was, now four years on from seeing a pretty young nurse flee in horror at the sight of my charred face and hands. Now I was living lavishly in the community of film celebrities. In the midst of the world's most perfect party I was imbibing the dearest dreams of millions of lonely soldiers fighting on a thousand different battle-fronts.

It was a sobering moment, evoking memories of burning gasoline kindled by the Luftwaffe tracer bullets that shot me down and out of the Battle of Britain; of wondering, too, whether anyone, let alone a girl, would have looked at me ever again if Archie McIndoe and the Queen Victoria Cottage Hospital, East Grinstead, had not been there to make me appear acceptably human once more.

Indeed, Archie McIndoe had done far more than that for me. He had seen me through the worst moments of my life; he had given me hope and encouragement, as he did to all his "guinea pigs"; he had unwittingly repaired me so well that I had been able to return to operational flying and avenge my injuries in renewed combat.

The reality now staring me in the face focused on returning to war and leaving the joys and pleasures of California, where my tour of the United States, lecturing on the Royal Air Force, had ended. But my approach to combat was not what it had been at the Royal Air Force College, Cranwell, during the winter of 1939 – the winter of the Phoney War.

As an officer cadet of nineteen, my thoughts were boyishly clear and simple. All I wanted was to be a fighter pilot like my hero, Captain Albert Ball – the man who had made a speciality out of penetrating far behind the enemy lines alone during the Great War, as we called it then, and who, in his search for prey, had shot down forty-seven German aircraft before he himself was shot down and killed.

I knew practically all there was to know about Albert Ball: how he flew, how he fought, how he won his Victoria Cross, how he died. I also thought I knew about war in the air. I imagined it to be Arthurian – about chivalry.

Paradoxically, death and injury had no part in it. In the innocence of youth, I had not yet seen the other side of the coin, with its images of hideous violence, fear, pain and death. I did not know then about vengeance. Neither did I know about the ecstasy of victory. Nor did I remotely suspect the presence within my being of a dormant lust for killing.

I was about five when my interest in airplanes first arose, and I vividly remember the disappointment I expressed because the flying model I was given for my ninth birthday looked nothing like the real thing. I modified it and made it work, which has led me to believe that I had an instinct about flying.

Aviation did of course feature commercially in the family. My uncle was an aircraft manufacturer and I played on the kinship for all it was worth – as any schoolboy in my position would have done. My locker at Cheltenham College was filled with Handley-Page aircraft brochures and I sometimes obtained wind-tunnel models from the firm for the exhibitions we ran. But my interest went beyond the family products at a fairly early age to the Royal Air Force, which gave birth to an ambition to make my career in it as a pilot.

My parents had lived apart for as long as I could remember. I only occasionally saw my father, usually for afternoon tea at his rather dark and musty London Club. These tended to be somewhat stiff and monosyllabic occasions, until the conversation turned to my studies and career. I would inevitably be filled with trepidation as I sensed his hackles rise at the mention of my ambition to be a pilot in the R.A.F. But I refused to be put off – until the time, that is, when he turned on me with greater severity than usual.

"I have spoken to your uncle at length about your desire to be a pilot," he said, "and he has advised me strongly against it.

"Pilots, he tells me, are two a penny. Hundreds are chasing a handful of jobs. Some of the best and most experienced have applied to join his firm. So what makes you think you'll be any better than they are and can walk straight into a job?"

Frustrated to the point of tears, I tried to explain that I wanted to go through the R.A.F. College at Cranwell and to make the Service my career. "There's no question of leaving the Air Force. I want a permanent commission. I want to fly!"

But he was adamant. " Now listen to me, my lad. Your uncle is prepared to find you a place in the Company if you qualify as an engineer. And that is precisely what I would do if I were in your shoes.

"Of course, if you insist on going to Cranwell, you'll have to pay for it yourself, as I don't intend to provide the money for such stupidity!"

It was only later that I understood the real reason he and my uncle were so opposed to my becoming a pilot. Their own younger brother had been one; and he was dead.

My mother was of little help. Besides having no more than a pittance from an ungenerous husband she refused to let her darling boy risk life and limb in "one of those terrible flying machines." And yet, she would have robbed to give me anything else I might have set my heart on.

With opposition like that, I reluctantly capitulated and joined London University. My father was pleased, of course.

But it never occurred to him that I might have inherited facets of his own determined character, nor that Hitler's Germany was causing aviation to encroach upon traditional institutions of learning. At Imperial College I discovered that free R.A.F. flying training was available to anyone who could pass the rigorous medical examination for admission to the University Air Squadron. I also saw that its exclusive standing among university clubs was the pretext I needed to persuade my mother to sign the parental authority required to allow me to fly.

From then on, whenever the weather permitted, I abandoned my books and headed for Northolt airport. By the end of my second year at London University I had become a very competent pilot –but I had failed my Inter-B.Sc. exams!

Faced with a parental ultimatum – to continue my studies without the distractions of flying, or to leave the university to make my own way in the world – the summer of 1939 was a bewildering one. Happily for me, or so I thought, Hitler overstepped himself.

Two

The university air squadrons that were established between the wars were intended to do two things: encourage undergraduates to take up the Royal Air Force as a career and create a reserve of partially trained officer pilots who could quickly be brought to operational standards in the event of war.

Within two weeks of Hitler's march on Poland on September 1, 1939, I received my call-up papers. Because of my London University Air Squadron affiliations, they were addressed to Acting Pilot Officer Alan Geoffrey Page, Royal Air Force. I was proud of that. I hoped the postman had noticed and gossiped.

By mid-October, I had reported to the newly opened Aircrew Receiving Centre at Hastings, the Sussex seaside holiday resort, together with several hundred other products of Oxford, Cambridge and London Universities, all of them resplendent in new officers' uniforms bought from Air Ministry allowances.

In Hastings the Air Ministry had requisitioned all the suitable hotels and apartment blocks to lodge, administer and knock us into shape for the dispersed flying schools we were to attend.

We were split into squads of about forty strong and the senior member of each group was placed in charge. My own was commanded by Flying Officer Michael Maw, with whom I had travelled from London by train. He was older than most of us by about three years, which accounted for his higher rank. This, combined with early marriage and fatherhood, gave him a maturity that belied his age. I looked up to him and would frequently seek his counsel in moments of hesitation on the road from youth to manhood.

But even his seniority was no protection against the obvious contempt with which the commissioned breed was held by the N.C.O. physical training and drill instructors assigned to each squad. No one escaped the sarcasm in their spat commands to march and countermarch over the seaside promenade that was used as a parade ground, or urge us to greater gymnastic effort. Almost any insult was permissible, as long as the regulation compliment was paid to the King's commission at the end of each diatribe.

"When I say right turn, I mean right turn – air force right turn – not some fancy university right turn … SIR!"

As greenhorns, we tolerated the situation.

It was, of course, essential to mould a band of individualistic students into acceptably fit and disciplined military units, and the N.C.Os did astonishingly well to create some order out of the chaos of our first few days in uniform, when we could hardly be said to know our left feet from our elbows. Now, with the tolerance of hindsight, I suppose that their contempt was more apparent than real.

At the end of the first week the Medical Branch claimed our attention. We joined a slow-moving line of young men with tunics off, their right arms bared to the shoulder, filing past a pair of bored-looking medical orderlies playing darts with a couple of hypodermic needles, the older of the two prefacing each jab with a muttered "just a little prick."

As my turn to be injected approached, the "tiny little prick" took on monumental proportions and I began to feel sick. But instead of looking away when the figure in front of me offered his arm for inoculation, I made the fatal mistake of watching the needle plunge deep into his flesh.

I never felt my injection!

When I recovered consciousness, the two orderlies were supporting me. There was no sympathy in their faces.

"What's going to happen when he sees reeeal blood?"

Wiping the moisture from my forehead with the back of my hand, I did indeed wonder. Was I really cut out to be a pilot, let alone a cool, efficient killer? At that moment I could have thrown in my hand and run home to mother.

I felt too shaky to argue when Michael Maw took me considerately by the left arm and led me into the fresh air.

"You'll feel better in a minute or two," he said.

I was too overcome with shame to say anything, and for a while we sat watching the grey caps foaming on the swollen sea.

Eventually Michael broke the silence.

"I know someone who can't bear to go to the top of a tall building." He seemed to be addressing himself, rather than me. "And yet, he was one of the best pilots in the squadron."

I turned and looked at him.

"Thank you. I needed that. 'Fraid I lost my sense of proportion. I feel better now – let's go."

Wherever we gathered over the next few days the medical orderlies' score was plain to see. Saluting was agony and it seemed to us that N.C.O.s and men were deliberately going out of their way to make us return their obligatory compliments. The bastards!

The evidence was just as marked when we were off duty. In the bar of the Grand Hotel everyone, with the exception of the rare civilian, clutched his glass with the left hand and winced at the slightest collision of right arms. But the tenderness did nothing to dampen our spirits.

Our conversation varied little. Though serious at times, it was more often lighthearted. Flying and airplanes predominated. Without exception we all knew that the majority of R.A.F. squadrons were sadly lacking in modern equipment. We also knew from Army friends that Britain's land forces were in the same boat – dangerously short of the sort of equipment needed to stand up to an assault by a modern military machine.

But youth has a wonderful facility for switching away from the unpleasant. We would almost inevitably drift into talking about sex, of which we knew and had experienced as little as we had of flying, and yet we held forth with the authority of Socrates! Our parents would have been left speechless had they even caught snatches of the conversations that drifted through the babble in the bar: ". . . all she said was that sexual intercourse was not a socially accepted form of introduction!"

The barmaids responded to the passes, ribaldry and invitations with marvellous humour.

"Oh you raf boys are all the same. If you're not doing it, you're talking about it!"

Many of the "raf" boys, like me, had only recently left the protective shelter of home for the first time, and despite the brave phrases and the jargon, we were very unsure of ourselves.

I have since wondered about the underlying motive that led us to don uniform without hesitation to range the skies in defence of the

homeland. Was it for King and Country? Or was it more fundamen-
tal than this well-worn recruiting cliche would have anyone believe?

Most of them, I knew, had learned to fly because of an insatiable urge
that is peculiar to all airmen – not because they wanted to go to war,
but because they wanted to fly. And yet, it did not explain our readiness
to man the front lines and sacrifice our high-spirited and joyful lives
without asking why. I never once heard anyone voice a motive for fighting the enemy. I tried to analyze my own reasons for taking up arms.
But I never did produce a satisfactory answer.

Early in November, postings to flying school were announced and
the inexplicable workings of fate exploded on me like a bombshell.
After years of dreaming, part of my life's ambition was coming to pass.
Just two months earlier, it had seemed an impossibility. Of all places
in Training Command, I was going to Cranwell.

After that, it only remained for me to become a fighter pilot.

Three

Twenty-four of us drew Cranwell for training and by the time we left Hastings, winter was setting in. The skies were overcast and the air was grey with the sort of wet mist that makes lights yellow and leafless trees all shiny. With Britain at war, there were of course no lights; only the blackout during those long, dark afternoons and coal-black nights. But even though the landscape we travelled through looked dismal from an overcrowded and unheated train, I was not depressed. To the contrary, I was as excited as a schoolboy.

Michael Maw was one of our Cranwell group and I was glad of his companionship, not only to share my excitement, but because deep down, I was apprehensive. I knew I was going to be a fighter pilot, but I also sensed that something, somewhere – I could not put a finger on it – was trying to divert me onto a different course. Was it something about me, in me? I did not have an answer, but at least I had a friend like Michael to lean on if Cranwell did not give me what I most desperately wanted.

R.A.F. transport had been laid on to meet us at Sleaford Station, and within half an hour had dropped us in front of the sweeping steps that lead up to the College's main entrance hall. Here we were pleasantly surprised to find a group of civilian batmen ready to unload our cases and show us to our quarters. The war did not seem to have reached Cranwell.' And inside the majestic hallway the orderly officer was quick to make us welcome and show us where to get the hot meal that had been prepared for us.

I awoke on my first morning to the surprising sight of a cup of tea brought in by my civilian batman. This was unexpected bliss. Above me Derek Dunn, my room-mate, stirred. He had been at Hastings too. We were the same age and of very similar nature, except that Derek bad a beautiful tenor voice.

"This is the life," he sang out. "Bring on the dancing girls!"

I was none too certain, despite my joy.

"From the amount I've read about this institution over the past ten years," I said, "I have the impression that the comforts are only to make the rest of it seem worse by comparison."

"I hope you're wrong," replied Derek. "So do I."

Our first appointment, we discovered from the notice board, was with the commanding officer. He wanted to talk to us immediately after breakfast.

He was short and square and looked as if he had been crushed by a sledgehammer. Legend had it that his spine had been compressed after a serious flying accident. His words of welcome were few but to the point. He outlined the curriculum and then, politely, clearly and concisely warned us of the penalties he would introduce if friction occurred between us and the last cadets at the college.

These cadets, he said, had been groomed under the severest Air Force discipline and a disorderly bunch of undergraduates, even though we were members of the volunteer reserve, could create havoc.

"Relative ranks are another possible source of friction," he explained. "You all hold the King's Commission, whereas the cadets are members of the rank and file until graduation. Differences in pay, prestige and perks are bound to cause trouble. So please, Gentlemen, respect my wishes."

With that, we were dismissed.

The chief flying instructor, Wing Commander Speedy Holmes, had captained Sussex at cricket before the war. A soft-spoken man, he radiated confidence and authority and was very popular. Apart from him and the C.O., we tended to treat the rest of the teaching staff as equals – and some of them with undisguised contempt.

Apart from some friction over haircuts – the "Byron Look" was not appreciated at Cranwell – all went moderately well. The weeks passed quickly enough, but I wanted to get at the enemy; not so much because I wanted to get into combat, but because I wanted to fly modem airplanes. The aircraft being used to train pilots for fighter command, training command and Army co-operation were relics of a bygone age – the Hawker Hind biplane which, without flaps or retractable undercarriage, could hardly be regarded as an adequate stepping stone to Spitfires and Hurricanes. And yet it was delightful to fly and it gave me enormous pleasure.

Those destined for bomber and coastal commands were better off. They were trained on the twin-engined Airspeed Oxford whose performance was not far short of the aircraft which formed the backbone of bomber command: Bristol Blenheims, Handley-Page Hampdens, Armstrong Whitworth Whitleys and Fairey Battles.

By mid-December 1939, I had officially qualified as a pilot by day and by night, although my night-flying experience had gone no further than some dual instruction and a single solo circuit on a pitch-black night. It was considered adequate.

Girls had played little part in my life up to then, except for a few platonic dates with a pretty showgirl named Yvonne Ortner, who later married Richard Hearne – Television's Mr. Pastry. I had concentrated all my love on airplanes. So, when the adjutant asked for a volunteer to take over orderly officer duties during the Christmas break, I offered to do so.

I knew my mother would have preferred me to go home, but I also knew she would understand that this was a unique opportunity for me to soak up the historical atmosphere of the place I had dreamt about for so long, unhindered by the disciplinary and academic pressures of training. And so it was that, except for taking the flag-raising and lowering parades, dealing with any complaints about food that arose in the airmen's Mess and joining my fellow officers in the tradition of serving the airmen's Christmas dinner I vanished into the portrait gallery and library of the college to read, to think and to lose myself in reverie, and to dream of emulating my heroes of the Great War.

The outside world was white with snow and for me, inside the great college, the solitude and quiet was bliss.

With the graduation and departure of the last of the pre-war cadets at the end of January 1940, Cranwell's training programme went onto a solid war footing. We replaced the cadets in the advanced flying training school and a new batch of reserve officers took over from us in the elementary flying training school.

The aircraft, however, did not change. We went on flying the Hawker Hinds, except that the ones we now used were fitted with a single, fixed machine gun, synchronized to fire through the propeller. They also had bomb racks under the wings.

They were not entirely useless. We did learn something about deflection-shooting in them, but as I have said before, they were hardly an adequate stepping stone to the aircraft in which we would actually have to go to war. Nevertheless, the enthusiasm with which we flew them more than made up for the handicap Stanley Baldwin and his political cronies had placed upon us. But we paid the price in the blood of those who died during the invasion of France in outdated Blenheim and Battle bombers.

By the spring it was our turn to muster for Wings Parade. How I glowed with pride over those wings. I had dreamt about them since I was barely ten years old and I had worked damned hard to make sure no one could find an excuse for scrubbing me off the course before I was awarded them.

The glow, however, was short-lived. No sooner had those wings been pinned ceremoniously to my tunic, than I found myself posted to Training Command – the last command a self-respecting fighter pilot wanted to end up in.

The prelude to this appalling development was delivered to us two weeks before the end of the course in the shape of an official form which asked us quite simply to choose, in order of preference, which three out of five commands we wished to serve in: Army Co-operation, Bomber, Coastal, Fighter or Training.

We all reacted differently to the document. My only difficulty was finding a second or third choice. A short life dreaming that I would one day become a fighter pilot did not include any alternatives. So I left numbers two and three blank and any further selection to fate.

Derek Dunn's philosophy was ahead of its time.

"It's dead easy," he said. "Select the Commands you don't want and you'll be posted to the one you do want."

His hope, but unwritten wish, was to be a bomber pilot.

The night our course ended, the Adjutant pinned the list of names to the notice board in the main hall and within minutes it was surrounded by a milling, eager throng hellbent on finding out what fate had decreed for them. Some turned away from the board yelping with excitement, others serious and deep in thought. The reality of war meeting them face to face for the first time.

Derek was not surprised. His theory had worked. Bomber Command was attached to his name. Poor Derek; he did not enjoy his happiness for long. He failed to return from a raid on Germany only four months later.

I was stunned. Reeling from the notice board, I turned and groped my way through the crowd and into the cool night air. At first, the blow did not register too deeply. I was convinced that I had misread the posting. So I returned to look at the list again. But I had not misread it; Training Command was clearly set down against my name.

All my thoughts and aspirations had been geared to leaving Cranwell for a fighter squadron and I became obsessed by the conviction that a terrible mistake had been made. Tormented, angry and frustrated over this obvious blunder, I decided that the earliest I could seek an explanation and have the posting changed was at the farewell cocktail party that traditionally ends every course. As I washed and changed in my room, I rehearsed again and again what I would say to the chief flying instructor.

As drinks were "on the house," the whole of the teaching staff turned up to give us a send-off, led by the commanding officer who moved in stately fashion around the anteroom, just like royalty, saying a few chosen words to each of the departing pilots.

I had no stomach for drink that night. I clutched a half-pint tankard of beer, but barely took a sip as I stood, as a man in a trance, waiting for the opportunity to speak to the C.F.I. Like a movie fan watching a film star, I kept my eyes riveted on him as he went around the room.

At last an opportunity opened for me and I advanced on him to plead my case. Patiently he listened to my torrent of words. They were not the first he had heard that evening, but perhaps none had been delivered with such earnestness and he was obviously sorry I was taking so unkindly to my posting.

"I think I know how you feel, Page," he said, "but unfortunately in wartime personal feelings go by the board."

I must have looked desperately miserable, because he became quite fatherly. Gently, he began to explain. "You must remember that to be sent to central flying school to be trained as an instructor for future instructors is about the highest compliment the Air Force can pay a pilot. We didn't give you an exceptional assessment just to get you shot down! And another thing to remember," he went on, "You're not going to like this, but good pilots are often bad fighter pilots."

For the first time since he began talking, I raised my eyes from gazing at a fixed spot on the carpet.

"A fighter pilot needs to be very ham-fisted on occasions and you're just not made that way. Sorry,"

He moved on, leaving me with some sensation of pride, but it was soon overpowered by my initial depression. I hardly slept that night, and next day I left for Meir airport near Stoke-on-Trent to keep in flying practice until my specialized instructor training could begin.

Four

Meir, set amid the sordid slag-heaps of the Potteries, did nothing for my crumpled spirit. Nor did the fresh green shoots of spring or the lengthening days lighten the obscurity engulfing my disillusioned heart. But suddenly, for the second time in my life, Hitler came to the rescue. Ignoring the neutrality of the Low Countries, he launched his offensive and swept through Holland and Belgium and into France, shaking the Allies out of the torpor of the Phoney War.

Responding to the attack, the Air Ministry took swift action. To my astonishment and delight they cancelled my posting to instructor training and ordered me to report to No. 66 Fighter Squadron at Horsham St. Faith airport, near Norwich.

There was no sipping from a half-pint tankard that night. Wine flowed so freely that a monumental hangover only made the slow train to Norwich the next day worse torture than it need have been. But I was happy, although the closer I got to my destination, the more I questioned my ability to do the job I had set my heart on. Indeed, at the halfway stage in the journey I was convinced that when the squadron commander met me at the station, he would be very disappointed in his latest recruit. The words of Wing Commander Speedy Holmes kept on coming back to me. "A fighter pilot needs to be ham-fisted on occasions, and you're just not made that way."

By the time the train had steamed into Norwich Station, I had reduced myself to a nervous wreck, and it only occurred to me as I lifted my kit from the baggage rack and began straightening my tie that a squadron commander would never turn out to meet a junior officer. He would delegate that job to one of his deputies. In a way, I was relieved.

As it turned out, no one was delegated to meet me at all, and after kicking my heels around the station yard for half an hour I telephoned the adjutant at the airport.

"Pilot Officer Page here," I explained. The reply was none too encouraging.

"What the hell d'you want?"

"Well, I'm the new pilot and I'm at Norwich Station."

"We're not expecting any new pilots! Sure you're onto the right squadron?"

"Just a moment." I fished out the telegram from an inside pocket. "Hello!"

"Yes."

"You're Sixty-Six, aren't you?"

"That's right."

"Well," I said, "my posting notice definitely states Sixty-Six squadron."

There was silence from the other end. I said nothing, since it was up to him to make the next move. Then, reluctantly it seemed to me, he said, "all right, I'll send someone to get you."

The driver of the van that eventually turned up was an affable, ginger-haired pilot officer, Dizzy Allen by name. A cheerful personality, he drove quickly and surely and by the time he swerved off the main road toward several neat rows of wooden huts surrounded by carefully tended grass, he had told me quite a lot about the squadron and its organization.

These wooden huts were the squadron's quarters. They stood on either side of a cul-de-sac, at the end of which was the officers' Mess. Allen drove up to it, brought the van to a violent halt, leapt out and shouted over his shoulder, "here's the C.O., I'll introduce you."

A group of officers stood outside in the afternoon sun playing with a large, white bull-terrier, and as I jumped out to follow Allen, they stopped for an instant to look at me. Like any new boy, I became acutely conscious of being an outsider who had yet to be accepted by the pack.

"The new pilot, sir," said Allen.

Squadron Leader R.H.A. Leigh removed an old pipe from his mouth, nodded at Allen and turned a cold eye on me as I saluted in the best Cranwell manner.

"Pilot Officer Page reporting for duty, sir."

The C.O. returned the compliment by raising the stem of his pipe languidly in the direction of his right eyebrow. The other officers went quiet.

"Oh yes, the Adj' has just told me about you," he said. "As a matter of fact, no one told us to expect you. Allen here will find you a bed and we'll have a chat in the morning."

"Yes sir. Thank you sir," I replied.

The squadron commander turned away towards the others and then, curiosity getting the better of him, turned back to ask me what aircraft I had trained on.

"Tutors, Harts and Hinds, sir," I replied.

"No, I mean since those types."

"Nothing, sir. Hinds were the last."

"Christ!" he said, and turned his back on me. "What will they be sending us next?"

Oblivious of the real crisis brewing, the Exceptional category I had been given at Cranwell seemed more than ever to be a burden rather than an asset. It was only that evening, when I had time to sit down and think through the events of the day, that I realized how much of a mistake I had made in reacting as I did. Squadron Leader Leigh had no idea, yet, that Cranwell did not think I was made like a fighter pilot. And now that I had achieved the ambition of my life and joined a fighter squadron, I was determined to show that I was born to be one.

Next morning "B" Flight jumped into the squadron van outside the Mess. I had not yet been assigned to a flight, so, like a young child, I stuck with the one person I knew, Dizzy Allen. On the way to the airport he explained that the Mess was dispersed away from the aircraft to save possible casualties in case of attack. Every night, however, one of the flights slept in the hangar crew room on the airfield so as to be available for take-off at first light. "B" Flight was now relieving "A" Flight.

The airport turned out to be one of the last on which construction had started prior to the declaration of war. Builders were still at work on the hangars, and the control tower in the middle of the airfield was surrounded by scaffolding. There were no runways, but the grass surface was reasonably smooth.

The van pulled up with a lurch in front of the hangar nearest to completion and the pilots jumped out to exchange friendly insults with "A" Flight, who took over the van and disappeared for breakfast. Dizzy rushed off to join the rest of the flight and prepare the aircraft, leaving me to my own devices.

Standing on the grass outside the hangar, my eager eyes took in the beautiful lines of the Spitfires dispersed around the airfield. The maxim I had picked up at Cranwell, "if it looks right, it flies right," had to apply to this surprisingly small fighter.

But approaching footsteps soon dissipated my excited reverie. The sergeant pilot came to a halt and saluted.

"Excuse me, sir," he said, "the C.O. would like to see you in his office."

As I entered and saluted, the squadron commander slammed down the telephone receiver.

"How the hell do they expect me to run a fighter squadron and a training school at the same time?" he said more to himself than to me. "Damned disgrace sending along a young boy who's never flown anything more advanced than a Hind. If you get killed," he added, looking at me severely in the eye, "it will be Group's fault. I've done my best to warn them."

The squadron commander lit his pipe carefully and deliberately in an obvious effort to regain a composure Group Headquarters had ruffled by refusing to supply an advanced training aircraft on which to convert his newest pilot onto Spitfires. For a moment he disappeared behind a cloud of smoke. When he emerged, he was leaning across the desk pointing an accusing pipe stem at me.

"For a start," he said, "we may as well establish the fact that you're a damn nuisance."

I gulped. "Yes, sir."

"The fact of the matter is that two weeks ago some clod crashed our Miles Master, so we haven't got an airplane in which to give you some dual before going off solo in a Spit. As you've never flown anything that has a retractable undercarriage or variable pitch airscrew, or that travels at more than a hundred and twenty, you qualify to become a damn nuisance."

Realizing that the fault was not really mine, I felt better.

But not for long. "In which case," continued the squadron commander, "I think it might be wiser if I sent you away for a conversion course."

The effect of these words was as stunning as the blow I once received on the head from a cricket ball at school; and he registered the impact without knowing for certain whether my deathly pallor was due to disappointment or immense relief.

"Please, sir," I stammered, "don't post me away from the squadron. Why, I ... it's just that I've so wanted to be a fighter pilot that ..." My voice trailed away as my numbed mind refused to think about the rest of the sentence.

The C.O. leaned back and blew a long, thoughtful cloud of smoke towards the ceiling. Then suddenly the pipestem was pointing at me across the bare office.

"Page! You're about to fly a Spitfire. But if you break your neck, don't blame me!"

Half an hour later I reported back to Squadron Leader Leigh. "Happy about it, Page?"

"I think so, thank you, sir." The C.O. grunted and knocked his pipe out on the machined piston head that served as an ashtray. "Let's have the take-off drill again."

"R-A-F-T-P. Radiator, airscrew, flaps, trim and petrol."

I had been sitting in the cockpit of a Spitfire for half an hour memorizing the cockpit procedures for take-off, flight and landing. I was now back for my final examination before being let loose with a machine.

The C.O. asked a few more questions; then, satisfied that at least I understood the theory, he stood up, and, with pipe firmly clenched between his teeth, beckoned me to follow him to the aircraft. He stood by while I stepped onto the port wing and into the small cockpit. An airman climbed onto the wing behind me to help me with my parachute and harness.

Word spread swiftly that an unusual first solo on type was taking place and soon ground and air crews were gathering to watch with morbid interest.

As soon as I was properly strapped in, the squadron commander climbed onto the wing for a final word. "Don't forget," he said, "taxi out quickly and turn her into wind – do a quick check and then get off. If you don't, the glycol will boil and so will my blood. Good luck!"

I responded with a nervous smile, closed the tiny door and turned to face the mass of dials, buttons and levers. For a moment panic seized me and the temptation to undo the straps and get out was very great – but it was quickly replaced by a strong desire to urinate!

The enquiring voice of the airman standing by the starter battery reminded me of the engine starting procedure, and my nervous feeling passed with the need for concentrated action. Carefully I recalled the squadron commander's words of instruction: throttle about half an inch open – gas on – nine full strokes in the KI – gas hand priming pump for a cold engine – propeller in fine pitch –brakes on – stick held back – press the starter button. I raised my thumb, the waiting airman replied with a similar sign, and I pressed the starter button firmly – the propeller began to rotate as the motor turned the twenty-four cylinders of the large Merlin engine.

A trickle of sweat ran down my forehead. Suddenly the powerful engine coughed loudly, blew a short stream of purply-white smoke into a small cloud and roared into life. Remembering that I had little time to spare before the temperature reached the danger mark of 110°, I waved my hands across my face. The waiting airman quickly ducked under the wing and pulled away the restraining chocks. Glancing down, I was alarmed to see that the glycol coolant temperature had risen from zero to 70°. Releasing the brake, I eased the throttle open and the surge of power carried the aircraft forward rapidly over the grass.

Was everything ready for a quick take-off? I wondered. I figured I'd better call up Flying Control and get permission to scramble*. Pushing over the switch on the VHF box, I tried to transmit. "Idiot!" I said to myself, "switch the damn thing on." Another glance at the temperature showed 95° and still a long way to go before turning into the wind. The radio came to life with a whine, and contact was made with a fellow human being. The controller's voice was soothing and

*Take-off immediately.

for the first time since strapping into the narrow cockpit, I relaxed slightly. But I was still none too happy.

The temperature now read 105° and there were still a few yards to go, plus the final check. Softly I prayed for help.

Temperature 107° ....

To hell with it, turn the damn aircraft into wind here. It looked like a long enough run.

Temperature 108° ....

Now for the drill: R-A-F-T-P-R – the radiator – God alone knows how many times I'd vainly tried to open it beyond its normal point to try to keep the temperature down. A – airscrew in the fine pitch – that's okay. F – flaps.

Temperature 109° ....

I abandoned the remainder of the cockpit drill and, opening the throttle firmly, started the take-off run. The initial kick from the rapid acceleration drove the worry of the engine temperature away for a while. Working the rudder hard with both feet to keep the sensitive little machine straight, I was too busy for other thoughts. Easing the stick forward, I was startled by the rapidity with which she responded to the elevator controls. The long nose in front of me obscured the rapidly approaching head at the end of the airport, but by looking out at an angle, I was able to get an idea of how far away it was. If the glycol boiled now at this critical stage, the aircraft would be enveloped in a cloud of white smoke that would prevent me from seeing the ground when the inevitable engine seizure and crash landing followed. Looking back into the cockpit again, I saw the hated instrument leering at me.

110° ....

Accompanying the feeling of fear was a new sound. The wheels had stopped drumming and a whistling note filled the air. The Spitfire soared gracefully into the air, thankful, as I was, to be away from her earthly bonds.

Inside the cockpit I worked desperately to get the undercarriage raised. The C.O. had explained to me that because the starboard aircraft leg hung down in front of the radiator when the wheels were lowered, this affects the cooling effect by the airstream. By raising the wheels the air would pass unhindered through the radiator to do its work. But here I fell into trouble again. To raise the wheels, I had to move the selector lever and this was on the right hand of the seat. I then had to pump them up with twenty movements by a long handle, also on the right. To do all this while flying the very sensitive aircraft meant using my left hand for the control column, while the right hand struggled with the undercarriage mechanism.

The Spitfire was now about twenty feet up, gaining speed rapidly and skimming over the trees and hedges. I selected "wheels up" and gave the handle a first stroke. The engine cut out for an instant and the nose plunged earthwards. Being unused to the technique of keeping my left hand absolutely still while the right one moved forward, I had inadvertently pushed the control column forward simultaneously with the first pumping stroke, thus causing the machine to dip suddenly. The negative gee placed on the carburettor had caused a temporary fuel stoppage. Some trees flashed by alongside the aircraft as a frightened pilot hauled back on the stick, and soon I was soaring skyward again, pumping frantically after removing my left hand from the control column. At this stage it was obvious that the Spitfire could handle herself better than I could. After this nightmare, the green light finally shone on the instrument panel, indicating that the wheels were in the locked-up position, and the engine temperature gauge showed a healthy fall. I took a moment to utter another silent prayer, this time of thanks.

Now I had some breathing space, so I was able to look about and concentrate on the other aspects of flying the airplane. Throttling back the engine and placing the propeller in coarse pitch, I allowed myself the luxury of relaxing slightly and looked down on the beauties of the Norfolk Broads. However, the pleasures of the English countryside didn't last long. Glancing down and behind me, I was horrified to discover that the airport was nowhere in sight. The swiftness of the Spitfire had soon taken me out of sight of the landing ground, and although homing facilities were available over the R/T, pride stopped me from calling the flying control tower for assistance. Instead, a worried young man flew about the sky in circles anxiously peering down for a sign of home. Ten minutes later, relief flooded through me when the unmistakable outlines of Norwich Cathedral appeared out of the summer haze, and from there the airport was easy to find. A minute later the graceful plane was banking round the circuit preparatory to landing.

Again I recalled the cockpit procedure given to me by the squadron commander: R-U-P-F – radiator, undercarriage, pitch and flaps. This time the pumping down of the wheels came quite simply, and the other essential procedures prior to the final touchdown followed. The exhausts crackled delightfully as the engine was throttled back and the plane came in gliding fast over the boundary hedge. In the cockpit, I eased the stick back and the long streamlined nose rose up and cut out the forward view of the landing run. Looking out to the left, I carefully judged the height as the Spitfire floated gracefully a foot or two above the green grass, then losing speed she settled down on the ground to the steady rumble of the wheels. As soon as the machine had come to a halt I raised the flaps and thankfully undid the tight-fitting oxygen mask. The pool of sweat that had collected trickled down my neck. With a newly-born confidence, I taxied the machine back towards the waving airman near the hangar. Just as I removed my helmet and undid the confining harness and parachute straps, Dizzy Allen walked up.

"Back in one piece, I see. How'd you get on?"

Trying to appear nonchalant, I replied, "Loved every minute of it. She certainly handles beautifully." The feeling of achievement obliterated the memory of the fear I'd felt during most of the flight, and now I felt justified in taking a place among my fellow fighter pilots.

My heart was singing.

Five

The only sound that disturbed the contented chirps of the unseen chorus of birds was the occasional interruption of a cuckoo. Bees buzzed busily across the sweet-scented grass in the warm sunshine. Half a dozen figures were stretched out in their yellow Mae West life-saving jackets, adding spots of colour to the predominantly green background. "B" Flight had returned to a state of "readiness". Fighter squadrons were usually kept in one of four states: "Standby," in which the pilots sat strapped in their aircraft ready for instantaneous starting and departure; "Readiness," whereby they remained at the most only a few yards from their machines, and could usually be taking off in under two minutes; "Available," which allowed them to leave the dispersal point and return to the Mess, but they were liable to recall to "Readiness" within a stated time such as half an hour. Squadrons were allowed relaxation in the form of "Release," but these usually only resulted during daylight hours from impossible flying weather conditions, and otherwise were only granted after dark to pre-dawn. During the "Phoney" war period before the Germans overthrew the Low Countries, the "Flight" or half-squadron only was used to meet any emergency. Quite often in the event of an alarm a section of three (half a Flight) was dispatched to investigate what usually turned out to be a false alarm.

Now the rumble of distant warfare had commenced in earnest on the Continent, but the lazy English countryside was still at peace with mankind and herself.

Lying on my back in the cool caressing grass, I looked up at the blue sky through the mesh of lashes formed through half opened eyes, quietly sucking a perfumed leaf of clover. At that point the only problem that existed in my young life was the disposal of a persistent fly that considered my nose the best available landing space in the immediate neighbourhood.

No one spoke. In the sleepy distance the rattle of a farm tractor added to the lulling chorus of the birds. Garn, the bull terrier, was the first to hear the new note, and her ears flicked sensitively. Pilots all, we were not long after the animal in detecting the distant hum of an approaching air engine. Still maintaining silence, eyes opened and heads were raised to enable better appreciation of the rising sound.

"Kestrel engine," I called out, and as soon as I'd uttered the words I regretted them. Interpreting the continued silence that greeted my remark as reproval for a show-off statement, I hated myself.

When the Hind trainer appeared skimming over the treetops I felt little satisfaction at the correctness of my hearing. Desperately I wanted to explain that after flying them for so long at Cranwell, it came as second nature to be able to detect the peculiar beat of a Kestrel engine.

The brightly painted yellow machine did a tight circuit inside the perimeter of the airport and descended smoothly for a neat landing. Dizzy called to me, "That's the Doc."

"The Doc?"

"Yes, Wing Commander Comer, the Sector Medical Officer."

I was very impressed. "That's pretty keen for the Sector M.O. to fly himself about from place to place, isn't it?

Dizzy laughed. 'To be keener than the Doc, you'd have to sprout wings and become an angel. The old boy's come over to scrounge a trip in a Spit, I'll bet."

The new arrival was evidently a popular figure, for in a single movement the reclining figures rose and strolled out to meet the taxi-ing airplane. Turning the machine neatly into wind before switching off the engine, the pilot lowered himself agilely to the ground and advanced youthfully to greet the approaching pilots. I was surprised to find on meeting the grey-headed wing commander a short time later, that he was not a young man by any standards, but I became even more impressed when the doctor later painstakingly enquired into my past history with genuine interest. In later years I was to recall the memory of Corner as a man with the bigness of a Catholic priest, but unhindered by the narrowness of the religion.

The squadron commander emerged from the hangar office in

shirtsleeves. Greeting the M.O. amiably, he stabbed a pipe stem in my direction. "You're just the man I'm looking for, Doc. Page, here, has just been posted in, but he's got quite a lot to do before we can put him operational.* How'd you like to stay with us for a few days and show him and Mounsden the ropes?"

Mark Mounsden had arrived at the squadron from an operational training unit only a few days before I had.

The question was practically unnecessary. The doctor enjoyed medicine, but lived – and died – for flying. Unable to resist the call of the air he persuaded higher command to allow him to participate in operational sorties. Later he was to attempt to bail out of his crippled Spitfire at a low altitude over the Channel, but didn't survive.

During the week that followed, I found out that there was little about fighter command and fighter pilots with which the Air Force doctor was not familiar. Imparting the sympathetic air of the medical practitioner, he was able to draw from his newly found pupils all that was puzzling them. Being overawed by the experienced pilots who made up the squadron, I had been too shy to ask those questions that were uppermost in my mind, but in the doctor I found a sympathetic listener and a teacher who was willing to answer queries and impart knowledge.

Fortunately for the pair of us, there were extra airplanes available for our use, owing to the aerial inactivity existing at that stage of the war. Together Mark and I would take to the air with the wing commander flying patiently along, allowing his protegees to practice formation flying on his machine. The days passed all too rapidly for us, and at the end of the first week we were looping and rolling in formation like an experienced aerobatic team.

Landing one afternoon from a particularly exhilarating flight, the doctor walked over to the other aircraft and met this happy pilot as I jumped off the wing.

"I think that that just about does it, Page."

For a moment I was puzzled by the remark. "Does it, sir?"

"Yes, I'm going to recommend to your C.O. that he make you op-

*Qualified for combat duties.

erational."

My heart was too full to mutter more than a " thank YOU, sir!"

Coming out to meet us from the hangar I could see the figure of the squadron commander. Even anyone not knowing him could have seen that he was not in the best of tempers.

We sensed his mood and waited for the outburst which soon followed.

"Bloody Command, what the hell do they think they're doing? Fighting a war or running a training unit … ?"

I'd heard these words before.

"… they give me a pilot for five minutes, then post him away again."

"What's up?" asked the wing commander.

"Finger trouble! They've just discovered that they've made a mistake with Mounsden and Page's postings and that they should've been sent to 56 Squadron instead."

"Command running true to form, eh," remarked Corner laconically.

The squadron commander then held a dissertation on the doubtful merits of staff officers in general, but only one member of the audience was listening to his scathing words. Stunned by the news that I was on the move again, I could think of nothing except that I had to leave my newly found friends. It was then that I realized how much the squadron had come to mean to me even during the few days since my cheerless arrival at Norwich.

Unwittingly the C.O. turned the knife in the wound. "Good unit, 56. You'll like them, Page. They're at North Weald flying Hurricanes."

My depression deepened at the idea of changing over to Hurricanes after flying Spitfires. It was supposed to be a very good airplane, that I knew, but after Spitfires … NO!

The only advantage I could find in my new posting was that when the real fighting started, my new Squadron, stationed on the outskirts of London, would be in the thick of it. Fate had also kept faith with me, and I was going to join 56 Squadron, the squadron my childhood idol, Captain Albert Ball, V.C., had served in during the first World War.

Six

The merry month of May brought with it the end to Allied complacency. Retreat was the order of the day. On land and in the air the situation was the same; we were outnumbered and ill-equipped. Unlike their sister bomber and Army co-operation units, the few fighter squadrons based in Europe did have the advantage of Hurricane fighters, but the odds were still hopeless. For the pilots sent to war in Fairey Battles and Blenheims, the best thing to say for them was a quiet "Amen". Their spilt blood and battered bodies bore fitting testimony to the crime of disarmament in time of peace. Although aircraft and crews were available in England to send to the Continent, this would not have been possible without seriously endangering the safety of the island. As a result some units were used from the United Kingdom on offensive sorties against the rapidly advancing enemy.

My reception at North Weald was even more bleak than the one at Norwich. Walking up to the Mess from the nearby railway station, I had time to take stock of the airport layout. To the right of the rising road lay the large hangars and the squat group of headquarters buildings. Beyond the hangars towered the high pylons of a nearby international transmitting station. The perimeter track of the airfield was studded with U-shaped pens made of high banks of earth; these being for the protection of the aircraft in case of sudden aerial attack. Standing back from the road on the left hand side stood the shape of the officers' Mess surrounded by well laid out gardens. Only the camouflaged appearance of the buildings lent a warlike touch to the picture of a peacetime Air Force station.

Deciding to leave my suitcase in the Mess before reporting to headquarters, I turned into the driveway that led to the main entrance. An air of desertion imparted itself from the officers' quarters. Entering the hall and depositing the heavy bag with a feeling of relief, I noticed the forsaken atmosphere of the place increase. Puzzled, I looked about for a sign of life, but all was still. Signing the arrivals book on the square oak table in the hall and leaving my suitcase trustingly by the telephone booth, I stepped out of the empty Mess into the warm sunshine. Crossing the road and about to enter the main camp, I was surprised to find a zealous sentry blocking the way and demanding identification. Producing a Form 1250 to the guard's satisfaction, I proceeded towards the station headquarters building.

Reporting to the station adjutant's office, I explained my presence and asked to be directed to my new squadron. The same keenness of spirit that the sentry at the gate had displayed exuded from the adjutant. Rapidly he provided me with my bedroom number in the Mess and appeared to know all about my past history and capabilities. Having discharged the official side of his job, the adjutant relaxed a bit and volunteered some information. Watching him, I felt that here was a man who was on tenterhooks lest he be caught slacking at his job. Somehow the deserted Mess, the zealous sentry and now this efficient adjutant seemed incongruous.

"Pity you arrived today, Page," he began. "Your squadron has been up at Digby for a couple of weeks doing gunnery practice, and they aren't due back until Friday."

This, I realized, partially explained the empty Mess.

"However," the adjutant continued, "The next three days before they return will give you a chance to settle down. By the way, I don't see on your papers that you've flown Hurricanes?"

Employing a miracle of understatement, I replied, "No, only Spitfires."

The other man appeared none too impressed. "You shouldn't have much difficulty with the old Hurribox then."

Noticing the administrative officer's lack of wings, I refrained from comment. "A pity he wasn't with me on my first flight in a Spitfire," was my only thought.

Leaving the adjutant to his paperwork, I thankfully left the overtidy office and went in search of the squadron offices. Leaving the headquarters block I walked towards the hangars, hoping to find a Hurricane undergoing an inspection. It takes a poor pilot to miss the opportunity of sitting in the cockpit of a strange type of airplane.

Rounding the corner of a wooden hut bearing the title "Parachute Section," I was delighted to find two Hurricanes standing on the tarmac between the two hangars. Although the Spitfire and the Hurricane were basically alike, inasmuch as they were low-wing, single-seater monoplanes, powered by Rolls-Royce "Merlin" engines, to the fighter pilot's eye, the similarity ended there. Whereas the Spitfire had all the speed and grace of the greyhound in its sleek appearance, the Hurricane portrayed the excellent qualities of the bulldog, being slower but much more solidly built than the other. To the Spitfire pilot there will be only one machine, and similarly to the man who flew the Hurricane. To the fortunate ones who often took to the skies in both types, there will be an everlasting love for both that borders on sweet-sadness that these aircraft, like human beings, last but a little while and then are gone. I was about to place a foot in the stirrup step protruding below the fuselage, when a voice behind me called, "Do you want something?"

Hastily removing the raised foot, I turned to meet the approaching figure. Apologetically I explained the fact that I was a new pilot to 56 Squadron, and that I wanted to see inside a Hurricane for the first time. At this the other man introduced himself as the 56 Squadron engineering officer.

"I think you'd better wait until the C.O. returns," he said. "I haven't the authority to allow you to go crawling over the aircraft. Besides, these ones are brand new and haven't even had the armour plating installed yet."

I contented myself with a walk around the machines before setting out across the airport to the dispersal huts. Minutes later I found myself crossing the centre of the airfield, ankle deep in rich grass bespeckled with a myriad of tiny daisies. Runways had not yet been laid and the background of trees from Epping Forest gave the airport a peaceful, rural air. Making an appreciation of the landing ground as such, I noted that the ground sloped downwards from south to north, and that a take-off from west to east necessitated passing between the hangars and the 300-foot pylons of the transmitting station. As opposed to the empty U-pens of 56 Squadron on the west side of the airport, those on the commanding high ground of the south were oc-

cupied by the rugged outlines of Hurricanes. In the secluded corner
at the bottom of the landing ground to the north stood the outdated
forms of twin-engined Blenheim night-fighters. Crossing the grass in
the summery stillness of the afternoon, I found it difficult to envisage
the slaughter that was taking place across the Channel. I was still a
boy playing at war, and apart from the death of a cadet night-flying
at Cranwell, none of the grim reality had yet been brought home to
me.

Reaching the perimeter track, I headed for the northernmost of
two long wooden huts that stood three hundred yards apart behind
the pens. This hut, according to the engineering officer, was the home
of "B" Flight, the flight in need of a replacement pilot. Climbing up
two steps, I opened the door in the end of the one-storied wooden
building. On either side of the entrance door was a small office, one
marked "Flight Commander" and the other, "Get out and keep out."
On closer inspection the latter revealed itself to be a sparsely furnished room consisting of a wooden table and chair, three telephones,
a Very pistol and a picture of a nude stuck on the wall. Above the
naked lady was the caption, "Time spent on reconnaissance is never
wasted." This was the telephone room into which vital messages were
relayed direct from the sector operations control. Beyond the short
corridor dividing the two offices lay the main part of the hut. Two
rows of iron beds covered with dull grey blankets lay on either side
with their heads resting against the cream-painted walls. Two iron
stoves with flues passing up through the roof added a touch of ugli-
ness from their positions in the centre and at either end of the room.
A few uncomfortable upright wooden chairs that stood clustered
round the stoves supplied the seating accommodation. Halfway
down the long room on the right hand side stood a rickety wooden
table covered with playing cards and bits and pieces of flying equipment. Shelves lined the walls between the many windows, and the
assorted contents on them would have done credit to a Chelsea jum-
ble sale. After inspecting my new home I took the opportunity to inspect the flight commander's office. This was the same size as the
telephone room, but had the extra luxury of a bed besides the inevitable wooden table and chair. On the wall above the table was a

blackboard bearing the inscription "B" Flight, and below it a list of pilots painted in white enamel.

I was glad to get out into the sunshine again as somehow the unoccupied dispersal hut exuded a ghostly quality. I felt that if one listened hard enough it might be possible to catch the boisterous echoes of young men who had filled its space until so recently.

On my return to the Mess I found a message to contact the squadron engineering officer. He had received instructions that the two new Hurricanes were to be flight-tested immediately. It appeared I was the only available pilot on the station, so despite the fact I'd never flown one before, I was given the job. After the Spitfire, the first thing I noticed was the added height of the plane off the ground, and the less restricted view directly forward along the nose. The cockpit itself appeared to be roomier, but the individual knobs and levers were not finished with quite the same quality as the other machine. However, I was happy to notice that the undercarriage system was automatically controlled once the position of the wheels had been selected, and the propeller was of the new constant speeding type. The engineering officer was very careful to point out that this particular plane was the latest of its kind, and was to be handled accordingly with due care. The engine-starting procedure was similar to that on Spitfires, with the added advantage that the engine kept cool almost indefinitely owing to the positioning of the radiator between the undercarriage legs.

Despite the strangeness of the airplane, I taxied her out confidently to the top end of the airfield, and after doing a thorough cockpit check and receiving the green "O.K." signal from control, I took off down the hill towards the parked Blenheims. The Hurricane rose gracefully and easily into the air, and I had the immediate sensation that here was a lady with very few vices. Climbing rapidly over the soft Essex countryside, I headed my aircraft eastwards to the North Sea. To the south below the wing tip shimmered the broad reaches of the Thames as they ran their course to meet the distant sea. Contentment filled my soul, and to show my appreciation of the day, I slowly and lazily rolled the Hurricane on to her back. Hanging upside down for a few seconds, I eased the stick back and pulled her vertically downwards with a rush of increasing speed. Far below me along the line of the aircraft's nose moved the tiny speck of a human being moving across the yard between a farmhouse and a barn. Moving the control column hard over, the responsive machine completed a hundred-and-eighty-degree aileron turn vertically downwards, then pulling firmly back on the stick with opening throttle, she climbed swiftly again into the sunlit sky and over into a wide loop. Singing happily to myself, I dived the plane back towards the hangars, no longer sorry that I was going to be flying Hurricanes.

Early next morning the sunny silence enveloping the airport was rudely shattered by the roaring sound of twelve Hurricanes diving low over the hangars in tight squadron formation. 56 Squadron had returned to its home base. Airmen seemingly appeared from nowhere in quantities, and as the aircraft landed and taxied towards the pens, the dispersal point came to life with running figures. Ribald greetings were passed between air and ground crews. A squadron develops a great attachment for its own airport, and a homecoming is always a welcome event. I stood outside the "B" Flight hut watching the pilots troop by with parachutes slung over their shoulders. One or two of them gave me a quizical look before passing on into the hut with their loads.

Having ascertained from one of the ground crew which was the senior "B" Flight officer – there was no flight commander; he had been killed in action – I approached a handsome blond flying officer. I introduced myself to Ereminsky.

"Where the hell have you been?"

His reply was hardly what I expected. I explained briefly my wrong posting to 66 Squadron. A few terse questions followed, and I was thankful I'd flown Spitfires when he enquired into my previous experience.

"Come and meet 'B' Flight." The interrogation was over.

Minny, as Ereminsky was known, introduced me to Flight Sergeant "Taffy" Higginson, the senior sergeant pilot in the squadron. From behind the bushy whiskers emitted a high-pitched voice entirely out of keeping with its formidable exit.

"Do you have a car, sir?" Taffy enquired with a faint trace of a

Welsh lilt.

"I'm afraid not."

The flight sergeant slapped his forehead in horror and dismay. "My God! Poor Esmerelda . . . there goes the last spring."

Ereminsky explained that Esmerelda was an ancient old car that did the journey from North Weald to London practically every night overloaded with oversexed pilots. She could be relied on to get them back to the airport in time for dawn readiness, regardless of the condition of the occupants.

Then the telephone rang.

To my surprise all conversation ceased and all ears strained to hear the telephone orderly's voice talking in the far room. It was not until he had finished speaking that the general babble of conversation resumed. A minute later Minny bellowed down the hut, "'B' Flight released until half an hour before first light tomorrow."

The news was greeted with the same enthusiasm as an unexpected half-holiday would be received at a children's school, and a wild rush began for the dispersal hut door. Inwardly I was disappointed. It meant to me that time was being wasted.

I wanted to get in the air, and above all get at the enemy. At that time of innocence I don't really think my mind understood what getting at the enemy really meant. It was an intangible something that just had to be gotten on with, so strong was the burning desire.

Seven

Esmerelda came to a thankful juddering halt in a cul-de-sac alongside the pub, and twelve thirsty pilots unravelled themselves from her musty interior. In a wave of laughter and repartee, we poured through the green and yellow painted door, to swell the number of occupants in the well-filled bar.

Shepherds stands in a narrow street in the heart of Mayfair and practically forms the western boundary of Shepherd Market. This particular area of London is unique in itself. Society and vice rub shoulders together in the taverns and coffee shops. Dowager Duchesses in mink and prostitutes in slacks frequent the same butchers and greengrocers to do their weekly shopping. Homosexuals carry on their simpering small talk unheeded by the whore exercising her miniature poodle. It is an attitude of "Well, we all live together in the same neighbourhood, so let's make the best of it." Nations could take a lesson from Shepherd Market.

By almost unanimous decision the fighter command pilots established Shepherds pub as their unofficial headquarters during the war years. The announcements of marriages, births and deaths were heard in the mullion windowed bar literally only hours after the events had taken place. The marriages and births were relatively few. Keeping a strict fatherly eye over the whole scene was Oscar, ably assisted by George, the lounge waiter. Oscar was Swiss. Short, dark and dapper, his manner of speech was clipped and tinged with a European accent. Always smartly turned out in a black coat and grey-striped trousers, he smacked more of the Harley Street surgeon than the Shepherd Market publican. Despite his almost frozen-faced appearance, Oscar had a lively sense of humour and an agile brain. But woe to the person who didn't behave himself on his premises. His store of information on squadron locations, equipment and other secret matters, would have done credit to the R.A.F. Intelligence Branch.

Aircrew returning from overseas could trace service friends more rapidly through the friendly bar than by the usual Air Ministry channels. Often the information was more accurate as well.

The public house stands on a corner in Hertford Street and although possessing several floors, the bar on the ground floor is the only one in the small building. This room is decorated in the Regency style. Miniatures adorn the walls panelled in natural wood and a sedan chair at the end of the long room does service as a telephone booth.

Rectangular in shape, the bar lines one complete wall, while opposite, beneath the mullion bay windows, are window-seats for those not wishing to stand. Behind the bar stand recessed alcoves carrying attractive pieces of Dresden china on small shelves.

Calling greetings to Oscar and his friendly wife, our group of pilots formed a wedge and moved towards the bar. Pints of beer passed backwards on a human chain and soon our chatter was adding its note to the buzz of conversation in the crowded room. Outside the prostitutes marched up and down with the regularity of guardsmen on their beats. Prophetically a flash of lightning lit the sky, soon followed by the crash of thunder. Time was running short for the merry young men with their frothing pint pots. But I was content with my lot in 56 Squadron.

The squadron was going through a difficult period at this time. It was common knowledge that the commanding officer, "Fuhrer" Knowles was due for replacement, and this in itself created an atmosphere of unrest and uncertainty. "B" Flight had recently returned from France where it had suffered casualties, dead, wounded and missing.

Fortunately for 56, the station commander at North Weald was a man of outstanding calibre. Victor Beamish combined all the best qualities of efficiency, courage and boundless energy. A member of the famous Irish Rugby International family, his physical toughness and personal charm, topped off with the soft brogue of his native land, endeared all the pilots to this great man. Tragically, the war would claim him as its victim at a later date. Without attempting to mother us, Beamish kept a careful watch over the squadron's progress, and would lead us in the air as often as his ground duties would permit.

Meanwhile, "Minny" Ereminsky continued as acting flight commander. Although Nordic in appearance, Minny was a White Russian by derivation.

Other members of "B" Flight were Dopey Davies, so called because he had a passing resemblance to the last of the Seven Dwarfs. Barry Sutton, a tall, lean ex-journalist, was one of the older hands in the squadron, and later wrote a book on its adventures through the Battle of Britain. Bob Constable-Maxwell had the distinction of flying with 56 in the Second World War, while his older brother had commanded the same squadron in the first World War. Peter Hillwood, Smythe and others were also active flying members of "B" Flight at this time. Mark Mounsden, who had also been posted incorrectly to 66 Squadron with me, was now in "A" Flight.

If I were superstitious, I would probably feel that fate began to frown on me when I decided to try and buy the deceased flight commander's car. Ian Soden's Ford V8 lay unattended in the garage behind the officers' Mess. My inquiries revealed that his family wished to dispose of it quickly in order to lessen tragic memories. My offer of five pounds was accepted. Inspection of the log book revealed that Soden had purchased the car from another pilot, now also deceased. Two weeks later, shortage of cash forced me to sell the car to Mark Mounsden. We were to remember our car at a later date.

At breakfast one morning Minny came over to where some of us were struggling with our dehydrated kippers. Leaning across the backs of our chairs he spoke in a modulated voice. "Fighter sweep over France – take-off ten-thirty, so be at dispersal by nine-forty-five."

Everybody nodded. My fork was halfway up to my mouth when suddenly my appetite left me and in place came a sickly feeling. Pushing away the greasy plate in distaste I concentrated on the large cup of sugarless tea. The tea and the excitement induced by Minny's announcement sent me off post haste to answer nature's call. The others ploughed steadily on with their breakfast.

During the period before reporting to dispersal I sat down in a comfortable armchair in the anteroom and attempted to digest the morning news. The situation, despite nonsensical statements of retiring to previously prepared positions, was beginning to look desperate. The German army was sweeping on like a tidal wave, and those British troops that were not surrounded at Dunkirk were retiring rapidly southwards to St. Valéry. Notwithstanding the written word in the newspaper in my lap, I couldn't associate myself with the struggle in Europe. I found it impossible to realize that at ten-thirty the squadron would be taking off to fly over the swiftly changing battlefields. Giving up the mental struggle, I let my mind wander over more personal matters.

What would my mother think if she knew what her precious son was about to undertake? "Poor Mother," I thought, "If anything happens to me on this trip she'll be heartbroken despite my being a pretty useless son." The urge filled me to write to her a long letter declaring my devoted love. Getting up from the chair, I crossed to the writing table and sat down. Beyond writing "My darling Mother," I was incapable of going on. Struggle as I did, the words seemed hollow and false as the sentences fashioned themselves in my mind. Eventually in disgust I tore up the notepaper and hurled it into the wastepaper basket. "I'll try again tomorrow," I thought, and strode out of the Mess. Arriving early at the dispersal point I found Minny was already busy organizing aircraft and pilots for the morning's sortie. As I came into the flight commander's office the handsome Russian glanced over his shoulder. "Ah, just the man I want to see. You'll be flying as Number 3 in my section. I'm leading the flight today, and Dopey'll be Number 2."

I immediately felt better at the thought of being with Minny. There was something very reassuring about his whole personality.

"By the way," he added, "There's an aircraft to be collected from the maintenance hangar. It will also be the one you'll fly today, so how about fetching it?"

Pleased at the opportunity to keep active until take-off time, I set out across the airfield towards the big hangars. I was delighted to find that the aircraft awaiting collection on the tarmac was the same new machine I'd flown the first day I joined the squadron. I climbed into the cockpit and taxied the aircraft over to the dispersal pens. After some of the older planes I'd flown, I hoped fervently that this one might be allocated to me permanently.

As the squadron commander was still away on leave, the "A" Flight commander was acting in his stead. A short, stocky man with a close-cropped bullet head, Flight Lieutenant "Slim" Coghlan looked more like one of the dreaded enemy than a fellow countryman. The six "B" Flight pilots selected for duty reported to the "A" Flight hut for briefing. This in itself was short and to the point. "Slim" Coghlan didn't believe in making speeches.

"There's a hell of a lot of activity in the Somme area which we're going to have a look at. Mind your tails and watch the sun."

On our way back to "B" Flight, Minny enlarged on the subject. "Our job is to sweep the area north of Dieppe and try and keep the Hun fighters away so that our troops on the ground can have a breathing spell. It's not much of a spell, I'm afraid; with our fuel reserves we can only stay in the area half-an-hour. If we do have to fight you'll be lucky to get back to England, so check your tanks carefully before coming back over the Channel."

Taffy Higginson, who was to lead the rear section of three, chipped in, "Where would you like my section, sir?"

"Five hundred feet above and keep yourself between me and the sun."

From that point onward I was too busy to be nervous. Emptying my pockets carefully, I donned a yellow Mae West and carried my parachute out to the waiting aircraft. Helpful hands from the ground crews lifted it up and deposited the carefully packaged bundle of silk inside the bucket-seat. Returning to the hut I stuffed maps into the side of my black leather flying boots and a miniature compass into a breast pocket. Such items could be useful in the event of being shot down over hostile territory and with a long walk ahead. Satisfied that I had everything, I gave the room a farewell glance and then stepped out into the warm sunshine. About to step up onto the aircraft wing I realized a sudden desire to urinate. Knowing that the opportunity wouldn't present itself for at least an hour and a half, the grass it had to be. Blushing slightly at the nearness of the ground crews, I attempted to glance nonchalantly about. To my amusement I saw that practically every pilot in the squadron was at an almost similar stage in the proceedings. This was my initiation into what fighter pilots term "a last quick nervous pee." Climbing swiftly up into the cockpit, willing hands soon passed the parachute and Sutton harness straps over my shoulders. With helmet on and oxygen mask clipped across my face, I primed the engine and then waited for the signal from Minny. Soon an arm raised itself aloft from the deputy flight commander's cockpit, and seconds later the "B" Flight machines roared into deafening life. Already "A" Flight was moving away from their dispersal pens to the top end of the airfield, and soon Minny followed with his two sections in their wake. The twelve taxiing machines looked like brown beetles crawling across the grass playing follow-my-leader, until the foremost insect stretched its wings and buzzed its way aloft. Minny turned his aircraft into wind preparatory to the take-off and I swung my Hurricane round so that my wing tip lay barely inches behind that of the section leader's. Dopey's machine took up its corresponding position on the other side. Raising a thumb to each of us in turn and getting a similar response, the Russian opened up his engine slowly and steadily and the three planes moved rapidly forward as if tied together. Gathering flying speed we left the ground simultaneously with spinning wheels retracting inwards and upwards.

In individual vee sections of three aircraft, the twelve machines wheeled southward and commenced the climb towards the distant French coastline. As the English shoreline passed beneath our wings so did we spread out among ourselves, allowing us to relax from the concentration of close formation flying, and to devote our concentration on searching for the unseen enemy.

For us young airmen winging our way over the Channel, life had abruptly taken on a new meaning. Gone for a while was the "eat, drink and be merry" attitude – the eating and drinking were over and "to-morrow" was now, perhaps "today". All that remained of youth in those swiftly moving Hurricanes were the physical attributes of our bodies, the minds were no longer carefree and careless. The sordid reality of all that our task implied banished lighter thoughts for the time being. Those of us who returned safely would don the mantle of youth once again and carry on with the roistering as if no interruption had taken place. To strangers from the other services and the civilian in the towns, our exuberant foolishnesses appeared as the indulged whims of spoiled children. Those same strangers could not see that beneath this safety valve of rowdiness were stretched the jagged nerves of young boys, old before their time. Instead of a legacy of peaceful playing fields and happy contented hours, ours was the heritage of blazing streaks marring the summer skies while tortured flesh bled for those at home. Surely our boisterous activities could be suffered for a short while by those so eager to criticize?

Midway across the Channel I was learning a painful lesson. To my acute discomfort I was discovering that you cannot wear a collar and tie and fly on operational sorties. The continuous twisting of the head to search the skies called for something less cutting than the sharp edge of a semi-starched collar. With one hand endeavouring to grope beneath the many incumbrances and so remove the offending article, the other one attempted to keep the aircraft flying on a level keel. At last, in desperation I ripped the collar away, tearing the shirt at the same time. Sliding the hood back I dedicated the piece of cloth to the clawing demands of the slipstream, and then sat back tired from the struggle in the confines of the cockpit. No sooner had I returned to the ceaseless vigil of searching the skies above, below, ahead and behind, when I became aware of a subtle change taking place in the behaviour of the other aircraft. Unable to account for it at first as no warning messages had come over the R/T, I frantically searched the tense air for the reason. Then I saw what it was. Out of the summer haze hanging low on the sea below us appeared the yellow cliffs of the French coastline to the north of Dieppe. The sight of this ravaged land held me fascinated until only by sheer effort did I manage to drag my eyes away and continue the sweeping search. It was then that I noticed the other two aircraft in the section had drawn ahead some considerable distance. The Hurricane responded instantaneously to the throttle and slowly the wide gap began to close.

By now the squadron had crossed in over the coast and the smoking town of Abbeville lay behind as the wheeling aircraft sped southwestwards.

Then I saw something that at first was difficult to puzzle out. The whole flight up to the present moment had taken place beneath clear blue skies, but here in front of us were appearing the biggest and darkest thunder clouds I'd ever seen. The central part of the ominous cloud seemed almost jet black and for the first time since our take-off an uneasy feeling akin to fear filled my body. Rapidly the distance between the Hurricanes and the threatening cloud diminished, and suddenly I caught my breath in astonishment as I realized the significance of the black clouds. This was no arrangement of nature, but the result of a gigantic blaze issuing forth from burning oil storage tanks thousands of feet below. The thick column of ebony smoke belched its way upwards until the cooling effect of the upper air spread it out in billowing dark grey-black clouds. Although astounded by the destruction taking place below, my thoughts were rudely shattered by an excited voice crackling into my earphones. "Look out! 109s above!"

Inside my aircraft the situation was almost pandemonium. Startled out of my wits for an instant by the verbal warning of enemy fighters, my mind had immediately gone blank and my brain refused to issue instructions. All I was capable of doing was to look wildly about the sky for the deadly enemy aircraft until a shock that practically stopped my heart brought my numb brain back to life. Losing sight of Minny's machine in the excitement, I inadvertently flew through the slipstream of his airplane, resulting in an enormous jolt to my own machine which to my inexperienced mind registered as enemy cannon shells finding their mark. Anti-climax came in the form of another R/T message. "It's O.K., they're Hurricanes." Later we learned that the "enemy" aircraft were from our sister Squadron 151 from North Weald, also out on a sweep.

Seconds later I was in trouble again. Our formation flew into the dense black smoke pall overhanging Dieppe, and when I emerged, it was to find the sky empty of other aircraft. Nowhere in the smoky haze could I spot the friendly outline of another Hurricane, and a lonely fear crept into my spirits. Flying along for a few more minutes in the vain hope of seeing the others, I eventually rolled over on my back and dived to the calm sea thousands of feet below. Levelling out, I streaked for home barely inches above the waveless swell of the

Channel. My first sortie over enemy-held territory was over. I had grown a little older.

The days that followed were similar in their pattern. Either we would accompany formations of Blenheim bombers across to France, in our pitiful attempt to check the onslaught of German might, or else we would sweep the areas approaching the Dunkirk beaches. With the extremely limited range of our aircraft we could do no more than put up a token showing of strength, and as soon as we turned homewards the Luftwaffe continued its attacks on our troops on the unprotected beaches.

Later I was often asked the belligerent question by our soldiers, "Where the hell was the R.A.F. at Dunkirk?" The answer was simple. We were there, but in time and numbers that could have little effect. Somewhere in this is a great moral lesson for those who scream disarmament without realizing its effects when you have to tight a fully-armed foe.

Two days later, for the first time in my life, I saw someone killed. It was one of those stupid accidents that have continued to destroy pilots since the earliest days of flying. I was standing outside the dispersal hut and saw it happen. Not being detailed for flying duties that afternoon, I had taken the opportunity to catch up with some of my overdue correspondence. Hearing a shout from one of the ground crew, I walked to the door in time to see three Hurricanes diving low over the airport. The lettering on the sides of the aircraft showed they belonged to 151 Squadron.

The three machines pulled out of the dive and climbed steeply into the sky, the two outside planes breaking away from the leader as they roared upwards. The right-hand aircraft commenced to roll as it broke away, but when it became inverted the nose dropped rapidly and it dived into the ground with a loud explosion. Appalled by the scene, the onlookers stood transfixed while a hideous column of fire rose from a field beyond the airfield boundary. Then we all began to run like wild men, crashing through the long grass and weeds. Overhead the remaining two airplanes circled like puzzled birds watching one of their own kind after it had plummeted to earth.

Logic penetrated through my brain and I stopped running. Com-

mon sense exerted itself and refused to accept any possibility of survival. The deed was done and all the running in the world wouldn't
piece together the pulp that had once been a human being.

In the distance the clanging bells of the fire engine and ambulance
sounded as they bounced across the airfield. I didn't really know what
it was that drove me onward towards the crackling funeral pyre. The
pilot hadn't been a particular friend of mine, but somehow there was
this insatiable desire to look at the bits and pieces.

The ambulance went by, the bell clanging of its own accord as the
clapper rocked back and forth with the effect of the uneven ground.
Passing through a gateway in the hedge it swayed its way over the field
and came to rest near the wreckage. Arriving muddy and breathless,
I joined the impotent group that watched the medical officer and orderlies, assisted by the firemen as they kicked the smoking pieces of
metal aside in search of ghastly remains.

After I'd stood there for a while I was aware of two definite reac-
tions to the scene before me. The first was one of slight nausea from
the combined smell of charred wreckage and burnt flesh. The other
sensation was more powerful than that of a queasy stomach. I realized
with surprise that the death of this recent companion didn't disturb
me very much. It was as if a wave of shock radiated out from the man-
gled debris, but just as it approached, the wave passed by on either
side leaving the senses high and dry on a little island, erected by nature
to protect the occupant from the drowning effect of the horror of the
event.

"Oh, my God!"

I turned to find a white-faced and breathless Dopey gazing at the
smouldering pieces, with shock in his eyes.

"How odd," I thought, "I've just passed you in years, Dopey. You're
affected by what you see, but I'm immune and they can't shock me
any more." I didn't stop to wonder who "they" were. "How about a
drink?" I was surprised at the casualness in my own voice. Dopey's
eyes turned on me in surprise, which slowly changed to comprehen-
sion. For a second they flicked back to the tragic scene, then turning
abruptly and grabbing my elbow, he led us both away.

In the bar we practiced the noble art of medicine. We knew the sickness and the remedy. "Ailment – death of a close friend or companion: remedy – wash the brain wound well with alcohol until the infected area becomes numb to the touch. Continue the treatment until the wound closes. A scar will remain, but this will not show after a while."

The two doctors carried out the treatment until the probing shadowy fingers of twilight reached along the dewy grass, and caressed the jagged edges of the man-made fissure in the gentle English field.

Eight

Dunkirk was over and already history was turning the brilliant evacuation into a glorious victory, such was and is the power of wishful thinking. Victory and retreat are incompatible words. The remnants of the proud British Army returned to the homeland to lick their honourable wounds, and to curse the R.A.F. and politicians in the same breath.

The pilots of 56 Squadron were tired. Day after day during the Dunkirk period we had been called upon to rise after four hours of troubled sleep by the hateful sound of the shrill telephone. Our increasingly jangled nerves were becoming more and more sensitive to the shrill note of the ringing bells. Rising from our beds and groping a way through the night to the dispersal aircraft, we sat shivering in the cockpits warming up the engines in case of an emergency call. Although the days of continuous urgent summonses had not yet arrived, the situation called for constant preparedness. Hardly had our sleepy heads returned to the coarse blankets, than a commanding voice would warn us of an imminent operation to take place on the other side of the Channel. Again that cruel hand would seize our very insides and twist them slowly so that the anticipated breakfast became a sick-making sight, and strong tea the only item a nervous stomach would accept.

Day followed day of flying long distances over water to hostile shores, knowing that if the enemy chose to fight that regardless of the outcome, gas reserves were hardly sufficient to complete the homeward journey. Nerves that were frayed cried out, "Let the soldiers do their own damn fighting, this is none of our affair."

Next morning the jagged nerves climbed back into the aircraft knowing that the cold and miserable men huddling on the wet beaches had to be helped, even if the assistance bordered on the pitiful.

Then it was over.

The feeling was one of relief. No longer were the agile aircraft tied by invisible bonds of loyalty to the tiny specks on the beaches far below. It was now a fight of kind against kind, and pride rather than patriotism, the driving force behind the determination to vanquish the foe.

The fate of the country now lay in the hands of those young men spurned before the war for their fast cars and glamorous women. Unmindful of the criticism that had been poured upon us, we took to the air with eagerness, leaving beneath us, in every sense, the factory worker insisting on his rise in pay – or else! A far greater reward than money lay in the heavens above. Ours was to be the glorious prize of cleaving a way through the skies on flashing silver wings, killing and being killed in the manner of ancient knights tilting in the lists, reaping not the empty applause of posterity, but the excitement and thrill that made a short lifetime worth living.

The squadron commander never came back from his leave: he had been posted to a non-operational unit. Slim Coghlan was ordered to carry on until a replacement arrived, and it was he who summoned the pilots as the "release" signal came through after nightfall, to make the longest speech of his career. Standing with one foot on top of the empty stove he called for silence. He got it. Around him pale faces and dark ringed eyes told a clear story of the twenty-hour working day . . . that had become their lot for longer than their tired brains cared to remember.

Coghlan looked around at the unkempt crowd about him, before breaking into a wry smile. "How would you chaps like a lovely holiday with breakfast in bed every morning?"

Our tired eyes lit up as they looked eagerly at one another.

Coghlan continued. "The powers that be think that because we've put up a fairly good show, we're to have our breakfast sent down here to the huts every morning from the Mess!" Incredulous expressions registered on our faces. "In fact, they insist that we have every meal down here just so that we can be near our lovely little airplanes all day and all night."

The sarcasm of the senior flight commander's remarks dropped heavily. "Steady, old man! When do we get some time off?" one of the airmen asked.

He laughed sourly. "By the look of it you'll get time off when the war's over or you're dead."

Taffy twirled his bushy moustache and squeaked, "That won't be long, I'm half-dead already."

When the laughter had subsided Slim continued. "Apart from the usual procedure of being at readiness from half an hour before first light to half an hour after last light, we are to have one section at readiness throughout the night. There will also be night-flying practice for all concerned. The remainder of your spare time is yours to spend as you will."

A tremendous groan followed this pronouncement until a realist chimed in, "How do we get any beer?"

The problem was solved rapidly, and the aircrew transport was dispatched to the Mess to bring back crates of beer.

The Battle of Britain had begun.

Nine

Returning to the Mess one evening after a rare day off visiting my mother and sister in London, I learned that Minny had been killed in action that same morning. Somehow the news didn't register in my mind, but somewhere deep inside was a numb pain. It couldn't be said that we had become close friends, but his death was another stab into the dying body of my own youth.

Ereminsky's death spurred the authorities into posting a new flight commander to "B" Flight. Dopey Davies, Barry Sutton and I were standing in the sunshine outside our dispersal hut, when Flight Lieutenant Gracie waddled in our direction.

"Looks just like a baby elephant," muttered Barry.

Dopey clapped him on the back delightedly. "When he gets up to us, let's all shout 'Jumbo.' Are you ready? One – two – three – JUMBO!"

Barry had winked at me, and we remained silent as Dopey roared out the new nickname. However, it was to stick, and he carried the title until his death three years later.

Gracie was far from being the popular conception of a fighter pilot. Fat and pasty, with a high-pitched voice, he was more of a Billy Bunter than a knight of the air. For tenacity of purpose in his pursuit of the enemy he had few equals.

One night, through the veil of sleep I could hear muffled voices and stealthy footsteps. The faint gleam from a masked torch broke the blackness of the night in the dispersal hut. I struggled back to consciousness to make out Gracie's rotund figure at the end of the hut. The duty airman was handing him a mug of tea filled from a large urn. Obviously something unusual was happening.

"What's up, Jumbo?" asked Barry Sutton.

Someone switched the lights on, and tea was passed round. Jumbo took several quick sips of tea before replying. "We're off to Manston to do forward 'readiness'. There's a big convoy going through the Straits of Dover, and Command reckons Jerry will have a crack at it."

No one spoke for several minutes, then someone asked, "Are we coming back here tonight?"

"Don't know, anything may happen." Gracie looked at each of us in turn before speaking. "Our orders are to maintain strict R/T silence on our way to Manston. Anyone disobeying that order needn't bother about their future in the Air Force, because they won't have one!" He looked at his watch. "Five minutes to press-tits."

We drained our mugs before stamping out into the darkness. Dim flashing lights showed us where the erks* were getting the aircraft prepared. I walked quickly out to my machine. Fortune had been kind to me and I had managed to retain X for X-ray as my own aircraft. In my mind the plane was already christened "Little Willie".

An erk was standing near the wing shining a helpful ray of light on to the footstep. "Nice night for a spot of flying, sir."

I looked up into the sky for the first time and noticed that the heavens were pin-pricked with a myriad of winking little lights. I laughed shortly. "There's only one place to be at night, and that's in bed."

"What's bed, sir?" the airman asked with seeming innocence.

There was no answer to that and we both laughed together. Ground and air crews were both suffering from lack of sleep. Enthusiasm was at its lowest ebb as I strapped myself into the seat by the dim orange glow of the cockpit lights. A dull tiredness pervaded my body and the thought of seeing action later in the day meant little at this moment. Reproaching myself at being tired didn't help very much either. "After all," I thought, "What have I got to be tired about? A dozen flights over France without getting a chance to shoot at anything. What are you, man or mouse?" I couldn't put it into words at the time, but nervous tension was having its fatiguing influence on all of us.

Purple flames stabbed the darkness as Jumbo's engine roared into life, quickly followed by the echoing thunder of the five other aircraft rending the night assunder with violent sound. All six machines switched on their formation lights as we taxied out to the take-off position. Jumbo led the first section of three machines, and Dopey led the second section.

Detailed to fly in the number two position on Dopey's right, I fol-

*Affectionate pilot terminology for ground crew.

lowed my leader across the grass. Close behind came Sergeant Hill-wood, completing our trio in the second section. "A" Flight was to fol-low twenty minutes later to allow "B" Flight time to refuel and be at readiness before they landed, thus allowing six machines to be avail-able at all times. A vague thought passed through my mind as my air-craft raced across the grass in tight formation with the other two. "Here I am," I reflected, "going off to war in a Hurricane and I've never even flown one at night before." Fortunately my brain was too dulled to be very impressed by the fact, and with blind faith I concentrated on keeping position with my section leader. If I kept my wing two feet away from Dopey's throughout the journey I was bound to land intact at Manston – it was as easy as that!

After a while the coldness of the night air began to penetrate the warm cockpit and helped to keep me awake. Below our swift flying fighters the English countryside lay asleep. Neither hamlet nor town showed a glimmer of light and suddenly I became wide awake with a feeling of immense pride. "They trust us," I reasoned. "They trust us to look after them just as a little child goes to sleep secure in the knowledge of its parents' guardianship." The sensation felt good.

For the next ten minutes my mind remained blank as I automati-cally concentrated on keeping formation. Then the cold began to creep into my body and with surprise I noticed the altimeter reading twelve thousand feet, and we were still climbing. Normally we would fly the relatively short distance from North Weald to Manston at two or three thousand feet and our present, ever-increasing altitude didn't make much sense. We had been briefed to maintain strict R/T silence, so there was little else to do but curse Dopey and the cold night air.

At fifteen thousand feet we levelled out and then immediately commenced a steep dive towards the murky outline of the Thames Estuary.

Minutes later the white identification lights on Dopey's plane flashed the letter of the day, and I knew we had arrived over Manston. Glancing quickly downwards I was able to discern the feeble flickering rays of the flares on the airfield below. Hillwood's luminous exhausts floated beneath me as the sergeant moved from one side of the for-mation to the other, forming echelon starboard for the landing. Gracefully Dopey led us round the circuit, coming in for a neat touchdown on the undulating airfield, and soon we were taxiing rapidly to the waving light beckoning us towards the waiting gas bowsers.

Thankfully we switched off, and cold, numb and tired, we crawled from the cockpits. A duffle-coated engineering officer supervising the refuelling came up and told us of the breakfast awaiting in the nearby hut. Our visions of steaming platters of ham and eggs with hot coffee were rudely shattered on entering the dismal hut illuminated by a solitary lantern. On the rickety wooden table stood two thermos cans, one with lukewarm baked beans and the other containing tepid tea. Thick slices of bread and margarine on tin plates completed the repast. Two wooden kitchen chairs comprised the remainder of the furnishings in the wooden building.

Jumbo's piles, which formed the main part of his conversation when not discussing the enemy, were obviously giving him hell. He was in a foul mood.

"Where the bloody hell have you been?" he addressed Dopey. "We landed twenty minutes ago and you were meant to be behind me."

Then Dopey confessed. Leading our section on take-off, he concentrated his gaze on the white navigation light on the rudder of Jumbo's aircraft, or so he thought. He had, in fact, picked out a bright star as a focal point, and it wasn't until we got to fifteen thousand feet that he realized we'd never catch up with the shining white light in front!

Dopey had lived up to his name.

Dawn found the six of us wearily attempting to keep warm by walking around near the parked aircraft. Sleep was out of the question, as apart from the damp grass or the cold drafty hut floor, there was no place to rest our tired bodies. Four hundred yards away "A" Flight were being refuelled from the grey bowsers. The thump-thump-thump of the delivery pump came clearly to our ears on the crisp morning air. The breaking day promised to be clear to start with, but low woolly clouds were beginning to form a few miles away where sea and land met at the coast. The sun rose brightly in the east bringing its rays of warmth to us as we kept our early morning vigil.

Suddenly the crack of the Very pistol, followed by the soaring flight of two fiery red balls, brought about frantic action. The telephone orderly who'd fired the warning signal from the hut, yelled hoarsely, "Scramble 'B' Flight, Angels 10."*

Feverishly we strapped ourselves into the aircraft, assisted by the ground crews. A minute later the engines burst into life almost simultaneously, and without bothering about wind direction, Jumbo roared away across the grass and into the air. I followed behind with Barry. The second section led by Taffy was hot on our heels. Climbing up behind Jumbo with as much power as the engine would permit for a long haul, I prepared myself for action should it come. Carefully I switched on the gunsight, camera gun, and turned the firing button to "fire".

Then the ground controller's voice came to us clearly over the R/T. The suppressed excitement in his voice was apparent as we raced skywards with everything strained. "Ninety bandits approaching from Calais. Yorker BlueLeader. Twenty plus at about Angels six, remainder Angels twelve, over."

Jumbo's squeaky voice acknowledged the fantastic message. "Roger, Blue Leader listening out . . . Yorker Blue and Green, line astern – go."

The two sections immediately formed for the attack in line astern behind their respective leaders. Positioning myself behind and beneath Jumbo's tail, I had time only to think, "Six of us against ninety, hardly fair odds for someone going into his first fight. Why the devil don't they send up another squadron to give us a helping hand?"

My reflections were cut short by Jumbo's voice. "Bandits eleven o'clock above and below, about ten miles . . . Yorker Green One, you take the gaggle below and we'll look after the lot up top . . . Blue Leader over."

"Roger, and the best of luck." The sarcastic humour in Taffy's voice came clearly over the air.

The trips I had made over the Continent during the collapse of France had helped me train my eyes to pick out vital details, but it wasn't until Taffy's voice had finished that I spotted the enemy aircraft and the convoy steaming serenely below. Out of the corner of my eye I spotted the three machines of the other section diving to intercept

*In R/T parlance "Angels" signified height per thousand feet. Angels ten were, therefore ten thousand feet.

the now clearly visible formation of twenty Heinkel 111 bombers. Then I saw the fighter escort we were to engage. There was no mistaking the ugly outlines of the thirty Messerschmitt 110 twin-engine fighters, and above these another formation of about forty Messerschmitt 109s with their big spinners and wicked rakish lines.

My mouth went completely dry.

By this time our three Hurricanes had managed to climb above the level of the twin-engined Me. 110s, but we were still below the single seater Me. 109s.

Jumbo dived, leading us to attack the Me. 110 fighters below. As my machine gathered speed I noticed a strange occurrence. The Me. 110s were forming up into a defensive circle to protect themselves from the oncoming attack from our three British planes. Being uncertain as to the best way to assail this orbiting group, I decided to spray the area near two of the enemy before diving through the centre of the circle. The eight Browning machine guns chattered away happily in the wings when the firing button was pressed, and for a moment I was having the time of my life.

The enjoyment ceased the instant half the enemy rear gunners opened fire at my diving fighter. Fascinated for a second by the appearance of orange glowing electric light bulbs suspended in the air, I suddenly ducked my head at the frightening realization that the pretty little balls of fire were hundreds of deadly machine gun bullets aimed at Geoffrey Page personally.

Raising a timid head again I found I'd dived through the lethal zone. Climbing the Hurricane vertically I positioned myself for the second attack. This was executed with more discretion, and I dived at the circling formation again, but this time almost head on and in the opposite direction of flight to the enemy. Through lack of experience I began shooting wildly at the Me. 110s, but nonetheless achieved the object of making the enemy break formation.

At that point the fight became a nightmare. The forty Me. 109s came streaking down out of the sun to finish off the impertinent British fighters, and for the next few minutes I registered nothing but flashing wings bearing Iron Crosses and streaks of tracer searing the sunlit sky. Firing constantly but always a little too late, the satisfaction of seeing my bullets strike home was never realized.

For a moment the skies seemed to clear save for a solitary 109 circling towards my Hurricane in the distance. Both of us sensed the challenge and hurled our aircraft head on at each other, the distance between us closing with frightening rapidity as I sat intrigued by the winking lights appearing on the leading edge of the enemy's wing. Then realizing the German was firing I returned the compliment, but again too late. Both our aircraft roared by within inches of each other and I found myself almost alone over the Channel. The only other human being in sight was swinging seawards at the end of a mushrooming parachute, making his relentless progress towards the cold waters below.*

Circling the defenceless parachutist I attempted to contact ground control to send out a rescue launch. Silence greeted the several attempts at transmission, so trying to fix the position of the figure that was now struggling in the water, I dived back to Manston.

On entering the circuit I was quick to notice a pall of white smoke rising from a corner of the airfield. Nearby stood the fire engine and ambulance. Remembering the swimming figure in the sea, I landed hastily and taxied back to the place I'd left a lifetime ago. Barry Sutton greeted me. "How'd you get on, did you get any?"

"I fired at a hell of a lot but never saw any strikes," I replied.

Barry patted me on the shoulder in a fatherly manner. "Better luck next time, but that's not too bad. We got five for the loss of one machine."

"Who's had it?"

---

*Seventeen years later this extract of the same head-on attack appeared in the "Luftwaffe Diaries," quoted by the German pilot, Dau. "Dau, after shooting down a Spitfire, had seen a Hurricane turn in towards him. It then came straight at him, head-on and at the same height. Neither of them budged an inch, both fired their guns at the same instant, then missed a collision by a hair's breath. But while the German's fire was too low, that of the British pilot. 'A.G. Page of 56 Squadron' connected. Dau felt his aircraft shaken by violent thuds. It had been hit in the engine and rudder and he saw a piece of one wing come off. At once his engine started to seize up emitting a white plume of steaming glycol. "The coolant temperature rose quickly to 120°," he reported "The whole cockpit stank of burnt insulation. But I managed to stretch my glide to the coast, then made a belly landing close to Boulogne. As I jumped out, the machine was on fire and within seconds ammunition and fuel went up with a bang".

Barry laughed. "Don't look so worried. No one's dead. Jumbo had to crash land back here after his coolant system was hit, but he's O.K."

I remembered the white column of smoke I'd seen when flying round the circuit. Then excusing myself I ran to the phone and told Group about the pilot down in the Straits of Dover. The controller asked several pertinent questions before requesting me to take off in an attempt to locate the man in the drink. A rescue launch was being dispatched from Ramsgate.

Ten minutes later, my aircraft refuelled, I took off to assist in the rescue. Climbing away to the south I could see the broad wake of the high speed rescue boat already on its way out of Ramsgate Harbour. Soon my lonely Hurricane reached the spot where the parachutist had entered the water, but half an hour's search revealed nothing.

It was then that I spotted two aircraft several thousand feet above, moving in my direction from the enemy-held coast. Remembering that there hadn't been time to reload the guns, I dived down onto the water and pointed my nose towards Dover. Homewards I sped to the safety of the protective coastline – or so I was foolish enough to think. Getting within a mile of Dover Harbour a storm of light anti-aircraft fire came tearing up from the guns of the Royal Navy by way of welcome.

Besides the lack of ammunition for the Hurricane's machine guns, I recalled that the R/T was also useless, preventing me from sending a message to the rescue launch telling them of my failure to locate the pilot and to warn them of the two aircraft patrolling the Channel. Already the trim little craft was setting out bravely from the security of the home waters on its humane mission.

Quickly catching up with the vessel, I was at a loss as to how to impart the message to the men below. The next few minutes would have done credit to Houdini. Struggling beneath the straps and equipment I finally produced a pencil and the inside of a cigarette package while the airplane performed frightening gyrations near the surface of the water.

Laboriously the message was written, but then came the problem of dropping it to those below. The contortions that followed in the little cockpit left me in a muck sweat, but finally in triumph I removed one of my socks to act as a message container.

Coming up as slowly as possible behind the boat, I threw the sock over the side aiming to drop it ahead of the speeding launch. Luck was prevailing and the boat hove-to and retrieved the missive. To the exchange of hand waving and wing waggling, this exhausted pilot headed thankfully back to Manston.

Taxiing in to the dispersal point I found Jumbo and the other four pilots digging into a hot snack on the sunny grass. Joining the chatting group I picked up the thread of the conversation. Taffy was doing the talking. "Speaking of films," he was saying, "there's supposed to be a hell of an exciting film at the local flic house about submarines."

Dopey shook his head wonderingly. "Submarines! Now there's an awful way to earn a living."

Ten

As darkness fell that evening our eleven Hurricanes took off from Manston in the failing light to return to North Weald after an eventful seventeen-hour day. A few minutes after setting course for our home base, an unidentified voice crackled over the R/T. "How about opening up the taps, Red Leader. The local pub closes in twenty minutes." The formation leader didn't acknowledge the message, but the forward speed of the squadron increased noticeably immediately afterwards.

Eighteen minutes later eleven young men were standing in the bar of the King's Head quaffing pints of beer and flirting mildly with the W.A.A.F. operations girls relaxing in their off-duty moments.

After a couple of pints apiece the landlord called "Time." Thereupon Taffy's Welsh voice raised itself above the hubbub in the crowded little bar. "All aboard for the Skylark. Esmerelda leaves for London in five minutes."

Artificial groans greeted the announcement. "Not tonight Taffy. Give it a rest or it'll drop off!"

"Count me out. I'm too tired."

"That makes two of us."

Five minutes later eleven young men piled into Esmerelda and headed for the London night clubs. Four hours later we were due to be back at "Readiness" on the airfield.

The "B" Flight pilots refought the morning's air battle for the twentieth time while our "A" Flight colleagues listened in dismal silence. To their undying disgust their machines hadn't been refuelled in time to take part in the interception.... However, they had been the first to congratulate the six of us on our success at preventing the convoy from being attacked and causing the enemy to head for home in a hurry.

Soon the dim lights of the big city began to appear through the black night as Esmerelda chugged along protestingly through the dark streets. Almost without being steered, Es. headed for the "Bag of Nails," a nightclub of dubious quality often frequented by the squadron. A large garage off Regent Street accepted Esmerelda and our cheerful group noisily marched off to the "Bag."

Handing our caps to the cigarette girl who was wrapped mainly in her own thoughts, the group moved through hanging curtains in the direction of harsh dance music from the room beyond. The parting curtains revealed a scene familiar in most of the nightclubs of the world. A band of bored pasty-faced players sitting on a dias, a dance floor the size of a postage stamp, small tables illuminated by subdued lamps and customers in various stages of intoxication, helped on their way by blasé hostesses.

… Being established clientele and free with our money, our party was conducted to a comfortable table alongside the dance floor. Hardly had we been seated than four hostesses slinked their way across the room to greet us by our first names.

Bottles appeared with amazing rapidity and their contents disappeared at the same speed. I found myself next to a voluptuous brunette in a scarlet evening dress … which for some inexplicable reason boasted two enormous pockets at waist level. Taffy sitting on the other side of the hostess, took in the well-filled dress with appraising glances. To nobody in particular he remarked with an American twang, "It must be jelly'cos jam don't shake like that."

Unhesitatingly she reached up and tweaked one of the flowing moustaches. "Anything I possess serves a useful purpose," she said sarcastically.

"As earmuffs, I suppose," Taffy countered.

I felt it was time to intervene to keep the peace. "If you want my opinion, everything I can see looks all right."

The N.C.O. was a little drunk by now and once again he slipped into American jargon. "Shake on it, pardner, I agree."

Looking down in the gloomy light, I saw a large hand presented for me to shake. What surprised me was that the wrist appeared out of the girl's voluminous pocket nearest to me. Tracing the arm back. I saw that it entered the dress from the pocket on the other side. She didn't appear to be disturbed by what was going on, and turned and talked to me for the first time.

"I haven't seen you before. Are you new to the squadron?"

Our conversation started off with polite generalities, and a short while later we slipped away to dance on the crowded floor. I was thankful that the floor space was limited as it enabled me to shuffle about without demonstrating the limitations of my dancing capabilities.

By the time we arrived at the garage to collect Esmerelda, the whole group had joined the Welsh pilot in a series of bawdy Air Force songs. Sweeping into the garage we piled into Esmerelda, with the exception of the bald-headed Smythe. Sergeant Smythe, despite a slightly intoxicated condition, was still very much interested in all things mechanical, and the sight of a dismantled headlight on a nearby car proved to be too much. The bits and pieces of the headlamp lay carefully arranged along the bonnet, and one by one he picked them up for inspection. Just as he was in the act of replacing the bulb a voice close by bellowed, "Hey, you! What' jer think yer doin?"

Startled by the shout Smythe turned and he let go of the bulb and an instant later it lay shattered on the concrete floor of the garage. The bewildered little man scratched the top of his bald pate as the irate garage attendant approached with arms akimbo.

"Now look what yer've ruddy well done:"

"Sorry, chum," the apologetic sergeant replied. "Here's five bob. Buy a new bulb and get yourself a pint at the same time."

"Five bob," exclaimed the man testily. "There's a quid's worth of damage there."

Smythe was genuinely sorry about his actions, but he resented being "done." Taking out a ten shilling note he offered it to the attendant. "There's three times as much as the damned bulb's worth. Now does that make you happy, mate?"

Spluttering and banging in the background, Esmerelda roared into life.

"I've told you wot it'll cost to replace it," snarled the man, "One quid."

Esmerelda chugged her way towards the garage exit.

"Ten bob or nothing," insisted the bald-headed sergeant.

"A pound, or I'll have the law on yer."

Cries from the disappearing car reached the two arguing men. "Come on Smythey – pull your finger out."

Sergeant Smythe pocketed the note and produced a half-crown in its place which he slammed on the bonnet of the car. "That's what the damn thing's worth, and you're lucky to get that."

With that the chubby little pilot took to his heels out of the garage, hotly pursued by the livid garage attendant. Fifty yards down the road Esmerelda snorted her way along slowly, as the occupants shouted words of encouragement to the puffing Smythe who was being over-hauled rapidly by his brawny pursuer.

Willing hands dragged him head first into the chugging car and Taffy crashed his way through the gears, leaving the fist-shaking figure standing impotently in the middle of the road.

Everybody seized the opportunity on the journey back to snatch a little sleep, including the driver. It happened fortunately, that every time Taffy nodded off over the wheel Barry sitting next to him woke up and carried out some remote steering. Ten minutes before first light Esmerelda chugged to a dutiful halt before the challenging sentry at the main gate.

"Halt! Who goes there?"

"Santa Claus, eight reindeer and a couple of other silly buggers."

"Pass friends!"

Esmerelda chugged off towards the dispersal point, and the war was on again.

Eleven

It felt to me as if I'd hardly put on my pyjamas and lain down, than the telephone shrilled its harsh note throughout the hut. Discipline overcame the yearning desire to turn over and cover my head with the blanket. Dutifully I sat up in bed, hoping that it was merely a routine message being passed through from Sector Control. The slam of the phone receiver followed by the thump of the orderly's urgent footsteps told their own tale, and before the message was shouted out, I was struggling into the ever-ready flying boots.

"Scramble Blue section. Vector zero nine zero, Angels 18."

A flurry of sound came from two other dark shapes in the room where Jumbo and Barry were scrambling into their flying kit. Cursing at myself for being a fool for staying out so late in the nightclub and for changing into pyjamas, I ran out towards my airplane clad only in flying boots and a Mae West over the poplin night apparel. Despite the fatigue clogging my brain, I went through the ritual of getting strapped in and starting the engine. The process was automatic.

A smear of light tore by in the night that was slowly turning to dawn, as Jumbo took off across the narrow portion of the airfield. Barry roared past a second later and disappeared into the half-light. Blindly following their lead I opened my throttle wide and the willing Hurricane raced across the grass in eager pursuit.

A last rumble of the wheels and she was airborne. Sitting in the cockpit surrounded by a false calmness, I automatically raised the wheels and adjusted the engine and propeller controls for the long climb ahead. "Better have a look and see where the others are ... My God!"

Violently I banked the plane over on its side as one of the towering masts from the nearby radio station flashed by inches away from the port wing. Sweat broke out underneath my tight-fitting helmet, and I was fully awake for the first time since the telephone had rung in the hut.

Recovering composure and settling the machine on the ordered course of 90°, I looked ahead for signs of my two companions. The next instant I was in cloud and had to concentrate on the blind flying instruments.

Emerging three minutes later at ten thousand feet, I found the night had departed and the new day had arrived at the higher altitude. Ahead and to one side were the friendly outlines of the other two Hurricanes silhouetted against another cloud layer several thousand feet above.

The calm voice of the controller came clearly through the headphones. "One bandit – Angels 18 on vector two seven zero –maintain your present course Blue Leader."

Jumbo's sleepy voice acknowledged the message.

I was wide awake. With chattering teeth I thought, "What a stupid way to fight a war, eighteen thousand feet up wearing pyjamas. Why the devil can't that damned Hun come over at a gentlemanly height?"

Now the controller's voice was urgent. "One thousand feel above you Blue Leader and very near."

Instinctively the three of us, now fairly close together, looked up. The text book interception had been carried out, for at that instant the twin-engined Junker's 88 dived out of the cloud layer above.

Swiftly our fighters turned to chase our quarry, hoping that he would stay out of cloud sufficiently long to allow us to close the gap. The German pilot spotted his pursuers and either from arrogance or ignorance, decided to outpace the Hurricanes to the safety of the cloud layer below, rather than retreating to the protecting cover so short a way above. The four machines tore downwards and with the natural prerogative of the leader Jumbo opened the attack. From a position on the flank awaiting my turn to attack, I could see that the distance between attacker and attacked was too great to allow for accurate marksmanship. Expending his ammunition, Jumbo broke away and Barry joined with the enemy.

The haven of cloud layer rushed up towards the diving Ju. 88. In my cockpit I thumped a knee with schoolboyish excitement. The excitement died in a flash as the second Hurricane broke off the attack and I realized that the enemy aircraft was still in one piece and that now it was up to me.

My mouth went dry as it had done before that first fight. Turning sharply in to carry out the attack my mind flashed back to the first engagement which now seemed a lifetime ago. Then I remembered that it was only yesterday. The eight machine guns broke out in their muffled chatter. One second we were flying in clear sky, and the next we were groping through the misty world of cloudland. Ahead of me I could still make out the faint blur of the enemy aircraft as the range between us closed rapidly. A thump warned me that my own aircraft had been hit. Bearing a blinding resentment for anyone foul enough to hurt my beloved machine, I kept the firing button pressed until comparative silence and the hiss of escaping air told me that ammunition was expended.

Kicking on rudder and breaking away from the engagement, I dived out of the cloud to find myself a few miles out to sea off the coast near Clacton. Then for the first time for several minutes I registered the urgent voice calling over the R/T. "Hello, Blue three – Blue one here – are you receiving?"

Composing myself I answered lazily. "Loud and clear, Blue one – Blue three over."

The relief in Jumbo's voice was obvious. "Good show. How'd you get on Blue three?"

"Quite a few strikes, Blue one, but he was still flying when I left him – Blue three out."

"Roger, Blue three – return to base."

Disappointedly I turned my airplane landwards and headed for home. Gloom and remorse filled my mind. "An enemy aircraft fifty yards away," I thought, "and you can't shoot the damned thing down. What will the rest of the squadron say when they hear that the three of you couldn't shoot down one lone weather reconnaissance machine?"

The controller's voice interrupted my thoughts. "Hello, Blue Leader – your bandit has been reported as crash landing on the coast near Clacton. Well done!"

One of the three Hurricanes returning to its base rolled continuously for the last forty miles of its journey in sheer delight.

We learned later that the rear gunner died from mortal wounds, as one of us had shot off one of his arms. The rest of the crew survived.

After an uneventful morning the following day, the squadron was ordered to take off and proceed to Hawkinge airport on the south Kent coast for refuelling. As usual Slim Coghlan led the Squadron, and Jumbo Gracie in "B" Flight brought up the rear six machines.

The ground organization was excellent. Hardly had the first Hurricane switched off its engine, than the gas bowser drew up in front and poured fuel into the thirsty tanks. Transport was waiting, and within ten minutes of landing we were seated in the officers' and sergeants' Messes enjoying a large tea. To all the questions put to him, Jumbo gave the same reply, "Haven't got a clue, old boy. Your guess is as good as mine as to why we're here."

A fatherly intelligence officer watched over our physical needs. As soon as he'd seen that we had had enough tea he guided us back to the airplanes. Lying on the grass in the soft summer evening with the birds twittering in the hedgerows and trees nearby, the war seemed very far away to me.

In spite of the ever-present spectre of death, I knew that this present life I was leading was the pleasantest I'd ever known. That strange bond, unknown in peacetime, that draws men together in times of physical danger had me in its grip, and I loved my fellow pilots. The idea of laying down my life to save one of them presented no problems right at this moment. An objective glance at my own life brought only confusing answers. "After all," I thought, "what is a life spent flying fast airplanes, drinking too much and sleeping too little, worth in the end?" It wasn't as if the company I kept was particularly intelligent – remarks varied little from the basic "wizard," "good show," "bang on" and other Air Force terminologies, but somehow I knew that it all added up to drinking the red wine of youth – enjoying it to the full while it lasted, which wasn't long. So much of the blood-red wine was spilling on the ground from the blue vapour-trailed sky above.

The I.O. came back in his little van and told Slim his orders. The squadron was to take off and patrol the French coast near Calais at twelve thousand feet. Five minutes later the twelve brown and green camouflaged machines taxied out and took off in sections of three. Barry, myself and Peter Hillwood formed the first "B" Flight section, and Taffy and his section brought up the rear.

The evening was calm and the air smooth as we climbed on the journey towards enemy held shores. In keeping with the evening, the placid voice of the controller came floating through the air from the friendly coast we were leaving behind. He had nothing specific to tell us, but suggested that we sweep southwards from Calais keeping about three miles out to sea. The atmosphere created by these instructions suggested that the controller was working on either secret information or guesswork, with the hope of surprising some enemy aircraft. Fifteen minutes of fruitless eye straining brought no rewards.

Then the controller's voice came sharply to our ears. "Turn 180° back to Calais, Red Leader. Something's going on there – that's all I can tell you."

Swiftly the Hurricanes wheeled about onto the reciprocal course and the speed of the formation increased rapidly. I closed in a little nearer to Barry and quickly checked my gunsight, camera and firing button. Seven minutes of strained flying followed until suddenly the cry went out.

"Tally ho – there they are – 12 o'clock ahead."

Ahead of us and slightly below were nine Junkers' 87 Stuka dive bombers setting out from the French coast in the direction of England. The shark's nose, gull wings, and claw-like undercarriage lent them a predatory air. As the twelve Hurricanes dived to the attack a warning voice called out, "Watch it, fighters above." I looked up swiftly and saw the twelve enemy Me. 109 fighters flying above and behind the formation of Stukas.

I caught my breath in astonishment on realizing that the enemy hadn't yet spotted the attacking British fighters. The Stuka formation flew calmly onwards.

From my position in the third section I had an excellent view of Slim's initial attack. The dive bomber selected by the Hurricane Leader emitted a large puff of smoke which was followed by orange flames. Gracefully the Ju. 87 dropped slowly away from the rest of the formation. There was a momentary period of inaction until the enemy aircraft realized what had caused the annihilation of their companion, then with one accord they jettisoned their wicked load of bombs before rolling on their backs and diving vertically for the grey sea beneath. The Hurricanes were immediately among them like a pack of yapping and snapping foxhounds.

I rolled my machine over on its back, pulled the stick hard into my stomach and aileron turned vertically downwards onto the tail of an 87. Sighting quickly I fired a long burst at the Stuka. "Take that, you dirty bastard, for Minny," I yelled into the oxygen mask.

A large piece flew off the German aircraft, but I was unable to notice the extent of the damage as my rapidly accelerating fighter dived past the slow bomber. Pulling out low over the water I looked about for another target to attack. Spotting a Me. 109 fighter turning in the distance at the same height, I closed the range to give battle. Our two machines circled warily like boxers in a ring sizing each other up.

Intent on watching my adversary, I didn't realize the presence of another enemy fighter until the white streaks of the tracer bullet flashed past the cockpit. Throwing my machine into a tight turn I pulled out of the lethal zone of fire and looked about for friendly assistance. None was visible.

Still turning tightly, I quickly checked the contents of my gas tanks and realized it was high time to head for the invisible shores of England. The two enemy aircraft had other ideas on the subject. Knowing that the Hurricane had used up a considerable amount of fuel already, they were content to climb up a few hundred feet and wait. Whenever I straightened out to fly home, they dived down from their advantageous position with the idea of sitting on my tail. This meant my Hurricane had to turn each time to meet the new attack without perceptibly getting any nearer to home. As I turned for the fifth time to meet the attacking Messerschmitts, I spotted a grey shape out of the corner of my eye which filled me with new hope. Pulling the "Tit"* as the enemy fighters broke away again, I pushed the nose of the Hurricane down and raced towards the distant outline of the

*An emergency knob for supplying additional power to the engine.

steaming destroyer. Praying hard that the ship would be sailing under the White Ensign, I cast fearful glances over my shoulder as the faster Me. 109s tore after me.

Risking my life on the assumption that the Royal Navy still had command of the high seas, I led my pursuers straight towards the businesslike shape of the destroyer. Seemingly the Luftwaffe pilots had no stomach for the match and soon they broke off the chase and headed back to France.

A challenging signal light flashed from the ship, but my knowledge of the Morse code had long since rusted. By way of reply I rolled the Hurricane happily and continued on my way home at a more leisurely pace. Having some time to think about it as the fighter slipped lightly over the swell, I pieced the whole puzzle together for the first time.

It was obvious now that the destroyer was operating so close to the enemy-held shoreline for special reasons, and that the British squadron had been patrolling to intercept any air attack the Germans might launch. This of course had come in the shape of the Stuka formation escorted by the Messerschmitt fighters.

In the Mess that night Dopey had difficulty in understanding why all of a sudden Pilot Officer Page should insist on buying him free drinks all evening to the toast of "the Royal Navy."

Twelve

Early morning light seeped into the dispersal hut and probed its fingers into the dusty corners. Youth was undisturbed by nature's gentle reminders of a new day being born. Youth slept on. Then the phone rang.

With one accord every figure tensed beneath its blankets as we strained to catch the words issuing from the small office. "Telephonitis" had us in its grip, and the shrill bell was eating away at our nerve coverings, leaving the raw edges exposed. The click of the receiver being replaced followed by silence filled us with relief. Perhaps another half-hour's sleep if we were lucky. Those who had not dropped off again heard the duty phone clerk tap on the flight commander's door and enter his office. Mumbled voices exuded followed by the sound of heavy bare feet – the click of the phone being lifted – another mumbled conversation – another click – and silence. It didn't much matter after that everyone was asleep again.

The high pitched voice penetrated into our sleep drugged bodies, unused to the luxury of five hours comparatively undisturbed relaxation. "Wake up, you lazy sods," piped the flight commander.

Disbelievingly the tousled figures roused themselves and looked at their watches. Surely the war wasn't over? Seven o'clock and still in bed. Something must be wrong!

Finally the sleepers had roused themselves sufficiently to satisfy Jumbo. Suspiciously he looked about him, his pasty face personifying concern and constipation. Waiting for the effect of a prolonged silence, he began to talk.

"For your information, gentlemen, the squadron was released from first light this morning until thirteen hundred hours this afternoon." Disappointed at the stolid glances that responded to what would normally have been exciting news, Jumbo continued. "His Majesty the King will be inspecting the squadron at eleven hundred hours this morning, and so I ..."

For a while his words were lost in the undisciplined murmur that followed the announcement.

"SILENCE!" He glowered as the hub-bub subsided. "And so I expect all of you to be turned out in your best blue by ten hundred hours with your buttons polished. I will hold an inspection parade at ten-thirty hours to make sure you're properly dressed. Respirators will be worn."

The importance of George the Sixth visiting the squadron removed the war from our minds. That, and the problem of remembering where we'd last seen our respirators. An hour later the hut smelled of nothing but Silvo and Duraglit as dark brown buttons transformed themselves into shining crested metal mirrors.

Soon we hardly recognized ourselves, and the babble of excited pointless chatter would have done credit to a bunch of debutantes preparing for their first dance.

"For the benefit of you ignorant R.A.F. types," Dopey ventured, "Your sailor King learned to fly and get his wings at Cranwell."

"Never knew that. Good for him."

"I hear he stutters very badly," I said. "Won't it be awful if he starts to say something and can't finish."

And so the conversation went.

The formality of the parade drawn up on the tarmac between the two hangars acted as a tonic on the tired actors taking part. Over-tired from constant strain and lack of sleep, the pomp and ceremony of the occasion, slight as it was, acted as soothing balm to our tired bodies. The ceremony itself was focused on the presentation of two Distinguished Flying Crosses. After the simple but impressive ceremony the slight figure in Air Force Blue walked down the line of pilots, chatting to each in his turn.

Bringing my eyes back from the far distance I focused them on the friendly face looking straight at me. Away in the distance droned Slim's voice carrying out the necessary introduction. "Pilot Officer Page, sir. A fairly recent arrival to the squadron."

A handshake given and one received. The first enthusiastically because it had to be remembered for a lifetime, and the other dutifully because it was part of a lifetime's work.

"How long have you been flying, Page?" The calm voice inquired.

"Tut . . . tut . . . two years, Ssss . . . sir," came my stammered reply.

"Shot down any aircraft?"

"Nun . . . nunn . . . not yet, sir. Only a sh . . . share in one I'm afraid."

"Never mind, there's plenty of time yet." Royalty smiled kindly and moved on.

Taffy, who had stood beside me during the parade, remarked later, "I'm so glad for your sake he didn't stammer too much!"

But I was to get my own back on King George at a later date.

The squadron returned to duty that afternoon with the feeling that it had just completed two weeks of well-earned rest. Such is the power of a truly loved sovereign.

Thirteen

Despite the distractions of motor cars and royalty, the intensity of the air fighting gained momentum and the lighthearted battles became sordid reality. Less and less time between flights was spent in idle talk. Sleep became the "Be-all" and "End-all" in life. Climbing out of our machines we threw ourselves on the nearest piece of grass and were asleep within seconds of touching the ground. High-powered engines could be ground-tested near our sleeping figures without disturbing us, but the smallest tinkle of the field telephone found us staggering bleary-eyed to our feet.

"Scramble – Angels 15 – 0 plus bandits approaching Dover."

"Scramble – Angels 12 – 90 plus off Ramsgate."

"Scramble – scramble – scramble ..."

Life became a nightmare, the centre of which was a telephone bell, and the only sure escape was death.

But it had its compensations.

Squadron Leader Manton, recently posted to command the squadron, addressed the ragged assortment of men gathered about him. Looking at us with our long hair and crumpled uniforms beneath the yellow Mae West, he must have smiled wryly to himself. If only some of the dowager duchesses and landed gentry could see what stood between the rape of their estates and the enemy hordes.

Quickly he briefed us for the patrol duty that had just been ordered by Group Control. Although most of us were in our late teens and early twenties, the past few weeks had turned us into hardened veterans, and so his briefing was confined to the barest essentials. We all knew how to conduct ourselves in the face of enemy fire.

Shortly afterwards the twelve machines roared into the air and climbed steadily towards the south coast. The day itself was conspicuous for its cloudiness, most of the previous days having had continuous sunshine. Reaching the cloud base at ten thousand feet our

Hurricanes droned back and forth along the coast between Dungeness and Dover. In spite of the cloudy conditions prevailing, visibility was excellent and the patrolling pilots had a ringside view of the drama taking place in mid-Channel. The surface of the calm sea was scarred with the multiple triangular wakes of fast motor torpedo boats and enemy "E" boats, as they engaged in a battle of the little ships. From the nearness of the Royal Navy vessels to the enemy coast, it was apparent that they had been out on a raid and were now fighting rearguard action against the "E" boats. To the northeast of the engagement two destroyers raced out from Dover to assist the withdrawing M.T.B.s, their creaming bows lending the painter's dash of white to the grey picture. One moment the naval engagement seemed distant and impersonal to the airmen, and the next we were drawn into it by a calm voice announcing, "Forty bandits approaching from the south – they are most probably after our friends down below."

Our Hurricanes wheeled outwards off our patrol line and headed toward the destroyers. It was while we were still about ten miles away from the ships that we spotted the large enemy formation. The make-up of the German aircraft left little doubt as to their intentions. The spearhead of the coming attack consisted of a dozen Stuka dive bombers strongly escorted by a large formation of Me. 109 fighters. It was plain to see that the British aircraft would arrive over the ships almost simultaneously with the Ju. 87 dive bombers. The battle of the little boats was forgotten in the race to protect the destroyers.

Manton issued his orders calmly as the gap between the two formations closed rapidly. "'A' Flight will take the fighters, and 'B' Flight the Stukas."

Jumbo squeaked his acknowledgement and "A" Flight climbed away to carry out their allotted task. Orange streaks flecked the grey sky as the light naval anti-aircraft guns opened fire on the approaching vultures.

Our six Hurricanes of "B" Flight came within firing range just as the Stukas peeled off into their screaming vertical dives onto the targets below. Realizing the presence of the British fighters, the sailors courageously held their fire and prepared to meet the inevitable attack.

Hurricanes and Ju. 87s intermingled in the stream of diving air-craft, and the chattering of machine guns added their notes to the scream of the enemy aircraft. Unsettled by the presence of fighters sitting on their tails, the dive bombers missed their mark with the ex-ception of their leader, his bomb scoring a direct hit on one of the ships. Registering a flash of pity for those aboard, I concentrated on the task ahead. Arriving a little too late to cause any damage before the attack, I watched the Stukas' tactics before dedicating my machine to a course of action. After releasing their bombs the Ju. 87s levelled out and headed homewards in a long line one behind the other, flying just a few feet above the placid sea. In this way any attacking fighter would be sandwiched between a pair of them, and would be open to the fire from the rear gun of one aircraft, and the front guns of the other. Seeing them skimming safely southward for the shelter of the French coast, an irrepressible anger rose up inside me and unhesitat-ingly I pointed the nose of my fighter downwards and dived to the attack.

Perhaps it was on account of the bombed sailors tending their stricken ship, or perhaps it was in remembrance of Minny and those others whose names were now forming a long list in my memory. Who knows? Whatever the reason, my Hurricane dived unwaver-ingly into the stream of enemy aircraft and settled solidly behind the selected victim before opening fire.

Grimly savouring the situation, I watched the flashing light ema-nating from the rear gunner's weapon ahead, while streaks of tracer warned me that the machine behind me was not being idle with its fire power. Closing the gap steadily, I waited until the range closed to about a hundred yards. Then, like a man yelling at the top of his voice to relieve pent-up feelings, I pressed the firing button and kept it de-pressed even after the Stuka had become a flaming inferno in front of my eyes. Almost regretfully I pulled away and watched the burning funeral pyre lose speed before plunging into the quenching sea that awaited.

Any German fighter attacking my Hurricane as it turned for home would have had an easy prey. Sitting dazed in the cockpit I flew the aircraft home mechanically. Again and again the sight of the flaming

Stuka presented itself to my mind's eye. Again and again I registered the horror and fascination of destroying the two human beings in the light grey airplane. Somehow it had been different in all the other fights, including the one in which the mortally wounded gunner had lost his arm. Then it had been a completely impersonal affair and I hadn't witnessed the death throes of the doomed plane.

Twenty minutes later, physically and mentally exhausted, I landed and taxied back to the dispersal pen, a different person. I had taken off from the same airfield an innocent, and returned a bloodied fighter pilot, or was it a murderer hiding behind the shield of official approval?

"Six enemy aircraft destroyed without loss calls for a party," Jumbo was saying. "Is the game on?"

The game was on, and the inevitable race up to London ensued. For our good behaviour in the air that day Group had bestowed the bounty of an earlier release than usual. With the one-track mindedness of our kind we headed up to the "Big Smoke" to spend our meager pennies. What was there to save for? The Reaper was too busy with his flashing Scythe to let us bolster up false hopes of "afterwards!" Hackneyed though it was, "eat, drink and be merry ..." had become the order of the day.

Arriving back at the dispersal hut in a maudlin frame of mind, I spent the short time remaining before first light in writing to my old friend, Michael Maw. I knew I would feel better after it was all down on paper, even if the letter was never posted. Sitting up in bed in the dark, I began to write with the aid of a torch.

"... it is difficult to know where to take up the threads again after so long. I sometimes wonder if our time together at Cranwell ever happened, and if this whole war isn't a ghastly nightmare from which we'll soon wake up. I know all of this sounds like nonsense, but I'm slightly tight and it's only an hour to dawn. Dawn ... it's a lovely sounding word isn't it? It personifies new hope – a second chance, at least that's what it should mean. To me it means nothing but another day of butchery. Oscar Wilde said it of fox hunting, and it applies to us. 'The pursuit of the uneatable by the unspeakable.' I know what you'd say in your kind understanding way. You'd say that it's all a terrible mess and that I mustn't blame myself personally for the chaos of the world. Maybe I am a bit sorry for myself at this moment, but, and it's a great big but, I enjoy killing. It fascinates me beyond belief to see my bullets striking home and then to see the Hun blow up before me. It also makes me feel sick. Where are we going and how will it all end? I feel as if I'm selling my soul to the Devil. If only you were here. I need someone to talk to who isn't tied up in this game of legalized murder.

> Look after yourself,
> Geoffrey."

Carefully I re-read all I'd written. It was never posted, nor did it need to be. Michael Maw had been killed in a training accident.

Fourteen

"You've got to hand it to Jumbo," Barry was saying. "He may be a miserable bastard at times, but he's got plenty of guts."

"He's blind as a bat in the air," I said.

"That may be," Barry persisted, "which is most probably the reason why he always takes you in his section."

I was pleased at the reference to my eyesight which, combined with an uncanny knack for spotting other aircraft in the sky, was gaining me a reputation in the squadron.

"I don't know about that, but I must confess he grows on you after a while."

Dopey nodded sagely. "If you want my opinion, he had a roaring inferiority complex when he arrived, which he tried to cover over with a thick layer of heifer-dust. Here comes the Doc. Ask him if I'm not right."

Looking round from where we sat cross-legged on the grass we watched the approach of the station medical officer. Like most of his breed, the S.M.O. disguised his true feelings under a non-commital professional mask. He was, however, a perplexed individual. A year's pre-war practice after qualifying had shown him that doctors as a species were usually held in high esteem by the community. The advent of war had shattered his carefully laid plans for the future, but worse than this had been the rude shock awaiting him in the Royal Air Force among the members of aircrew. The respect for his medical knowledge still existed, but somehow the pilots took no notice of the studied professional pose, and struck at the human being beneath who had taken healing as a career.

Cheerfully we greeted him. "Wot cheer, Doc. How many have you killed today?"

The M.O. winced. Here it was again, this attitude of tolerating him as an essential nuisance. It made it particularly difficult for him to carry out his present mission if the right note of respect wasn't struck. "I want to have a serious talk with you chaps," he began.

"Don't tell us there's a W.A.A.F. in the family way?"

"Not guilty !"

"Nor I."

Dopey shook his head sadly. "I wish I were guilty, but I haven't the energy to raise my eyebrows these days."

The M.O. pounced on the opening offered. "That's just what I've come here to talk to you about. I've been watching you all pretty closely these past few weeks and quite frankly I'm worried at what I see going on."

Our silence gratified his professional ego, but he should have been warned by the innocence of our expressions.

"It's no good this business of flying all day and whooping it up all night. The next thing is you'll get sick and then where will you be?"

"In bed with a pretty little nurse."

A few more years of experience would show the worthy doctor that we couldn't take ill-health seriously, although in the long term he was quite right. The drawback was that it was impossible for us to think in terms of the future with the hazards of our daily occupation.

The quivering figure of the flight commander came waddling into view. "There you are, Doc. There's a patient for you. Make him 'regular.'"

"It's all very well for you types," piped Jumbo. "You get so nervous you don't need a laxative."

"You don't need a laxative," Dopey remarked. "What you need is a tame ferret."

The M.O. threw up his hands in despair. "You deserve to die, the lot of you."

"Come to think of it," said Barry, "who'd care to join me in a pint of that deathly brew served at the King's Head?"

Protesting violently, the medical officer was led off to the pub and plied with quantities of ale. Later that night a group of pilots undressed the M.O. and put his inert body to bed.

He had given his last talk to the pilots on the subject of over-indulgence. There was another member of the squadron who, like the doctor, had to be taught a simple lesson.

Sergeant Pilot Baker was, fortunately for "B" Flight, a member of "A" Flight. As someone remarked, a trifle unkindly perhaps, that the reason he was so dim was because his mother had been frightened by a nightlight when pregnant. Not unnaturally he acquired the name of "Finger" – a title earned by having his digit firmly wedged, but unlike the little Dutch boy, he wasn't credited with having it stuck in the dyke.

Unfortunately 'Finger' was quite a loveable character and although a dead loss in the air, his activities never failed to amuse the other members of the squadron. Squadron Leader Manton summed the situation up one day by remarking, "The Huns have got the Italians to slow them down, and we've got Finger."

Sergeant Pilot Baker was five feet, four inches in height, with china blue eyes, a fair moustache struggling for survival, and a medal. His simple nature and good humour, combined with a Winnie-the-Pooh brain, took the leg-pulling in good grace. In fact he would often retaliate by pointing out to the practical jokers that he, Sergeant Pilot Baker, had a medal, whereas they had not been recognized by His Majesty.

Everyone knew, of course, that the decoration worn so proudly beneath his wings was the Coronation Medal earned for standing stiffly at attention along the Royal route when George VI and his Queen drove to the Abbey to be crowned. Each and every pilot played up to the importance of "Finger's" medal and a respectful atmosphere was maintained whenever the topic was mentioned.

But alas, despite the recognition by his King and Country, Finger still remained incorrigible in the air. In his first air battle he forgot where the switch was to turn on the reflector gunsight. In the second he remembered the gunsight, but left the gun button on "safe" much to the joy of a sitting target of a German bomber just in front of him. The third time Finger was so happy at remembering his switch on both gun sight and guns, that he forgot to look behind and a few seconds later he found himself floating down in a parachute.

Then Finger went to war for the fourth time. For a while the cloudless skies were streaked with condensation trails and lethal missiles, and suddenly, as always, the skies were clear of gyrating airplanes as both sides mutually agreed to go home. Eleven Hurricanes landed back at their airfield within a few minutes of each other. Laughingly we joked over the not-unusual tardiness of the twelfth. One of the "A" Flight pilots checked off the points on his fingers.

"Let me see now, he's remembered to switch on the gun sight, so it can't be that. He's learned about turning the gun button on to 'fire,' and I hope he's remembered to look behind ... I know! He's forgotten to pull the ripcord on his parachute!"

The laughter turned to concern as the hours passed by and no message was received from the missing pilot.

Inquiries through Group Operations revealed nothing. No one had seen an aircraft crash and the only parachutists had been Jerries. His loss took a great deal of the sunshine and laughter out of our lives for a time.

Taffy summed up our feelings after the next flight following Baker's disappearance. Giving his combat report, he said, "I gave the Me. 109 a short burst and he blew up, and I thought that evens it up for Finger."

Five days later one of the pilots landed in a state of great excitement. The last to land after the recent fight, he rushed over to our group standing around the tea urn outside the hut. "I've just seen Finger's plane," he shouted. "Down near Romney Marshes."

Inquiries through the local police soon traced Finger to his comfortable lodgings in a pub near Rye. It never occurred to him to report his whereabouts to the squadron. Instead he waited for us to find him!

Inside the hut a solemn stillness reigned. Beds had been cleared away to allow space for the ceremony, and standing rigidly to attention with their backs to the walls, stood the squadron pilots. Standing on a dais, looking suspiciously like an aircraft chock, stood the "A" Flight commander. Behind him and slightly to the right stood another pilot reading from a scroll of toilet paper. Facing the dais stood a puzzled Sergeant Finger Baker. The citation was read aloud for the assembled squadron to hear.

"It is hereby decreed that you, Sergeant Pilot 'F' Baker, having displayed outstanding finger trouble even for one so well-versed in the art of digital dexterity, inasmuch that on Tuesday afternoon of last week you did, after being mildly shot down, crash-land your aircraft and thereafter repair to the local tavern. Whence from this abode of rest your only communication with your fellow human beings was, "another pint, please." This monotonous chant being upheld until by chance one Sergeant Pilot – may he be forgiven –did espy your air-craft from the air and lead us to your humble lodgings. Not content with this, you did then touch your rescuing officers for the sum of two pounds, ten shillings and a tanner, to settle with mine host for the vast quantities of ale quaffed in his posting house. You will now be invested with the Bar to your superlatively won Coronation Medal."

Solemnly the insignia of merit was placed about Sergeant Baker's neck: the unmistakable handle swung loosely at the end of a metal chain. Two minutes later Finger was deposited, medal and all, into the nearby static water tank. Squadron life resumed its normal tempo again for a while.

Fifteen

Hardly a day was now passing without some striking event taking place. The death of a friend or enemy provided food for a few moments of thought, before the next swirling dogfight began to distract the cogitating mind from stupid thoughts such as sadness or pity – remorse had long since died. It was the act of living that perhaps became the most exciting form of occupation. Any fool could be killed; that was being proved all the time. No, the art was to cheat the Reaper and merely blunt his Scythe a little. After all, it was only a game and he was bound to win, but it was fun while it lasted.

Simple escapes from death such as Finger's were too commonplace to be mentioned. Something more spectacular was necessary to draw anything greater than a passing comment. It was the more sensational of these flirtations with posterity that placed milestones in our lives. Events happened with such rapidity that the day before yesterday seemed a lifetime ago, and ten seconds of close attention by an enemy fighter could also feel like a lifetime.

Flight Lieutenant Ironside, from 151 Squadron, better known as "Tinribs," was one of the first to set a high standard in the sport of "Juggling with Jesus." The cause itself was simple enough, but the effect almost disastrous. Tinribs and a German youth in a Me. 109 fighter indulged in a duel to the death which consisted of charging at each other head-on with guns blazing. Doing little harm to each other on the first occasion, they wheeled about and returned to "tilt" in the lists. The British pilot never had the satisfaction of seeing the results of his fire upon the enemy aircraft. Instead, a cannonshell from the Me. 109 struck the Hurricane in the centre of the bulletproof windscreen, shattering it to fragments, but fortunately for the pilot, not passing through. Another shell wrought its share of damage to the engine. Tinribs discovered three unfortunate occurrences: first, a large fragment of glass had penetrated his left eye, damaging it irreparably; secondly, the engine was behaving in a manner that indicated fire or almost immediate seizure; and thirdly, the distortion to the windscreen prevented the sliding hood from being moved should he wish to abandon the machine in a hurry. Bleeding profusely from the face, and landing at the nearest airfield became another problem with which to contend. The engine instruments in the cockpit gave readings that would have caused most pilots under easier circumstances to have had nightmares, but there was little he could do about it except to try and land. Just within gliding distance of an airfield, the engine seized and the Hurricane was brought in safely over the hedge by the semi-conscious, one-eyed pilot. Twenty minutes later the ground crew succeeded in hacking their way through the canopy with an axe to release the trapped occupant.

There were other small milestones besides those passed in the air. One of them was the day when I received a small registered package. On opening it I found inside a beautiful silver hip flask sent to me as a present from my mother. Firmly I declared my intention to the other members of the flight that the flask was to be filled with brandy and kept for an "emergency." After release that night, I and my brother officers repaired to the Mess bar where the flask was solemnly filled with Three Star Brandy. Then placing it in the breast pocket of my tunic, I announced that there it would remain until the "emergency." We remained at the bar drinking beer until the barman refused all further orders.

Five minutes later my thirsty companions declared that a state of "emergency" existed. Only by obstinate refusal did I manage to save the contents of the flask for another day.

Sixteen

The day eventually had to arrive, and when it did it dawned with the sun rising in a cloudless blue sky, like its predecessors for the past weeks. The order of the day was that the squadron had to proceed to Rochford after an early lunch, to relieve the sister squadron which was doing the morning shift from the forward airfield. Soon after mid-day our twelve machines were winging their way eastward, and ten minutes later we were diving into the small airfield like wild geese settling into a potato field. Taxiing across the grass we parked our airplanes in the allocated area at the farthest corner of the airfield away from the main buildings. As we arrived the other squadron taxied out and departed, leaving us the facilities of the solitary bell tent, with its field telephone. Chairs or tables were non-existent.

After ensuring that my machine had been properly refuelled and that everything in the cockpit was ready for a quick getaway, I climbed down and joined my companions on the grass outside the tent. Throwing myself full length on the cool sward, I lay on my back with closed eyes listening to the nearby songs of the birds. The murmur of nearby voices came to me in snatches, and I had the pleasant sensation of knowing that sleep wasn't very far away and that half the things I was hearing might be figments of the imagination.

"...there's only one decent way to die – drunk on the job."

"...why on earth do you Catholics conduct your services in a language that most of you don't understand, and that Christ never spoke?" A distant rattling sound followed by a loud voice brought me back to partial consciousness. "Wake up, Geoffrey, you lazy bastard. Tea's up."

Slowly my surroundings began to make sense as the drugged effects of a deep sleep receded by degrees. Rolling over on my stomach I watched the scene about me. From my low view-point, the grass airfield had the appearance of stretching for miles until distant buildings and hangars formed a bumpy horizon. Lending an air of artificiality in the far distance were the barrage balloons protecting the town of Southend.

The screeching brake drums of the tea wagon brought my mind back to the immediate surroundings. Willing figures were jumping up from the ground to help unload the heavy thermos flasks of tea and plates of food. Guiltily I thought, "I should be there giving a helping hand, but they most probably don't feel as tired as I do." My muscles felt drained of energy and although the spirit was willing, the flesh was very, very weak. Soon the tea things were laid out on the grass about the telephone. Sitting there like a pagan idol surrounded by its worshippers sat the instrument of our destiny. One ring of its small bell and the lives of individuals altered course: unborn generations owed their stillness to its fearful sound.

Lying on my stomach I gazed with burning hatred at the black instrument: the instrument that made me want to retch every time it rang its shrill imperative cry. So great was the feeling that only fatigue stopped me from getting up and ripping the leads from their terminals. It started from a minute spark from somewhere deep inside and grew as it moved towards the surface. Its origin may have been attributable to being disturbed from a heavy sleep, or just the results of overstrain from the preceding weeks of battle. Whatever the cause, an unreasonable desire to destroy welled up inside and took me to join the others in the hope that somehow these unworthy feelings might be expressed. Sitting cross-legged in front of the spread of bread and butter aided by a large jar of strawberry jam, I munched away taciturnly while the others chattered away in the language of airmen.

Then the raid started, but this time the attackers came without any warning sirens to precede them. Beating their tiny wings, the yellow striped raiders swooped down and attached themselves to various parts of the jam pot. This afforded me the relief I had been seeking. Without hesitation I plunged a spoon into the sticky red mass and removed a mound of jam. With this I started the first round of a personal game. Explaining it to Bob Constable-Maxwell and Taffy, I pointed out that the wasps in the jampot represented ground targets and that the spoon and its contents were the bomber with its

load. Passing the spoon in a steady movement over the top
of the jar, part of its contents was allowed to drop from a height of
eighteen inches and bomb the enemy below.

Despite the action which smacked of a schoolboy pulling the
wings off flies, I felt a great deal better after the destruction of ten of
the insects clad in football jerseys.

The telephone shrilled just before a missile was released on wasp
number eleven.

The spoon was arrested in mid-air, and for an instant I had the
doubtful pleasure of watching my hand shake as a result of the high
pitched urgent note. "Page, my boy," I thought, "you're getting the twitch.
You'd better watch it."

Jumbo slammed down the receiver. "Scramble ... seventy plus approaching Manston, Angels fifteen ..."

Gone was the feeling of lethargy as nervous energy supplied the
power to my legs to cover the fifty yards to the waiting machine. Gone
also was the nauseating feeling in the pit of my stomach now that the
mind had physical actions to control. One foot up into the stirrup
step, second one onto the wing, then a short step along the wing, right
foot up into the step in the side of the fuselage and so –into the cockpit. A nimble-fingered rigger passing parachute straps across my
shoulders, followed by the Sutton harness straps – one –two – three
– four – pin through – tighten the adjusting pieces –mask clipped
across – oxygen on – prime the engine – switches on – thumbs up
– press the starter button – there she goes. Almost with one accord
the twelve engines roared into life flattening the dancing grass behind
them with their violent slipstreams. Nearby I noticed one of the
whirling propellers slow down and stop. Ground crews rushed up to
assist, but then the scene was gone as I taxied swiftly out behind
Jumbo's aircraft. Today the "B" Flight commander was leading the
squadron, giving Squadron Leader Manton one day's holiday. Bob
Constable-Maxwell formed the third member of the section. With
myself to his right and Bob on the left, Jumbo opened up and our
Hurricanes tore across the grass. Close behind came the remaining
eight machines.

Sweltering in the greenhouse heat of the closed cockpit, I slid back the hood and allowed the whipping wind to cool my sweating body. The Hurricanes raced upwards with little R/T chatter except for a word from the controller confirming the numbers and the height of the German raiders. Automatically now I went through the ritual of preparing the airplane for action. A voice broke the radio silence and announced that lack of oil pressure was sending him home. The ten Hurricanes tore onwards to intercept the seventy enemy aircraft. 'Odds of seven to one,' I thought. "No better or worse than usual." I remembered that early morning interception when we had outnumbered the solitary reconnaissance machine by three to one, and what a job it had been to shoot him down. The altimeter read ten thousand feet, and below us the coastline of North Kent followed our track as we raced to intercept the raid approaching from the southeast towards Manston and Margate.

At eleven thousand feet I closed the cockpit hood again and a shiver ran through my body. Keeping sufficiently close to Jumbo to be able to follow him at short notice, I still kept far enough away to be able to devote time to searching the sky for trouble. This was known as battle formation.

At first they appeared as a swarm of midges in the top half of my bulletproof windscreen, but closer inspection showed them to be more deadly than any tiny insects. Still several thousand feet below our opponents, our climbing fighters had the disadvantage of a lower altitude. As the gap lessened, we saw that the huge formation consisted of about thirty Dornier 215 bombers escorted by forty Messerschmitt 109 single-seater fighters.

"Not unlike wasps at a distance," I thought, although the markings were different. Swastikas and iron crosses instead of yellow and black stripes. I laughed with nervous anticipation. "Damn stupid if our guns happened to fire strawberry jam."

Jumbo's unmistakable voice came piping through the headphones in the helmet. "... echelon starboard – go."

Out of the left-hand corner of my eye I saw Bob's machine slide below Jumbo's and my own to take up the new position to my right and slightly astern. By way of habit, I pulled the sliding hood back and locked it in the open position. This facilitated a hurried exit.

In front of us the enemy armada was turning northwards and setting out over the sea. The Hurricanes banked in pursuit as we continued our climb to reach the slender bombers. High above, the Me.
109s weaved like hawks waiting to swoop on their victims.

The distance and height between hunter and prey was closing. At
last the Hurricanes arrived at the same height as the Dornier bombers
which allowed us to level off and build up some speed. The large
enemy aircraft were themselves flying in echelon to starboard formation as were our intercepting fighters.

To my surprise I saw that Jumbo was intending to attack the leading aircraft in the bomber formation. This necessitated flying past the
aircraft behind the leader's, and also meant running the gauntlet of
their rear gunner's fire.

Slowly we overhauled the heavy Luftwaffe machines, and I had
the impression of an express train overtaking a slower one. There was
time to inspect each other before passing onto the next one up the
line. Instinctively I glanced above and behind, but for some strange
reason the Me. 109s were still sitting aloft. The sweeping movement
of my trained eyes showed that Bob no longer stood between me
and the enemy. Momentarily reassured that nothing lethal was sitting
behind my aircraft, I settled down to the task of firing at one of the
leading machines although it was still about six hundred yards ahead.

Then the enemy rear gunners started firing....

Analyzing it later I realized that the fire power of the whole group
was obviously controlled by radio instructions from a gunnery officer
in one of the bombers.

One moment the sky between me and the thirty Dornier 215s
was clear; the next it was criss-crossed with streams of white tracer
from cannon shells converging on our Hurricanes.

Jumbo's machine peeled away from the attack. The distance between the German leaders and my solitary Hurricane was down to
three hundred yards. Strikes from my Brownings began to flash
around the port engine of one of the Dorniers.

The mass of fire from the bomber formation closed in as I fired
desperately in a race to destroy before being destroyed.

The first bang came as a shock. For an instant I couldn't believe

I'd been hit. Two more bangs followed in quick succession, and as if by magic a gaping hole suddenly appeared in my starboard wing.

Surprise quickly changed to fear, and as the instinct of self-preservation began to take over, the gas tank behind the engine blew up, and my cockpit became an inferno. Fear became blind terror, then agonized horror as the bare skin of my hands gripping the throttle and control column shrivelled up like burnt parchment under the intensity of the blast furnace temperature. Screaming at the top of my voice. I threw my head back to keep it away from the searing flames. Instinctively the tortured right hand groped for the release pin securing the restraining Sutton harness.

"Dear God, save me ... save me, dear God ... " I cried imploringly. Then, as suddenly as terror had overtaken me, it vanished with the knowledge that death was no longer to be feared. My fingers kept up their blind and bloody mechanical groping. Some large mechanical dark object disappeared between my legs and cool, relieving fresh air suddenly flowed across my burning face. I tumbled. Sky, sea, sky, over and over as a clearing brain issued instructions to outflung limbs. "Pull the ripcord – right hand to the ripcord." Watering eyes focused on an arm flung out in space with some strange meaty object attached at its end.

More tumbling – more sky and sea and sky, but with a blue clad arm forming a focal point in the foreground. "Pull the ripcord, hand," the brain again commanded. Slowly but obediently the elbow bent and the hand came across the body to rest on the chromium ring but bounced away quickly with the agony of contact.

More tumbling but at a slower rate now. The weight of the head was beginning to tell.

Realizing that pain or no pain, the ripcord had to be pulled, the brain overcame the reaction of the raw nerve endings and forced the mutilated fingers to grasp the ring and pull firmly.

It acted immediately. With a jerk the silken canopy billowed out in the clear summer sky.

Quickly I looked up to see if the dreaded flames had done their work, and it was with relief that I saw the shining material was unburned. Another fear rapidly followed. I heard the murmur of fading engines and firing guns, but it was the sun glinting on two pairs of wings that struck a chill through my heart. Stories of pilots being ma-chine-gunned as they parachuted down came flashing through my mind, and again I prayed for salvation. The two fighters straightened out and revealed themselves to be Hurricanes before turning away to continue the chase.

It was then that I noticed the smell. The odour of my burnt flesh was so loathsome that I wanted to vomit. But there was too much to attend to, even for that small luxury. Self-preservation was my first concern, and my chance for it looked slim. The coastline at Margate was just discernible six to ten miles away. Ten thousand feet below me lay the deserted sea. Not a ship or a seagull crossed its blank, grey surface.

Still looking down I began to laugh. The force of the exploding gas tank had blown every vestige of clothing off from my thighs downwards, including one shoe. Carefully I eased off the remaining shoe with the toes of the other foot and watched the tumbling footwear in the hope of seeing it strike the water far beneath. Now came the bad time.

The shock of my violent injuries was starting to take hold, and this combined with the cold air at the high altitude brought on a shivering attack that was quite uncontrollable. With that the parachute began to sway, setting up a violent oscillating movement with my teeth-chat-tering torso acting as a human pendulum. Besides its swinging move-ment it began a gentle turn and shortly afterwards the friendly shoreline disappeared behind my back. This brought with it an idée fixe that if survival was to be achieved, then the coast must be kept in sight. A combination of agonized curses and bleeding hands pulling on the shrouds finally brought about the desired effect, and I settled back to the pleasures of closing eyes and burnt flesh.

Looking down again I was surprised to find that the water had come up to meet me very rapidly since last I had taken stock of the situation. This called for some fairly swift action if the parachute was to be discarded a second or two before entering the water. The pro-cedure itself was quite simple. Lying over my stomach was a small metal release box which clasped the four ends of the parachute harness after they had passed down over the shoulders and up from the groin. On this box was a circular metal disc which had to be turned through 90°, banged, and presto! The occupant was released from the chute. All of this was extremely simple except in the case of fingers which refused to turn the little disc.

The struggle was still in progress when I plunged feet first into the water. Despite the beauties of the summer and the wealth of warm days that had occurred, the sea felt icy cold to my badly shocked body. Kicking madly, I came to the surface to find my arms entangled with the multiple shrouds holding me in an octopus-like grip. The battle with the metal disc still had to be won, or else the water-logged parachute would eventually drag me down to a watery grave. Spluttering with mouthfulls of salt water I struggled grimly with the vital release mechanism. Pieces of flesh flaked off and blood poured from the raw tissues.

Desperation, egged on by near panic, forced the decision, and with a sob of relief I found that the disc had surrendered the battle.

Kicking away blindly at the tentacles that still entwined arms and legs, I fought free and swam fiercely away from the nightmare surroundings of the parachute. Wild fear died away and the simple rules of procedure for continued existence exerted themselves again.

"Get rid of the 'chute, and then inflate your Mae West," said the book of rules, "and float about until rescued."

"That's all very well," I thought, "but unless I get near to the coast under my own steam, there's not much chance of being picked up." With that I trod water and extricated the long rubber tube with which to blow up the jacket. Unscrewing the valves between my teeth, I searched my panting lungs for extra air. The only result after several minutes of exertion was a feeling of dizziness and a string of bubbles from the bottom of the jacket. The fire had burnt a large hole through the rubber bladder.

Dismay was soon replaced by fatalism. There was the distant shore, unseen but positioned by reference to the sun, and only one method of getting there, so it appeared. Turning on my stomach I set out at a measured stroke. Ten minutes of acute misery passed by as the salt dried about my facial injuries and the contracting strap of the flying helmet cut into the raw surface of my chin. Buckle and leather had welded into one solid mass, preventing removal of the headgear.

Dumb despair then suddenly gave way to shining hope. The brandy flask, of course. This was it – the emergency for which it was kept. But the problem of undoing the tunic remained, not to mention that the tight-fitting Mae West covered the pocket as another formidable barrier. Hope and joy were running too high to be deterred by such mundane problems, and so turning with my face to the sky I set about the task of getting slightly tipsy on neat brandy. Inch by inch my ultra-sensitive fingers worked their way under the Mae West towards the breast pocket. Every movement brought with it indescribable agony, but the goal was too great to allow for weakness. At last the restraining copper button was reached – a deep breath to cope with the pain – and it was undone. Automatically my legs kept up their propulsive efforts while my hand had a rest from its labours. Then gingerly the flask was eased out of its home and brought to the surface of the water. Pain became conqueror for a while and the flask was transferred to a position between my wrists. Placing the screw stopper between my teeth, I undid it with a series of head-twists and finally the great moment arrived – the life-warming liquid was waiting to be drunk. Raising it to my mouth, I pursed my lips to drink. The flask slipped from between wet wrists and disappeared from sight. Genuine tears of rage followed this newest form of torture, which in turn gave place to a furious determination to swim to safety.

After the first few angry strokes despair returned in full force ably assisted by growing fatigue, cold and pain. Time went by unregistered. Was it minutes, hours or days since my flaming Hurricane disappeared between my legs? Was it getting dark or were my eyes closing up? How could I steer towards the shore if I couldn't see the sun? How could I see the sun if that rising pall of smoke obscured it from sight?

That rising pall of smoke . . . that rising pall of smoke. No, it couldn't be. I yelled, I splashed the water with my arms and legs until the pain brought me to a sobbing halt. Yes, the smoke was coming from a funnel – but supposing it passed without seeing me? Agony of mind was greater than agony of body and the shouting and splashing recommenced. Looking again, almost expecting that smoke and funnel had been an hallucination, I gave a fervent gasp of thanks to see that whatever ship it was, it had hove to.

All of the problems were fast disappearing and only one remained. It was one of keeping afloat for just another minute or two before all energy failed. Then I heard it – the unmistakable chug-chug of a small motor boat growing steadily louder. Soon it came into sight with a small bow wave pouring away to each side. In it sat two men in the strange garb peculiar to sailors of the British Merchant Service. The high revving note of the engine died to a steady throb as the man astride the engine throttled back. Slowly the boat circled without attempting to pick me up. A rough voice carried over the intervening water. "What are you? A Jerry or one of ours?"

My weak reply was gagged by a mouthful of water. The other man tried as the boat came full circle for the second time. "Are you a Jerry, mate?"

Anger flooded through me. Anger, not at these sailors who had every reason to let a German pilot drown, but anger at the steady chain of events since the explosion that had reduced my tortured mind and body to its present state of near collapse. And anger brought with it temporary energy. "You stupid pair of fucking bastards, pull me out! !"

The boat altered course and drew alongside. Strong arms leaned down and dragged my limp body over the side and into the bottom of the boat. "The minute you swore, mate," one of them explained, "we knew you was an R.A.F. Officer."

The sodden dripping bundle was deposited on a wooden seat athwart ships. A voice mumbled from an almost lifeless body as the charred helmet was removed. One of the sailors leaned down to catch the words. "What did you say, chum?"

The mumble was more distinct the second time. "Take me to the side. I want to be sick."

The other man answered in a friendly voice. "You do it in the bottom of the boat, and we'll clean up afterwards."

But habit died hard and pride wouldn't permit it, so keeping my head down between my knees, I was able to control the sensation of nausea. Allowing me a moment or two to feel better, the first sailor produced a large clasp knife. "Better get this wet stuff off you, mate. You don't want to catch your death of cold."

The absurdity of death from a chill struck me as funny and I chuckled for the first time in a long while. To prove the sailor's point the teeth chattering recommenced. Without further ado the man with the knife set to work and deftly removed pieces of life jacket and tunic with the skill of a surgeon. Then my naked body was wrapped up in a blanket produced from the seat locker.

One of them went forward to the engine and seconds later the little boat was churning her way back to the mother ship. The other sailor sat down beside me in silence, anxious to help but not knowing what to do next. I sensed the kindness of his attitude and felt that it was up to me to somehow offer him a lead. The feeling of sickness was still there from the revolting smell of burnt flesh, but I managed to gulp out "Been a lovely . . . summer,
hasn't it?"

The man nodded. "Aye."

No further efforts at conversation were necessary as by now the tall sides of the old tramp steamer were looming above the little boat as they lined the rail looking down at me. A voice hailed us. "What you got there, Bill? A Jerry?"

The man with the knife cupped his hands and called back, "No, one of our boys."

Swiftly a gangway was lowered and two pairs of strong arms formed a hand chair and carried me to the deck aloft. The grizzled captain came forward to greet me with out-stretched hand. Clasp knife spoke quietly. "He can't, Skipper. Both hands badly burned."

"Bad luck, lad," the captain said. "But never mind, we'll soon have you fixed up." To the sailors he said, "Bring him into the galley."

They carried me down the gently heaving deck and through a door into the galley. The warmth of the room struck me immediately and I asked to be allowed to stand. Reluctantly they deposited me on my feet and a brew of hot ship's tea was held to my lips. New life began to course through my frozen body as the fluid and the warmth of the room took effect. The captain, who had disappeared, came back with a metal first-aid kit. "We'll have you fixed up in a jiffy, and the Margate lifeboat's on its way out here to take you ashore. Right, off with the blanket." Naked and unashamed I stood there while the old man cast a swift look over my body. "You got shot in the leg as well." The skipper shook his head sadly. Surprised, I looked down and for the first time became aware of the bleeding wound in my left calf.

Quickly the captain cut up large squares of pink lint, and made fingerless gloves for my injured hands. Another strip of lint was tied across the raw forehead. "That's the best I can do, I'm afraid," the old man said.

My thanks were cut short by a hail from the deck. "Lifeboat alongside, Skipper."

With the blanket back around my shoulders they led me out through the door in time to meet the coxswain of the lifeboat. Two of his crew followed carrying a stretcher. A quick exchange of information took place between the two captains, then the coxswain bade me lie down on the stretcher. Feeling rather much the admired hero, I refused at first, but the common sense of the two skippers prevailed, and I lay down. The instant my head touched the canvas I knew how exhausted I really was.

Warm blankets were tucked about me and soft coverings placed round my hands. A sensation of swaying followed by tilting, the lapping sound of water, and then the gentle lowering of the stretcher into the centre of the long boat.

"Smoke, chum?" My head nodded weakly. "Afraid it's only a Woodbine."

Lying on my back looking up at the blue sky through swollen watery eyes, I became aware of the cigarette placed between my lips. Deeply inhaling the smoke, a sense of complete relaxation prevailed and for the first time my tired muscles relaxed.

However, the sensation of well-being passed almost as quickly as it had arrived. The warmth of the galley and the steaming tea had brought back life and feeling, and feeling brought with it the intense pain of burnt hands.

Roughly the crew attempted to console me as whimpers of suffering escaped through my lips. It was obvious that their inability to ease the suffering was causing them acute mental discomfort.

Nature offered her own relief-valve, and for a few minutes I escaped into unconsciousness.

When I came round again the boat was only half a mile away from the quayside and I insisted on being propped up to watch our arrival. Apart from a group of about a dozen people, the town had an air of desertion about it that struck me immediately. Behind the group on the quayside stood a white ambulance. On coming alongside the stone steps that led from the water's edge to the promenade, the same query was called down to the boat. "Is it a Jerry?"

Dimly I wondered what would have been my chances of survival had I been an officer of the Luftwaffe. British people were kind-hearted, but there was a snapping point after they had been goaded too far.

The reception committee was waiting at the top of the steps. The blurred image of a figure stooped over the stretcher which made polite sounds about being the Mayor, and that he would be only too delighted to help in any way. The figure was replaced by two uniformed representatives of the law offering more practical suggestions of help. "Would I like my Unit and next of kin informed, and where were they to be found ?"

Dim recollections of an ambulance ride, the outside of the general hospital, followed by a long journey down endless corridors on a trolley, a heave, and I was lying on top of a comfortable bed in a small private room. Soon blessed relief from pain was injected into my arm. The matron bustled in and displayed her singular charm. She informed me that I was the sole occupant of the large hospital and an honoured guest. Pride at being one of the nation's heroes rose in my breast, but an instant later the "hero" was mortified to hear that he was to receive an enema before being wheeled into the operating room. Such was the price of glory.

In spite of my protestations about keeping singularly good health, the procedure was insisted upon. It was pointed out to me that burns ran a grave danger of septicemia and that the blood must be kept cleansed.

After the indignity had been completed by a singularly pretty

nurse – just to make matters worse, I was trundled away to the operating room on a trolley. The surgeon, anaesthetist and a gowned
nurse comprised the skeleton staff for surgical cases. All three helped
to lift me onto the table beneath the huge over-hanging light.

The nurse and surgeon disappeared to scrub-up and the anaesthetist prepared his hypodermic syringe.

A sudden desire to know the extent of my facial injuries absorbed
me and I pleaded for a glance in a mirror. Sensibly the second doctor
refused the request and changed the subject to safer topics.

The masked and gloved surgeon returned with his assistant.
Neatly the anaesthetist tied a rubber cord round my bicep and
searched the hollow of the elbow joint for a suitable vein. Not wishing
to see the needle enter the skin, I looked away and upwards, catching
sight of myself in the reflector mirrors of the overhanging light. My
last conscious memory was of seeing the hideous mass of swollen,
burnt flesh that had once been a face.

The Battle of Britain had ended for me, but another long battle
was beginning.

Seventeen

The car approached at breakneck speed on the road below, its tyres screaming out in protest as it roared round the corner. The hood was down and the hair of the two occupants streamed in the wind. Both the young men looked up at the same time and waved. Although the car never slackened speed it seemed to take a long time getting past my high vantage point. Again they waved to me but this time it was an invitation to join them on their headlong journey. The parachute opened with a sharp crack and I floated gently down into the back seat. The driver turned round and laughed in sheer delight. "Welcome aboard! We've been waiting for you," said Minny.

I knew instinctively that sitting next to Minny was Ian Soden and that the three owners were tearing along in our Jonah car.

The dream passed on into more fantastic realms as the car sprouted wings and left the road far below. Above the roar of the engine and the whipping of the wind, Minny yelled back. "It shouldn't be too long before Mark Mounsdon joins us, eh?"

As if it were a great joke, the three of us roared with laughter. "Looks as if it might rain," remarked Soden as the car went into a climbing turn to avoid some clouds shaped suspiciously like the North Weald hangars. As it straightened out again, so did the hood rise from its folded position. I leaned over the two occupants in the front seat with the intention of clamping the rising hood into the erected position. Exactly how it happened did not matter. All I knew was that somehow my fingers had become clamped between hood and windshield and that the attendant agony was damnable. The excruciating pain accompanied a return to consciousness, and with an awareness of the fiendish torture taking place at the extremities of each arm.

"Sister's coming along with something to make you sleep." Soothingly the pretty nurse wiped the beads of sweat from my top lip with a piece of gauze.

The saliva between my lips was as sticky as boiled rice water as I tried to utter words. The sentence was formed politely in the mind, but the only word that came forth from the body was "drink!" Neatly and efficiently the blurred white shape turned to the large jug of lemon juice standing on the bedside locker. A firm arm supported my weak head while the cool liquid flowed down my eager throat. Her attractive face flashed into focus for an instant, but just long enough for me to register her look of revulsion. At that point I hated her and I hated myself with the illogical reasoning of a drunken man.

The bustle of female starch announced the arrival of the Sister with her kidney dish of physical relief. The stab of the hypodermic needle into the sensitive flesh came as a welcome pin-prick to remind me of blessed escape. Hardly had the needle been withdrawn than the thirst returned with renewed vigour. Again the cool white arm supported the leaden weight as the greedy body absorbed the drink.

The Sister's outline was hazy at the end of the bed, preventing me from seeing her facial expression, but the embarrassment in her voice was undisguised. "I'm sorry to trouble you, Pilot Officer Page, but I'm afraid I've got to get one or two particulars from you."

The swollen lump of flesh produced what it fondly believed to be an impish grin. The result was devastating.

"I should like to know…" she faltered, "the address of your next of kin, and your religion."

A ghastly chuckle preceded the answer. "I'm going to disappoint you I'm afraid, Sister. I'm going to live."

The mortified woman beat a hasty retreat leaving the bestial form demanding more fluid from the pretty attendant.

The effort of conversation and the effect of morphia soon had me back in a state of blissful unconsciousness, and pain no longer ruled the day. The night consisted of a series of disjointed photographic impressions of an elderly nurse sitting knitting by the light of a hooded table lamp, and of vast quantities of lemonade being poured into my porous body. For good measure, vivid nightmares occupied the short moments of restless sleep.

Although the worthy woman never said it in as many words, it struck the patient that she wouldn't be sorry to see me die quickly so that she could get back to the comfort of her lodgings.

Dawn had just lightened the sky when it started.

Dozing fitfully between conscious pain and subconscious nightmare, the fantastic bang as the gun discharged near the window practically completed the task the enemy rear gunners had set out upon the day before.

Jagged nerves responded violently to the discharge of the anti-aircraft gun placed just a stone's throw from my window as the defences opened up. Windows rattled violently and the curtains flapped protestingly as each round discharged itself heavenwards.

Added to the crack of the ack-ack guns was the fiendish shriek of the dive-bombing Stukas. If my physique had not been at such a low ebb, I might have laughed at being at the receiving end of a noisy air-raid.

After three solid days of pain, gunfire and bombs, I implored the matron to be moved to a quieter spot. Heroics had died a swift death after the first day's treatment of high explosive sounds. Together with her charm ran a great efficiency and soon the matron brought the glad tidings that an ambulance would arrive the next morning to transfer me up to London.

My sister Daphne, living in London, somehow managed to find her way to Margate, despite chaotic rail communications. The shock expressed on her lovely face at the sight of me, gave a message beyond words.

The following day, true to its promise but an hour late, came the ambulance driven by two ineffectual young females in F.A.N.N.Y. uniform.

Another trolley ride, a heave, and I was stacked in the lower of two stretcher racks. It then appeared that there was to be another occupant for the journey, and departure was delayed for his arrival. Fifteen minutes later a sitting-up stretcher case slid into the upper birth, consisting of an army sergeant with a badly sprained ankle.

Five minutes of flirtatious repartee followed between the over-permed drivers and the sergeant, before the rear doors were shut on the two stretcher cases, my sister Daphne and a Sister from the hospital. The long journey to London began.

Lying there looking up at the slope of the sergeant's posterior outlined by the canvas of the stretcher, I imagined that every bump in
the road was at least a miniature tank trap. At the end of half an hour
the Sister jabbed me with pain-killing morphia.

One hour after they started the two girls were hopelessly lost. In
spite of the injection I began to feel very ill after the second hour had
passed, and just when I felt about all in, the ambulance drew up in
front of the hospital.

Gaily one of the girls came back to inform me that this was the
sergeant's disembarkation point, and that London was still a long way
off. Lurching and jerking, they set off again after the detour to deposit
the N.C.O., and the Sister had to administer another injection to keep
her whimpering patient under control. My sister did her best to console
me with comforting words, but despite her loving efforts, I was beyond
that stage. Another series of stops and starts ensued as the drivers inquired the way, but finally the girls found the place they were looking
for. This consisted of a house ten miles off the London road where they
duly deposited a package entrusted to their care. The journey resumed.

Five hours after setting out, the ambulance approached the Royal
Masonic Hospital in Hammersmith, recently taken over for partial
use by the Royal Air Force.

Eventually the bouncing ambulance came to a lurching halt in
front of the hospital, and after what felt like an eternity, the double
doors were opened. The two flighty attendants poked their noses inside before disappearing. "Bet you thought we'd never get here," giggled Flat Chested.

"See you in church," sallied Square Rump.

Satisfied with their war effort, the two members of the appropri-
ately named corps toddled off, leaving the Sister to help the male hospital porter unload the body.

I thank my lucky stars for the little woman's presence. The porter
gave the impression of having served his apprenticeship in Smithfield
Market, such was his attitude towards a hunk of flesh. Between them
they at last managed to lay the stretcher on the trolley, and the three
of us proceeded towards the main entrance.

The patient was oblivious to the surroundings. Life consisted of two gigantic pumps forcing liquid pain into my arms with each beat of my heart. Above the thumping note I was aware that an exchange of information was going on between the resident nursing staff and my Sister-in-waiting. She came to the side of the trolley to say her farewell and quickly stroked my hair with a gentle touch. Before I could summon up the strength to thank her she was gone.

Pushed by the solid weight of the porter, the trolley trundled down the inevitably long hospital corridors, round corners and eventually finished up alongside the bed in an immaculate private patient's room. The escort of three young nurses prepared to lift me onto the bed by a combined effort, but the porter had ideas of his own. Reaching an arm under my back until it appeared the other side, he took his other arm over the top of my body and joined hands. With this grip firmly established, he squeezed hard and raised the prostrate figure from the stretcher. The scream of agony that issued from my lips as the porter's full strength took my injured hands in his vice-like grip resounded round the hospital.

For the first time in my life in front of women, I used the filthiest stream of language of which I was capable to lash the half-witted attendant. Sulkily the man retired from the room as a senior nurse arrived to find out the cause of the trouble.

When I came round for the fourth time that day, it was to find her handsome young face looking down at the mass of burnt flesh with compassion. Then her face disappeared into the watery blur that existed most of the time. Soothingly she spoke to me and the painlessly administered injection brought swift relief.

Time slipped by to a fairly familiar pattern. Drugged sleep brought with it nightmares that always ended up in burning aircraft. Awakeness brought with it attendant pain and misery before the cure-all needle did its work. The drugged semi-conscious state was perhaps the worst of all. The creeping effect of the morphia caused me to nod off until suddenly I came awake again with a jerk of nerves. This violent nervous twitch would cause my hands to flick quickly, bringing with it a sensation that surmounted even the numbing qualities of the drug. Like the fog lifting from the sea, so did the lazy passage of time suddenly end. I awoke for the first time aware that despite physical discomfort, I was back in the living world again. The instant she walked into the room, the nurse knew that a change had taken place and she walked over to the windows to draw the heavy curtains apart. Warm sunshine filled the clean white room.

"You've been a sick boy," was her first remark. "Hungry?"

I was and said so. "I could eat a horse!"

She chuckled. "It's highly likely your wish will be granted."

Ten minutes later she returned with a tray and half a bottle of champagne. With a twinkle in her eye, she remarked, "They seem to think you need building-up, so the doctors have put you on a diet of champagne!"

The project however, had to be abandoned after two sips as the alcohol set the pumps in my hands working at full pressure again. She fed me tenderly as a mother would feed her newborn child, and I began to look forward to the meals as the great events of the day. Between mouthfuls, the conversation took on the tune of friendly railery. After a discussion as to which one of us was in charge of the eating operation, she insisted that she was captain of the ship and therefore to be obeyed. I promptly dubbed her "Skipper" and she answered to that name until I was transferred to another hospital.

Soon after that, visitors were permitted. My mother and sister had naturally been allowed to have glimpses of me during the delirious stage, but now others were allowed to come into the room for short intervals. My range of vision didn't extend beyond the edge of the bed, and only this far by squeezing my eyes tight to remove the ever present watery film over them.

Jumbo, Bob and Barry came as soon as operational commitments permitted. Their news stimulated me to a point of excitement that concerned the watchful Skipper. Despite their light-hearted manner, I could see that they were desperately tired, and that the gayness was only a pretence. Jokingly they passed off the deaths of friends as if it were a cricket score. When they had gone, the reaction set in, and for long moments I lay sobbing helplessly. Exactly what the tears were for, I didn't know myself. Perhaps for the deaths of my companions or from self-pity at no longer being a part of squadron life. As Skipper explained it to me later, she said it was a natural reaction to the strain of fighting and the violent shock to the system after sustaining extensive injuries. It all helped to clear the air and by next mealtime I was all smiles again for my personal nurse. But the next day I suffered the first of what were to be repetitious setbacks. One of the prettiest girls I'd seen in my life came into the room to help Skipper with the dressings. Attired in the cool, colourful uniform of a V.A.D. Red Cross nurse, she personified the wounded warrior's vision of the ideal angel of mercy. Standing beside the dressing trolley assisting the professional nurse, she was unable to hide the expression of horror and loathing that registered on her lovely face at the sight of my scorched flesh. From the depths of my soul I longed for Beauty to cast me a friendly glance, even if it came in the shabby guise of pity, but the first expression remained constant.

Following her hypnotized stare, I looked down watery-eyed at my arms. From the elbows to the wrists the bare forearms were one seething mass of pus-filled boils resulting from the disturbed condition of the blood. Then for the first time I noticed the hands themselves. From the wrist joints to the finger tips they were blacker than any negro's hand, but smaller in size than I had ever remembered them to be. I shared the V.A.D.'s expression of horror until Skipper intervened. "That black stuff's only tannic acid. It's not the colour of your skin."

Relief flooded through me and my face relaxed. Not so that of the V.A.D.'s.

Skipper turned to her assistant. "Gauze, please, Anne."

Dutifully the other girl passed the piece of dressing, and then suddenly she fled from the room. A deadly silence settled in the room, and it was half a minute before Skipper continued with her work. When I spoke it was with an icy edge to the command in my voice. "Get me a mirror please, nurse."

Deftly she dabbed away at the oozing matter issuing from underneath the black tannic acid about the wrists. She answered me in a soft undertone. "Anne is a brilliant pianist and an inexperienced nurse, and the sight of your wounds has obviously been a shock to her, poor child."

Coldly I repeated my request. "I should like a mirror please, nurse."

Flicking the dirty swab away and carefully selecting more sterile wool with the two pairs of forceps she continued, "You'll see yourself in a mirror all in good time."

"I want it now!"

Her voice took on a bantering tone as she appealed to my sense of humour. "Now then, don't be a silly boy. Remember you're a big brave fighter pilot."

The new tack failed to work, and unreasonably I reiterated the demand. It was then for the first time she looked up at me and the coldness in her voice matched mine. "You will be allowed to look in a mirror, Pilot Officer Page, when I see fit to permit it and not before."

An antagonistic silence descended between us, and the precise method by which she completed the dressing demonstrated her frame of mind. For my part I lay there hating her and with a fury born of frustration. Ten minutes later she dropped the tweezers with a final clank into the kidney dish and propelled the trolley out of the room without a parting word.

"Right, you miserable bitch," I thought. "I'll look in a mirror if it kills me."

The mirror itself presented no problem, hanging as it did over the washbasin alongside the bed. The only difficulty was that of getting out of bed and taking the two steps away to face my reflection. First came the task of throwing back the bedclothes, which with usual hospital efficiency, were tucked firmly in on each side under the mattress. Five minutes hard elbow work dislodged them slightly at the price of violently throbbing hands. After a rest I tried again and succeeded in moving them back as far as the cradle which kept the sheets off my injured leg. Stage number two merely consisted of sitting up and swinging my legs round over the side of the bed, a task none too easy in a weakened condition and without the aid of hands. Once I was sitting upright with my legs dangling over the edge of the bed, I felt a wave of dizziness pass through me. Pausing for it to pass, I attempted the long drop from the high hospital bed to the polished floor beneath. This had to be done by literally straightening my body and sliding feet-first to the floor, hoping not to lose balance on the way down. Taking a deep breath I straightened my back and slid downwards. Balance was maintained, but the jar of striking the ground buckled my knees, and I only saved myself from falling by virtue of an arresting elbow. The pain caused by the jolt necessitated another rest, but with every second of passing time my leg muscles became weaker.

At last there was nothing left but to leave the protecting solidarity of the bed, and take the two vital steps to the edge of the basin. The first one was completed with confidence, but the icy sweat that accompanied the second step forewarned disaster. Tottering in front of the mirror, I squeezed the moisture out of my eyes and surveyed the image in front of me. The shock of the swollen face three times its normal size was almost too great to comprehend, but it was weakness and not horror that caused me to faint away.

Skipper's shocked face appeared reflected in the mirror as the door opened behind me, and I was aware of a distant stab of pain as my hands struck the basin and my mind slipped into unconsciousness.

Eighteen

The days passed by rapidly and with them came the bombing raids on London itself. The sound of the warning siren even before the guns fired or the bombs dropped reduced me to a nervous wreck, and I would lie there cursing everything Teutonic and promising myself vengeance. Skipper and I were back on amicable terms again after she had picked me up inert from the floor, but it was becoming obvious that the air raids were impeding recovery. Skipper told me of a plan that was afoot to evacuate the few pilots in the hospital to another one in the country. I received the news with mixed feelings.

It was on Skipper's day off that I met him for the first time. Matron, a primly efficient older woman, walked into the room and brandishing a letter asked me if I felt up to receiving a visitor. Unable to read or smoke, I was happy in my stronger moments to have someone to talk to, especially in Skipper's absence. Leaving the letter face-downwards on top of the bed-cradle, Matron departed briskly. I lay there for a while conjecturing whom this strange visitor might be, until my eye caught sight of the white piece of paper lying above my legs. Easing myself gently up in the bed, I reached down and drew the letter towards me by gripping it between both elbows. Recovering my breath before the final effort of turning it over, I set about the last stage. Through the watery blur came the dull and formal words of the letter. "... Mr. Archibald McIndoe is hereby authorized by the Air Ministry to visit Pilot Officer A.G. Page at the ...."

I lay back exhausted.

An hour later the matron re-entered, followed by a young man, who looked to be in his late thirties. Having introduced him as Mr. McIndoe, she departed. The visitor had dark hair parted in the middle and brushed flat to the head, horn-rimmed spectacles, broad shoulders and a friendly mischievous grin. His whole appearance was not unlike that of Harold Lloyd, the film comedian.

Grasping a leather briefcase firmly inside a hand that would have done credit to a professional boxer, he advanced round to the left hand side of the patient's bed and seated himself on an upright chair. Extracting a sheet of paper and pencil he viewed me from over the top of his glasses. The eyes had an incredible depth behind them and seemed to exude great understanding. The words came out crisply with the slight flatness of note peculiar to New Zealanders.

"Hurricane or Spitfire?"

"Hurricane."

"Header tank?"

I laughed. "Yes. The wing tanks in my machine were self-sealing, but some bright type forgot to treat the tank in front of the pilot."

The eyes twinkled again. "Just can't trust anyone, can you?"

We both laughed.

He didn't stay long and during his short visit the conversation was lighthearted and dealt with seemingly inconsequential details. Was I wearing goggles and gloves? How long was I in the water, and how soon afterwards was the tannic acid treatment given?

The visitor rose and took a cheery farewell of me. He waved a large hamfisted hand as he passed rapidly through the door. "Good-bye, young fellow. See you again."

Little did I realize how often I would be seeing him.

The next day the authorities ordered the hospital to be evacuated. Skipper broke the news with forced cheerfulness, but it was obvious to both of us that the parting would be a wrench at the instinctive friendship that had grown between us.

"Besides," she added by way of making matters a little easier. "You'll get better more quickly in the country and can have a nice long convalescence."

"Convalescence be damned! I've got to get back flying as soon as possible. There's no time to waste sitting around ... deckchairs."

Skipper laughed heartily. "Silly boy, you'll never fly again."

My silence told her she had said the wrong thing.

After tea they dressed me up as much as possible in a new uniform forwarded from North Weald. My arms were placed in slings and a silk scarf wrapped about the neck bandages in lieu of a tie. The tunic was draped about my shoulders like a cloak. Finally the whole apparition, looking more like a scarecrow than an R.A.F. officer, was placed in a wheelchair and trundled out to the waiting ambulance. I never did discover why they dressed me up for the long journey between the two hospitals. Blinking watery eyes in the warm sunshine I was happy to see that the two ambulance crew were male Air Force orderlies and not F.A.N.N.Y. drivers. Gently but firmly they lifted me out of the chair and deposited me on a bunk in the back of the vehicle. Two minutes later two more pilots walked into view under their own steam. The taller of the two was somewhat Christ-like with his distinguished black beard and large deep-set eyes. The reason for the beard was the fact he had been burnt about the jaw and mouth, so shaving was impossible. His companion was slightly shorter and much broader by comparison with the slim-bearded figure. Wrapped about his neck was a thick bandage which caused him to carry his head cocked to one side. He had received an enemy bullet through the side of his neck.

Politely we introduced ourselves as the doors were closed and the ambulance drove away from the hospital grounds. Soon we were talking "shop" and comparing notes concerning our respective squadrons. All of us were Hurricane pilots, as were the majority of the Battle of Britain aircrew, and the first hour of the journey passed quickly enough.

P./O. D. H. Grice, the bearded flight lieutenant, looked at his watch.

"The pubs open in a couple of minutes. How about a pint?"

The other man and I looked at each other questioningly.

"I'm game," said Stephens.

I nodded in agreement. Although the thought of collapsing into bed appealed to me enormously, the idea of going into a "local" again as a normal human being, proved too great a temptation. Grice banged on the partition. The panel slid back and one of the attendants peered through.

"Pull up at the first decent-looking pub you see," Grice commanded.

The man hesitated for a moment and consulted with the driver before his grinning face reappeared.

"Is that an order, sir?"

"It is," said Grice firmly.

His conscience clear, the man grinned happily. "Very good, sir."

Five minutes later the ambulance rolled to a stop in front of a small whitewashed inn. Colourful chintz curtains showed through the gleaming glass of the mullioned bay windows.

Grice and Stephens gave me a friendly arm apiece as we passed through into the cosy bar parlour. The phlegmatic locals with their pints of beer and rough cloth caps could not have appeared more surprised if a bunch of Zulu warriors had walked in, in full regalia. We propped ourselves up by the bar and demanded pints of beer from the shaken landlord. Carefully Grice held up the glass tankard and poured some of its contents into my mouth. Weak though it was, the beer flavour brought back in full flood the atmosphere of my pre-injury life. For a brief moment I felt that once again I was a normal human being participating in everyday affairs.

At that point the landlord's wife joined her husband behind the bar. Her loud undertone to him soon jerked me back to the true state of affairs. "The poor dears, and them so young and all. Quite turns me stomach."

Grice caught our eyes, nodded and we rose to depart. As the door closed behind us, we could hear the babel of voices begin. Their stupid mutterings brought back Skipper's words with a bitter rush. "Silly boy, you'll never fly again."

The R.A.F. hospital at Halton was a pre-war establishment famous for one section that devoted its activities to the curing of unpleasant social diseases picked up by enthusiastic airmen. It looked like what it was – a cross between a barrack block and a prison. Regular service discipline and red tape were the order of the day. Medicine was a necessary nuisance that interrupted the parade ground alignment of the beds and the polishing of the floors, the latter being a vital factor in making life more difficult for the orthopedic patients. Fortunately for the inmates, the war brought with it a body of civilian doctors fresh from the struggle of London hospitals and abysmally ignorant of service ranks and procedures. Nevertheless, these men donned uniform and outwardly complied with the legion of futile regulations.

Unaware of the procedure in our new abode, the three of us entered the portals singing lustily in a tipsy condition. The beer, watery as it had been, had affected us quickly in our weakened state. A grinning medical orderly met us and led the way along innumerable bleak corridors before ascending to the first floor.

"You won't 'arf cop it, gentlemen, if Sister hears you."

"Fuck Sister, in that case," said Stephens in his best old Etonian voice.

The orderly was gifted with a sense of humour. "I don't think you'd want to, sir. You wait till you see the old battle-axe."

Fortunately for all concerned, the meeting was postponed until the following morning as this was Sister Risden's afternoon off. The ward contained about twenty beds, only half of which were occupied. Despite the permeating hospital aroma, the long sparsely furnished room created the impression of a public convenience with beds.

Our guide indicated three vacant beds, and with a genial "Make yourselves comfortable, gents," sloped off for his supper. I felt just about done in and gratefully accepted Grice's offer to undress me. Thankfully I tumbled into bed and fell asleep.

One glance at Sister Risden's face was enough to know that she and Florence Nightingale had little in common. Aptly named "Polly," her curved beak hung menacingly over tightly compressed thin lips. Without a word of greeting or the flicker of a smile, she took down the service details of name, rank and number from each of the three new arrivals. No questions were asked concerning our injuries or needs.

Having noted down these vital particulars she swept from the ward, but not soon enough to miss the well-timed sally that emanated from one of the occupied beds. "Relax, boys, now you can be sure of getting a funeral befitting your rank."

The instigator of the remark lay in his bed with one plastered leg pointing ceilingwards as it hung suspended from a series of ropes and pulleys. Johnny Walker was the humourist of the ward and one of the few people, patient or staff, who was not frightened by Polly Risden. Her hatred for him was apparent to all. Johnny Walker had a nervous way of sniggering every time he passed an amusing remark. "You may have thought the war was rough, chaps, but wait till you've had a few days of Polly's loving care and attention."

Despite a feeling of loneliness at my separation from Skipper, I felt this new ward sister couldn't be as bad as she was painted. "She can't be that poor a nurse," I protested. "Beneath that starched exterior most probably beats a heart of gold."

Walker giggled. "Where her heart should be is a copy of King's Regulations amended up to date."

For twenty-four hours I championed Polly Risden more from boyish goodwill than knowledge. The next day brought a change in my outlook.

Occupying the bed on my right was a flying officer with a broken arm encased in a plaster cast. The nervous condition of this young man far exceeded his physical injuries, and within a few hours of awakening on the first new day in the ward, I was subjected to my companion's tale of woe. It turned out that the flying officer had finished his honeymoon only the day before meeting with his injuries. His young bride, living as she did in the local inn on the edge of the airfield, was now more likely to encounter enemy action than her husband.

The anxious groom paced the floor beside my bed seeking words of solace to reassure him that his wife would come through safely. I did my best to soothe his troubled heart with expressions of comfort, but finally I realized that nothing but the sight or sound of his beloved would help the neurotic airman.

On the second day it happened.

A junior sister came rustling down the ward in good humour to collect the flying officer, who was struggling left-handedly to trim his moustache with a pair of blunt scissors.

"Don't worry about that," she advised him. "Your wife's on the phone, and she's had to wait seven hours to get the call through."

Everyone in earshot who knew about the F.O.'s circumstances felt happy. This was something he needed far more than medical attention. The sound of her voice would be the greatest cure of all. I heaved a luxurious sigh. The effect of a recent injection had elevated me to a land of well-being, and this good news for my companion topped it off beautifully.

Then the flying officer returned down the ward, a mop of black hair, sunken dazed eyes and a black moustache. Nothing more.

"What's up, old man?" For once Johnny Walker was serious and no snigger followed the question.

"The bitch ... the bloody bitch!"

It was only when he said it the second time, that the F.O. put any feeling into the words. Numbly he seated himself on the edge of his precision-made bed.

"Anything I can do to help?" I asked quietly.

Slowly the other man brought his eyes back from the distance. "She's been waiting by a phone box for seven hours to speak to me, and just before I could answer, that . . . that bloody bitch of a Sister, Polly Risden, told her that patients were not allowed to receive private calls and hung up."

It was the violent pumping of the blood in my hands that told me the extent of my anger, and for a minute I lay there gasping for air and control of my feelings. To feel angry was almost an unknown emotion for me. At school I had been accused of being too easygoing, but now I experienced a hatred that consumed normal reasoning in the heat of its fires.

Two days later I was able to strike a small blow in revenge.

Every morning I was visited by Wing Commander Cade (later Sir Stanford Cade), a soft-spoken Polish surgeon. Seating himself beside the bed, he would examine my hands with the gentleness of a kitten. Together we would discuss the changes and rate of discharge coming from under the tannic acid gauntlet. With scissors and forceps the surgeon would deftly snip away at the leathery casing where it showed signs of coming away from the tender flesh beneath. As each raw area became exposed, he would point it out to the sentinel figure of Polly Risden standing at the end of the bed, and instruct her to treat them with saline dressings.

Two days after the Ward Sister's cruel treatment of the flying officer's telephone call, I had sufficient reason to complain. Since Wing Commander Cade had first issued his instructions concerning the treatments, none had been carried out. So on the second morning I complained bitterly to the surgeon of the Sister's negligence, partly from good reason and partly from spite.

The occupants of the ward were startled to see the normally placid Polish officer explode and vent his wrath on the shattered Sister. Uttering dire threats if his orders were not obeyed in the future, he swept out followed by the protesting woman.

That night I was not given the cup of Ovaltine normally provided for those more seriously injured to help them sleep.

Polly Risden had struck back!

Days of snipping went by with no decrease in the throbbing in my hands, and the calm face of the Polish Wing Commander began to show traces of concern. Finally one morning he came to a decision. "I'm afraid, young man, that we must operate on these poor hands of yours and remove the tannic covering. It will be too painful to do it otherwise than under an anaesthetic."

A chill of fear entered the pit of my stomach at the surgeon's words spoken in precise English touched with its Polish intonation.

I raised a sickly grin. "You know best, sir."

The surgeon hoped the patient was right.

Masked faces with detached impersonal eyes gazed down on the trolley as the anaesthetist bared my arm for the sodium pentathol injection. A painful jab, the taste of onions, and then the nightmare ride in burning airplanes accompanied by distant pain slowly coming nearer and nearer. Memories of the blurred figure of a Sister beside the bed, a jab of a morphia injection and then oblivion and blessed relief from pain.

Following a deep sleep I finally awoke with a clear head. Apprehensively I looked down at the two unbandaged objects lying propped on a sterile pillow. The pinkness of the tissue paper thin skin covering my hands made me think of newborn babies. So sensitive were they that the slightest draught across the ward registered pain sharply, just as an indrawn breath hurts on the exposed nerve of an aching tooth.

However, the joy of seeing my hands unencumbered by the crippling effects of the tannic acid more than made up for the physical discomfort. The joy was short-lived.

Day by day my strength increased and with it the condition of my hands deteriorated.

Fraction by fraction the tendons contracted, bending the fingers downwards until finally the tips were in contact with the palms. Added to this the delicate skin toughened by degrees until it had the texture of a rhinoceros's hide, at the same time webbing my fingers together until they were undistinguishable as separate units. The Polish surgeon watched impotently as the cruel contractions continued. Then one morning he posed the question to his patient.

"If your hands continue to form this thick scar tissue, I'm afraid it will mean a series of skin grafting operations. Are you prepared to try and prevent that?"

I shuddered. "What is the alternative, sir?"

The wing commander looked out of the window into the distance. "We may be able to keep the skin soft by the use of hot molten wax baths, followed by massage."

The choice was appalling from my point of view. Either method conjured up visions of prolonged pain for my raw nerves. After a moment of silence I said, "I'd like you to decide for me."

Nodding briefly, the Pole turned on his heel and left the ward.

The hot wax bath treatment began that same afternoon.

Sister Risden strode triumphantly into the ward. Her words matched the starchy rustle of her white uniform. "In place of the commanding officer's inspection this morning, the hospital is being reviewed by Air Marshal Probert.."

Johnny Walker sniggered. "Good Lord, is that old clot still alive?"

Polly Risden turned a withering glance in his direction. "When I want your opinion, Flying Officer Walker, I shall ask for it." With upturned beak she strutted from the ward.

Male nursing orderlies stood stiffly to attention in their white surgical gowns as the visiting party approached. Accompanying the hospital commandant was the bowed figure of an elderly Air Marshal. Puffing cheeks worked like bellows in the shallow setting of his face. He listened disinterestedly to the commanding officer's self-satisfied comments. Passing down the row of beds, the senior Air Force officer asked questions of their occupants and passed on almost before receiving a reply. Pausing in front of Johnny Walker's bed he stopped to examine the many weird designs that adorned the plaster cast on the patient's injured leg. In a bored manner he enquired, "And how did you meet with your accident, my boy?"

Johnny, who had been shot down when outnumbered twenty to one, replied earnestly, "As a matter of fact, sir, it was no accident. It was a deliberate attempt on my life."

Receiving dirty looks from all of the inspecting party, Johnny retired sniggering to the depths of his pillow.

Sweat broke out on my forehead as the physiotherapy sister poured the molten wax into the enamel basin. "Don't forget," she said soothingly, "try and stand as much heat as you can."

Leaving me to judge the moment when I could bear to immerse my sensitive fingers in the hot fluid, the sister turned to her other patients. The wax baths were becoming more and more of a nightmare to me as time went by. Each day was rendered hideous until the hateful operation was completed, and the congealed wax peeled off. The torture was not to end there, however. Electrical machinery attempted to stretch the contracting tendons, and for half an hour my twitching fingers jerked under the effects as the electric shocks passed through them.

Despite the treatments, it became obvious to both medical staff and patient that the battle was being lost. Slowly but inexorably, the skin that had been paper-thin thickened and coarsened until it became as unpliable as heavy leather. The fears of the Polish surgeon were becoming fact, and eventually he voiced the words I had been dreading. "Your hands will have to be grafted. I will arrange for you to see Mr. McIndoe."

The precise words brought back the memory of the youngish man with horn-rimmed spectacles, visiting me in the London hospital.

"McIndoe?" I asked vaguely.

"Yes," answered the Pole. "He is the consultant plastic surgeon to the Royal Air Force."

Nineteen

The taxi driver was a talkative, friendly individual. Once he knew of his passenger's destination, he embarked on a long dissertation. "Nice little place, the Cottage Hospital, sir. Sort of friendly without too much starch, if you get my meaning." He prattled on.

Meanwhile, in the back of the car I cloaked myself in a mantle of dejection and self-pity. The beauties of the soft Sussex countryside did nothing to dispel the mood. The dragging down process had been slow but steady. For three months I had watched the gradual contraction of my fingers combined with the coarsening of the scar tissue. Painful treatments only increased my bitterness towards my lot. The mind rejected feeling gratitude for the life saved. Better to be dead I felt, than constantly tortured.

Forgotten were the beseeching words screamed out in agony from the cockpit of the burning plane for my creator to save me. Dark resentment ruled instead.

"'Ere we are, sir. The Queen Victoria Cottage Hospital. Neat but not gaudy, and I'm sure you'll find it an 'ome from 'ome . . . thank you, sir, and the best of luck."

The taxi drove away, leaving me standing outside the entrance doors to the trim little one-storied building that served as a hospital to the nearby town of East Grinstead. An island of flowers in front of the entrance and carefully tended lawns lent a tranquil air to the surroundings. Unable to lift the suitcases, I pushed through the glass doors and announced my presence at the inquiry desk. Soon a porter bearing my luggage was leading the way down spotless corridors to one of the small wards, named after the Kindersley family. A trim-figured Sister in a dark blue uniform surmounted by a white cap greeted me. She spoke with the soft brogue of southern Ireland. Efficiently she noted down details of my service particulars, and the extent and type of my injuries. Sister Hall placed down her pen carefully and looked at me with emotionless eyes. "Mr McIndoe will be doing a round of the wards this evening. Meanwhile I'll show you to your bed, and you can be getting unpacked."

Leading the way from her little office we passed through a door into the small bright ward. Large glass windows extending from floor to ceiling along the entire length of one wall let in a wealth of daylight. Outside, gently sloping lawns led down to bright flower beds beyond.

The peaceful garden scene was counterposed by a loud voice breaking the air. "You stupid bastard, Richard . . . oooops, sorry, Sister."

"Don't worry about Sister," another voice replied. "They're used to bastards in Ireland."

Sister Hall chose to ignore the sally. "This is your bed, Mr. Page. I'll have a nurse help you unpack." Without waiting she turned and left me.

"Let me give you a hand."

Turning from my struggles with the latch of my suitcase, I was confronted with the figure of a young man in his early twenties, bearing the livid red weals of fire about his forehead and eyes. A humorous mouth and twinkling eyes made the face very likeable at first sight. Deftly he opened the suitcase, talking as he did so.

"My name's Tollemache and that apology over there for an R.A.F. officer is Hillary."

I glanced over in the direction indicated and received the shock of my life. Standing at the foot of a bed stood one of the queerest apparitions I had ever seen. The tall figure was clad in a long, loose-fitting dressing gown that trailed to the floor. The head was thrown right back so that the owner appeared to be looking along the line of his nose. Where normally two eyes would be, were two large bloody red circles of raw skin. Horizontal slits in each showed that behind still lay the eyes. A pair of hands wrapped in large lint covers lay folded across his chest. Cigarette smoke curled up from the long holder clenched between the ghoul's teeth. The empty sleeves of the dressing gown hung limply, lending the apparition a sinister air. It evidently had a voice behind its mask. It was condescending in tone.

"Ah, another bloody cripple! Welcome to the home for the aged and infirm!" With that Richard Hillary limped painfully out of the ward.

Tony Tollemache laughed at the expression on my face.

"Most probably shook you a bit, his face I mean. Just had a new pair of eyelids grafted on and they look a bit odd for a day or two."

I gulped. "But they look raw and bleeding."

Tollemache patted me on the shoulder. "Only mercurochrome, old boy. It's a red antiseptic that looks a bit bloody, that's all." Left to my own devices, I felt lost and homesick like a small boy on his first day at boarding school. The ward was divided into three small sections by glass partitions that rose to shoulder height. In each section were four beds. I noticed for the first time that, of the other three beds near my own, only one was occupied.

"Good afternoon," I ventured cautiously to its occupant. Hillary's reception had been a trifle unnerving.

"Hello," replied the youth in bed cheerfully. "First time here?"

"Yes, it is."

The other grinned. "First two years are the worst. I'm Roy Lane."

I introduced myself. Years later I was saddened to hear that Lane had been beheaded by the Japs after bailing out of his aircraft. During the course of our conversation, Hillary's name was mentioned again.

"Don't let him get you down," Roy Lane advised. "He's a conceited young man with a sharp tongue and a large inferiority complex."

"How can you be conceited with an inferiority complex?"

"Simple," Lane answered. "For years he's been told by his mother what a wonderful boy he is, but in the service he's had his backside kicked. Not surprising he's a bit mixed up."

It was some weeks before I overcame my awe of Hillary. "This is Pilot Officer Page, sir. A new arrival."

Archie McIndoe looked at me over the top of his horn-rimmed spectacles. "We've met before."

I smiled. Somehow I always felt happier when talking to McIndoe. "Yes, sir, at the Royal Masonic Hospital."

The surgeon bent over my crippled hands, turning them over slowly as he examined the damage. Without raising his head he looked up over his glasses. "Long job, I'm afraid."

Hesitantly I asked, "you'll have to operate?"

This time his head went back and the dark eyes met mine firmly. "Yes. Many times I'm afraid. But you'll be all right in the end."

I believed him.

Gently the night nurse shook my shoulder. "Your tea and toast, Mr. Page."

Glad to be awakened from the chaotic nightmares that dogged my sleep, I propped myself up on an elbow and examined the scene. Heavy breathing and occasional snores floated across from the other beds as their occupants slept on. The night nurse and I were alone in a little world of our own.

"What time is it please, nurse?"

Guardedly she shone a flash of light onto her wrist. "Nearly five-thirty. Drink the tea before it gets cold and then try and get back to sleep."

She left me to the darkness of the ward and my own thoughts. I sipped the warm brew slowly. I could feel it going down to meet the tiny knot of fear bunched in my stomach. Today was it – the day I had been dreading so long was now here.

Five hours later they would wheel me into the operating room to have the mass of scar tissue removed. Skin grafts taken from the inside of my leg would then be sewn into place to cover the raw hands. I shuddered and lay back on the pillow, staring at the ceiling with sight-less eyes.

The toast grew cold and remained untouched.

The ward had been awake for two hours. Disjointed happenings diverted my mind away for minutes at a time from the main channel of my thoughts, but remorselessly the aching fear returned. At first the caustic repartee of Hillary and Tollemache had helped, but the arrival of an empty trolley brought me back to grim reality with a jolt.

The hours passed and with them every movement of the swing door into the ward brought my head round with a jerk. Then the lunch trays arrived and I realized how hungry I had become despite the apprehension. At last only I remained to be served and I looked at the V.A.D. nurse expectantly as she re-entered the ward. Guessing my thought, she wagged a reproving finger. "Nothing for you. You're the first case for surgery after lunch."

The icy chill of fear returned to freeze my marrow.

Then minutes later the businesslike figure of the young Irish Sister arrived at my bed. "Dressing gown and slippers on, Mr. Page, and along to the bathroom please. You have to be 'prepped.'"

I looked at her questioningly.

"Prepared for the operating room," she answered the unspoken query.

My cold feet never felt the chill of the tile floor as I slipped out of bed. A minute later I shuffled down the corridor in the Sister's wake. The bathroom smelled strongly of antiseptic. A solitary chair and a surgical dressing trolley stood as stark companions to the gleaming white bath.

The Sister didn't look up from her tasks at the trolley.

"Dressing gown and pyjama jacket off, please."

Slowly I peeled off the warm garments as if shedding my last friends in the world. Love seemed dead and all that was left was this unfeeling woman in these chill surroundings. Nothing but pain lay ahead. My soul whimpered.

"Right arm out straight." The command whipped out. Deftly the forceps grasped a large pad of cotton wool, immersed it swiftly in ether and lopped it over the outstretched hand. Involuntarily I gasped with the icy cold of the rapidly vaporizing fluid. Her eyes flicked upwards for a second.

"Don't be such a baby."

The sickly sweetness of the ether drove the reply away and I held my breath to avoid inhaling the anaesthetic. Soon the whole arm from finger to shoulder were sluiced and followed by a deft shaving of the masculine hairs from my forearm.

Again the ether treatment. This operation completed, the Sister opened a sterile drum and extracted squares of material which she proceeded to wrap round my naked arm. A fine gauze bandage was quickly wound over the top of the material to keep them in place. I gazed at the mummified appearance of the limb as if it were not my own, but produced from a tomb of one of the ancient Pharaohs.

"Wait here one moment." With that she disappeared with only the slight rustle of starch to mark her departure. Five minutes passed before the door reopened, admitting the white gowned figure of a male orderly.

The new arrival chuckled. "Poor old Sister, efficient as the devil, but she can't look a man in his parts unless he's unconscious."

I didn't understand.

The orderly bent over the trolley. "Now then, sir, trousers off, if you please."

The performance with the Sister was child's play compared to the ritual that followed. The icy cold douche of the ether on the most sensitive parts of my anatomy, followed by the sight of a razor so close to all that I held near and dear was unnerving. Shorn of hairs and those down to the knee on my right leg, left me feeling more naked than I had ever felt before in my life.

Happy to explain the reason for the extensive shave, the orderly chatted on. "Got to get rid of the hair – harbours germs, and germs is death to a skin graft. The donor area, the part where they get the new skin in this case, must be sterilized just the same as the hand where it's going to."

A few minutes later the leg matched the arm with its swathings. The pyjamas were replaced by a surgical gown tied together down the back by tapes. Feeling like a hamstrung horse, I hobbled down the ward and thankfully crawled into bed.

They hadn't finished with me yet. A V.A.D. arrived with a pair of the longest white, woollen stockings I had ever seen. "To keep your tootsies warm," she remarked.

A quick remembrance of my mother returned with her words, but the memory faded rapidly at the sight of the Sister advancing down the ward carrying a kidney dish containing a hypodermic syringe. Again the smell of ether as a small area on my left bicep was sterilized to accept the injection. The dragging seconds of anticipation made the slight prick of the needle an anticlimax. Expertly she removed the dart and wiped the minute puncture with the impregnated cotton wool. Impersonally she indicated the trolley lying behind surrounding bed screens.

"Onto the trolley, Mr. Page. They'll come for you later."

Awkwardly I clambered out of bed and climbed onto the narrow rack. Sister Hall tucked in the blankets with quick professional movements and then left me to my thoughts. Despite the woollen socks and the warm blankets, I lay there shivering. My teeth began to chatter. Then the injection began to take effect. Lightly at first, the pleasant sensation of well-being touched the back of my neck and spread slowly upwards to the top of the head. Gentle fingers seemed to be massaging my forehead and eyes and I no longer felt cold. The taut nerves relaxed and for the first time since awakening, fear left my body.

Sister Hall put her head round the screen. "Sleepy, Mr. Page?"

Drowsily I opened my eyes from the drugged coma. "Yes, but . . ." The words would not come out.

She nodded knowingly. "There's something in that injection to dry up the saliva in your mouth. That's why it's difficult to talk."

The words were wasted. The drug was doing its work.

At first I could not associate myself with my surroundings. Vaguely aware of a sensation of movements and the rumble of wheels, my mind refused to coordinate events. My eyes came down from the moving ceiling and took in the gowned and masked figure pushing the trolley from the end near my feet. The detached eyes smiled at me, but quickly became stern as I attempted to raise my head.

"Lie down, please," the nurse commanded. "We'll soon be there," she added in a softer voice.

Despite the drug, the blind fear was returning. Thinking back on it, I was really just a little boy dressed in a man's role, missing maternal protection. Only the nurse's presence stopped me from begging a reprieve from further pain. Swing doors parted and the trolley slid into a small anteroom beside the operating room.

Figures bustled around and words were exchanged in hushed voices. Suddenly the relative silence was broken by a hearty voice exclaiming, "Well, and what have we got here?"

The rotund figure in its white theatre gown appeared more like a

*R.A.F. jargon for someone who is crazy.

pork butcher than an anaesthetist. Above the large paunch was a friendly face consisting of chubby cheeks, double chin, rimless glasses and a small moustache. A few wisps of hair failed to hide much of the bald skin on his head.

"I'm John Hunter, better known as the Gasworks," he added cheerfully. "Which reminds me, have you heard the story of the girl called Virginia …?"

Giggles from the other occupants in the room attested to Doctor Hunter's popularity as a storyteller. The yarn failed to interrupt the anaesthetist's work, and as the story enlarged so did he continue with his preparations. Glass vials were robbed of their precious liquids and transferred to businesslike hypodermic syringes; gas cylinders were replaced on the anaesthetic trolley; and a general atmosphere of sterilized efficiency was maintained.

A muttered order from Hunter, and a male orderly placed a stool beside the patient's trolley, upon which the corpulent doctor seated himself. Neatly he stretched and tied a narrow piece of flexible tubing about my left bicep and massaged the arm in the direction of the elbow. Quickly the deep veins began to show as the blood pressure built up.

"Just a little prick, if you'll pardon the expression," said the doctor cheerfully.

I averted my gaze as I saw the large needle press into the flesh in the crook of my elbow. Almost instantly after the slight pain of the jab came a violent taste of onions at the back of my throat and a warm glow suffused my entire body.

Darkness engulfed me suddenly.

Lieutenant Patrick O'Conner of his Majesty's Highland Light Infantry was pleasantly round the bend. The abnormal to him was normal, and the Queen Victoria Cottage Hospital needed, in his opinion, livening up.

A collision between his platoon truck and a fire engine of the Glasgow Fire Brigade had resulted in several deaths and the departure of Lieutenant O'Conner for surgical treatment. Ironically, the first engine and the platoon truck were both dashing madly to put out the

Geoffrey Page, aged 17.

Top: Hurricanes in flight, Battle of Britain.

Above left: Flight Lieutenant E J "Jumbo" Gracie DFC, flight commander with 56 Squadron 1940. After long service in England and

Malta he was killed commanding a Mosquito squadron in 1944.

Above right: Flying Officer Bryan Wicks DFC, 56 Squadron in 1940, killed over Malta in October 1942.

Top: Geoffrey Page (second from left), briefing pilots before the first operational sortie into Germany.

Above left: North American Mustang 1a, similar to the type flown by Geoffrey on 29 June 1943 with ADFU.

Above: Squadron leader J A F MacLachlan's grave, Pont L'Eveque Communal Cemetery.

Top: Sitting in his Spitfire IX, France 1944, Geoffrey is bombed up and ready to go. Note his initials "A G P" and the Wingco's pennant, the prerogative of a Wing Leader. Note too the D-Day invasion stripes under the wings.

Above left: Geoffrey lecturing in the United States in 1945.

Above right: Geoffrey's future wife Pauline in the uniform of the Canadian equivalent of the W.A.A.F.s.

Top: Pauline with Lassie during the filming of "Son of Lassie" in Canada in 1943.

Left: C Aubrey Smith is best man at the wedding of the author and Pauline, Santa Barbara, California, 1946.

Top: Geoffrey's father-in-law, Nigel Bruce, in a fascinating publicity shot. From left to right. Rex Harrison, Nigel Bruce, David Niven and Clark Gable.

Above: A Guinea Pig Club re-union. Nigel Bruce is at left, Archie McIndoe second from right.

Top: A very rare postwar photo. With Geoffrey in the jeep are, in the front, Douglas Bader and back, Adolf Galland (left) and Bob Stanford Tuck.

Above: Family group: Geoffrey Page with Pauline and daughter Shelley and son Jamie.

Top: Another family grouping, this time without Jamie but with son Nigel (third from left, rear), Shelley (far left) and extended family.

Above: The Battle of Britain Memorial unveiled by the Queen Mother in July 1993. Seeing this to fruition had occupied a great deal of Geoffrey's time in the 1980s.

same batch of incendiary bombs in a field outside Glasgow, when they collided head-on.

His injuries were confined to his face and consisted of a broken jaw and a badly fractured right antrum. This latter injury resulted in the cheekbone being pushed inwards and a consequent drooping bulge to the eye above. Dental surgeons set to work and soon had the jaw back in shape. To keep it in position it was clamped to the upper jaw by means of a suitable brace; a solitary screw over the front teeth kept the metal casts afixed one to the other. McIndoe reset the fractured antrum, but was confronted with the problem of keeping the broken cheekbone in the correct position. To overcome this difficulty he wrapped a plaster cast about O'Conner's head, into which he inserted a three-inch iron bar, leaving it to protrude horizontally above the damaged area. From this yardarm was attached thin platinum wire that stretched down to enter minute holes drilled in the antrum.

Despite his dapper figure and locked jaws, Patrick O'Conner managed to produce a rich deep boom from his throat that would have done credit to his Regimental Sergeant Major. His first twenty-four hours in the hospital left their impression.

Walking jauntily into the ward in his uniform of white spats, tartan trousers, khaki tunic and glengarry perched on the side of his head, he commenced to inspect the ward. Finally with an air of faint disgust he left his bag on the bed and marched out without a word to anyone.

Shortly before midnight he returned, giving voice to a lively rendering of a bawdy Scottish song, hiccuped twice and went to sleep fully dressed. The efforts of the night nurse to undress him were of no avail.

The following morning Lieutenant O'Conner was wheeled into the operating room for surgery. But it was not to be. At the first incision of the scalpel a jet of blood under terrific pressure shot forth, and he was returned to the ward until the alcoholic content in his blood had dropped to reasonable levels.

Lieutenant O'Conner's tartan trousers disappeared mysteriously for the next two days, but reappeared when he returned from the operating room.

Now I had a glimmering of what Christ must have felt as they drove the nails through his hands. The nails were many and they were being hammered inexpertly through the same hand, only to be withdrawn agonizingly with huge pincers. The hammering torture came from a distance, or so it seemed, but it was there nevertheless. Wildly I tossed my head from side to side on the sweat damped pillow. " No . . . no . . . n . . . n . . ." The moan came as a disbelief that such things could be, were allowed to be. Like a frightened animal being stroked, I calmed down as gentle fingers wiped my wet forehead with gauze.

"Lie still and we'll give you something for the pain."

Fuzzily through the mists of the lingering anaesthetic I heard the words. A shuddering moan escaped my lips as the nails were wrenched out for the tenth time. My head started its wild tattoo. This time Sister Hall made no attempt to soothe her patient, but swiftly set about administering the injection of morphia. The prick of the needle was unfelt in the sea of pain. Soon my head stopped its senseless rolling and torture disappeared over the horizon as the drug began its calming effect.

Hillary paused at the end of the bed and stood silently watching what he thought was my unconscious body.

"You're not as tough as you try to make out, are you, Mr. Hillary?" There was something near to triumph in Sister Hall's voice.

Quickly recovering from the surprise of being caught unawares, the tall figure gave a contemptuous snort. "Bloody fool should have worn gloves."

She did not even bother to glance down. Hillary's hands were equally badly burned and for the same reason – no gloves.

An hour later the torture began again. Slightly less in intensity though the pain was, it needed another injection to allow me to retain my sanity. That evening McIndoe visited his surgical cases in the ward. I opened my eyes slowly at the sound of Sister Hall's voice.

". . . and this is Mr. Page, sir."

McIndoe grinned down sympathetically. "Bet it hurts like hell, eh?"

One minute before, and the remark would have been a miracle of understatement. Now however, the surgeon's presence brought a slowing down to the steam hammer pounding away in my right hand. "Oh, it's not too bad thank you, sir."

McIndoe's glance took in the dark blue circles under my eyes. Nodding a farewell, he passed on.

The steam hammer picked up speed again.

Days and nights followed each other in a slow agonizing shuffle. Time consisted of blessed stabs in the arm that brought temporary relief. Relief that seemed to be a period during which the next wave of pain built itself up to crash down pitilessly as the drug wore off. For five days it ebbed and flowed through the channel of my arm. Food was brought, remained untouched, and was silently removed without remonstration. It was a steady diet of morphia and throbbing liquid agony.

Feeling hollow-eyed and emaciated I watched the white-capped and gowned group approach on the afternoon of the fifth day – or was it the fifth year? McIndoe nodded his usual friendly greeting, but the face that took in my condition was serious.

"How goes it?"

The answer never came. I was too near to tears.

Rapidly the surgeon explained to the group my case history and explained the surgical steps he had taken to deal with the problem. A rattling of metal and glass announced the arrival of the dressing trolley. Still keeping up his running commentary, he lifted my heavily bandaged hand gently from its pillow rest, and removed the safety pin from the elastic crepe bandage. Removing several turns he bent his head swiftly and sniffed at the discoloured material now appearing. A grunt escaped from him and the flow of words ceased. As each of the lower layers of bandage were removed, I could feel the gigantic pressure on my hand being released and new life flowing into the member. With the sensation came the smell. It had the sickly sweet aroma of putrified flesh, and I knew it was my own.

Curtly McIndoe addressed the Sister. "Saline arm bath immediately."

One of the attendant group raised his operating mask into position as the stench polluted the air. The last of the bandage came off. I stared fearfully at the object holding everyone's attention. As I watched, McIndoe removed a flat wad of blood soaked yellow cotton wool from the back of my hand, to reveal something I failed to understand. My whole arm began to shiver nervously. Gently the bloody bundle was placed back on the sterile covered pillow.

"Have a little rest."

Thankfully I sank back into the pillow and relaxed the pent-up muscles of my body.

Curiosity exerted itself and I forced myself upwards to get a better view. Puzzlement must have shown in my face for McIndoe turned to explain.

"You want to know what I've been doing to you?" The cloak of seriousness had dropped away. "As you know," he continued, "the back of your hand was completely covered in thick scaly scar tissue – keloid scars. Well, I stripped all that off from the knuckles almost to the wrist. In its place I put a paper-thin layer of skin taken from the inside of your thigh. We call that a theirsch graft."

The pain from the hand during the past five days had also made me only dimly aware of the bulky dressing on my leg.

McIndoe went on. "This skin graft is sewn into position – in your case about sixty to seventy stitches – and long ends of thread are left hanging at regular intervals from quite a few of these stitches. After that, a dry sponge is cut and placed to fit exactly over the grafted area. The trailing ends of the stitches are then brought over the back of the sponge, and knotted together."

"What for?" I asked, almost automatically.

"Well, the sponge is then moistened which in turn causes it to swell, but as the thread restrains it, it can only exert pressure against the hand, forcing the new skin against the raw surface. That way the two surfaces join together."

There was silence in the ward for a moment.

"It's the pressure that causes most of the pain, I'm afraid, and the tightly wound elastic bandage only adds to the misery."

I smiled ruefully.

McIndoe resumed his serious air as quickly as it had been

dropped.

"Ready for some more?"

I nodded.

Again the gentle fingers raised the gory mass from its rest. "Stitch scissors!" It was a quiet command.

Instantly they were passed and the subdued sound of snipping was the only noise in the ward. Strand by strand the threads leading to the central knot were severed and the last of the cruel pressure removed.

"Tweezers !"

Gingerly the bloody sponge was eased up from its bed and lifted clear.

I turned my head away and went icy cold with nausea. All those days of fiendish torture couldn't result in this – this stinking pulp of rotten flesh and oozing pus. It wasn't . . . it wasn't fair. The tears were even closer. Meanwhile the careful examination had been continuing. The surgeon's voice brought me back from the land of self-pity.

"Luckier than I thought. That's about a fifty percent take, I should think."

I looked down again at the chunk of meat on the pillow. To my untutored mind it seemed surprising that McIndoe was not planning to amputate at the wrist, but here he was gaily talking of half the graft succeeding. How anything could live in the midst of that foul stench surprised me.

"Get the hand into the bath, Sister. Let it soak for half an hour, then the usual dressings – plenty of sulphanylamide powder. The rest of the stitches can come out tomorrow." The infectious grin appeared and with a pat on the shoulder for me he departed, a stocky, competent figure surrounded by white ghosts.

I lay back with a deep sigh, and for the first time felt the beads of sweat cooling on my forehead.

The removal of the stitches brought about a change in my life.

Despite having enjoyed the first pain-free night since the operation, my nerves were still jumpy and my hand ultra-sensitive.

It went badly from the moment the probationary nurse wheeled up the dressing trolley to the bedside. Sister Hall decided that her high standards were not being maintained and soundly berated the young girl. Following this a message came that McIndoe was sending one of the resident Air Force surgeons to remove the stitches.

I felt like a small child that is deprived of its mother's protective nearness. I did not wish to have my dressings done by this strange doctor, and in my mind began to think up excuses to cause a postponement. While my brain was frantically searching for a reason, Sister Hall reappeared accompanied by the surgeon. Feebly I began to suggest that perhaps the following day would be more propitious, but my pleas fell on deaf ears. Soon the bandages were peeled away, leaving the greasy tulle-gras strips lying next to the sensitive flesh. Deftly these were lifted off with forceps, their fatty nature not causing them to stick to the raw exposed areas.

Fascinated despite myself, I followed the quick, trained movements of the surgeon's hands. The pattern remained the same – surgical tweezers gripped the suture firmly and raised it sufficiently for the next action; a quiet but distinct snip as the stitch scissors cut through the black gut and the tweezers coming to grips again to lift clear the neatly tied little bows.

Life altered at the seventh stitch.

A nurse at the far end of the ward dropped a luncheon tray as the scream rang out. Heads raised themselves off pillows in curiosity. The R.A.F. doctor looked up from his task in surprise at his ashen-faced patient.

"Sorry, did I hurt you?"

It was a moment before my quivering lips could form an answer. "The stit … stitch must be through … through a nerve. Just like a red hot needle being pushed up my hand and arm."

Again the surgeon bent to his task, speaking as he poised his instrument for another attack. "Take a grip of yourself and it'll be over in a second."

Again the cry rang out, this time sounding like a medieval victim being stretched on the rack. The surgeon looked up impatiently, anger furrowing his brow.

"You've got to stand a little pain you know!"

The words came hissing from between by bloodless lips.

"You swine … you bloody filthy butchering swine. Get away from me and stay away."

The Sister's voice rose above the heavy racking sobs that followed. "I think perhaps he's had enough for one day, sir."

Without a word the irate uniformed doctor departed.

With my face buried in the pillow, I began to kindle up hatred for the first time in my life. I began by hating the surgeon for causing me the physical suffering, and this in turn extended to everyone about me. Then, as my mind and body calmed down, the hatred went back to original causes and the Germans became the focal point of my loathing and bitterness.

The seed was sown.

The following day Archie McIndoe did his normal rounds of the wards. Sister Hall explained the problem of the offending stitch. His reply personified the bigness of the man.

"Give him a sixth of morphia, and take it out yourself, Sister."

Half an hour later she removed it painlessly, and in my doped condition I wondered why the surgeon the previous day could not have resolved the problem with the same simplicity. Perhaps it's little touches like this that make great men.

Although the relief from the pressure bandages was great, days of painful dressings followed. Each time the dressings were removed and suffering returned, I indulged in dark thoughts of retribution for those who had brought me to this state. At the end of two weeks I was able to hobble about the ward and most of my cheerfulness had returned, except for the sombre moments during the daily dressings.

Two weeks lengthened into a month and by now I was badgering McIndoe to perform the next operation. The call to the air and the opportunity for revenge were ringing in my head.

Dreading the repetition of the previous operation and all its aftermath, I was wheeled into the operating room once again.

The second graft, this time to the left hand, proved to be as painful as the first. During the long hours of the night when pain and misery were at their height, I would at times console myself with thoughts of Richard Hillary. Hillary had undergone a serious grafting operation the previous week. A few days afterwards, as a probable result of his weakened condition, he contracted an infection of the middle ear which rapidly developed into an acute mastoid. A small two-bed wing existed off the ward and Hillary was put into this and given extra special nursing.

Two nights after my own operation I lay awake cursing life in general and Germans in particular. Then my trained ear caught the unmistakable beat of the enemy aircraft's engines. Automatically I identified it as a Junkers 88. Raising my head from the pillow my ears followed the path of the machine as it growled across the night sky. Steadily the uneven beat grew louder and I knew that it would pass directly over the hospital. As the whistle of the falling bomb commenced, the horrors of sound created during the first few days in Margate after being shot down came back vividly. Pain and self-pity, hatred and revenge were subjugated in the blind terror that rose in my throat as the projectile screamed earthwards.

Even if movement had been possible, it was all over too soon. The bomb struck the ground a few yards beyond the large plate glass windows. The building shook violently and the blackout curtains flapped inwards.

I lay there with my eyes and muscles screwed up tightly, waiting for the explosion that had not occurred. Hardly had I relaxed than the sleeping figures about me awoke and the night nurse came hurrying to the ward, her flashlight playing dancing patterns about the walls and ceilings. Her high-pitched voice contrasted oddly with the sleepy male voices that plied her with questions.

"Nothing to worry about … nothing to worry about … just a small air raid."

My laugh rang out bitterly. "It may be a small air raid, but there's a bloody great unexploded bomb a few yards away."

No one thought of going back to sleep that night. Within the hour air raid wardens, rescue squads and bomb disposal experts had taken a look at the situation and advised the same thing. The ward was to be evacuated.

It was decided by McIndoe in consultation with the bomb disposal squad that the risk of moving Hillary in his condition was greater than the chances of the bomb exploding. Soon a pen of sand-bags was being placed around the sick man's bed, while sleepy order-lies and nurses carried stretchers and organized the removal of the other patients from the danger area. Two hours later I found myself being lifted gently into a comfortable bed in a large country home several miles from the hospital. Dutton Homestall was the Sussex residence of John and Kathleen Dewar. John Dewar, as his name im-plied, derived his income from Scotch Whisky, much to everyone's satisfaction.

The original part of the house was a comparatively small section that had once been John O'Gaunt's shooting lodge in Ashdown For-est. Kathleen Dewar had, however, seen a large Tudor mansion that took her fancy in Cheshire, and had it moved stone by stone to join the shooting lodge in Sussex. Despite the new addition, the Dewars retired to the smaller original section of Dutton Homestall and of-fered the vast halls and bedrooms of the remainder to the Red Cross.

I found myself in a huge oak-beamed bedroom that contained as many beds as the hospital ward. Too tired to appreciate my surround-ings after the harrowing night and the bumpy ambulance ride, I soon fell asleep despite the thumping in my hand.

"Wotcher, me old cock sparrow!" The rich fruity voice from the next bed broke through my deep sleep. This was the first occasion I had come face to face with the notorious Lieutenant Patrick O'Conner.

"Don't be so bloody bumptious," I growled. The Army officer re-fused to be disheartened.

"Watch your step, my lad. Dutton Homestall is a haven of rest for tired Army types – none of this worship of an Air Force uniform here."

Hardly glancing at the occupant of the next bed, I asked with stud-ied boredom, "What are you in for, hemorrhoids or sex?" Despite myself and my bad temper, I warmed to the hearty laugh that escaped from O'Conner's locked jaws.

"Take a look around, you may become interested in sex yourself."

The door of the room had just opened and a troupe of extremely attractive V.A.D. nurses entered carrying breakfast trays.

O'Conner's deep chuckle gurgled out again. "Blanket baths are taking on a new significance in my mind."

I felt better.

Time slipped by pleasantly enough in the beautiful surroundings of Dutton Homestall. The unexploded bomb had been rendered harmless, but none of the patients was in any hurry to return to the hospital. Doctors and patients both saw the advantages of a short respite from the operating table, although no rest would be available for the surgeons with the steady influx of new injuries.

Patrick and I soon became friends, and the army officer's wild habits helped to take my mind away temporarily from morbid thoughts. O'Conner confessed to me one day that his love life had become complicated.

"You see, old boy," he explained. "I'm engaged to be married."

"And now there's someone else, I suppose?"

O'Conner tilted his head back and poured some fluid into his mouth from the spouted feeding cup before answering. He made a face. "Ugh! Too much soda." He poured more whisky into the cup from the bottle on his bedside. "No, no one else," he continued. "But the silly girl has got herself pregnant."

"Plain clumsy," I remarked dryly.

O'Conner ignored the sarcasm. "Now she's insisting we get married soon, and I'm getting an awful feeling of being dragged into marriage."

We started a lengthy discussion on shot-gun weddings. Finally we agreed that wedlock based only on the necessity of making the child legitimate was courting eventual unhappiness.

Patrick asked my aid in making his fiancee see the matter in the same light.

Patrick's next problem was connected with the seat of his precious tartan trousers. Returning to the ward one night, slightly the worse for wear after an evening in the local pub, he staggered down the narrow corridor, using the walls as assistance in remaining vertical. Unfortunately he had forgotten that one wall eventually gave way to a curtained partition screening the saline bath used for the very badly burned patients. Leaning his weight on the curtain, he crashed through the partition, to land sitting in a bucket of highly concentrated disinfectant. Cursing loudly, he extricated himself from the bucket and proceeded his weaving way into the main ward, and finally sat himself down on his bedtable.

I was awakened by his drunken screaming, as he dashed around the ward in a frenzy, clutching the seat of his pants. Lights were turned on, and the night nurse came bustling starchily down the ward.

"Now Mr. O'Conner, what seems to be the trouble?"

"My bottom," he yelled. "It's on fire!"

With quick efficiency she removed the offending tartan trousers and ordered him to lie face downwards on his bed.

A few terse questions, and she realized the cause of the trouble and took appropriate action.

"You'll probably spend the next few weeks sleeping on your stomach, Mr. O'Conner."

From my adjoining bed I could now see in the well-lit ward, Patrick's bedtable. Normally painted a light yellow colour, it was now a mass of blisters where the neat disinfectant had acted as a paint remover. Next morning, lying face downwards with an imperial hangover, Patrick's muttered words floated in my direction. "What a bugger! Come to a burns hospital with a few broken bones, and finish up getting my arse burnt."

The saga of Patrick O'Conner continued.

Despite the waning of the relationship between Patrick and his fiancee, the baby she was carrying waxed and was finally born without undue trouble. Patrick's next problem was whether he was to marry the girl or not. Despite my advice to the contrary, he announced his forthcoming marriage at Caxton Registry Office. As I was bedridden at the time, I was unable to attend the simple office ceremony. Patrick told me afterwards, amidst fruity giggles, what had transpired.

Arriving at the Registry Office for Marriages, Births and Deaths, the young couple was led by the uniformed doorman to the appropriate office on the ground floor. Inside they were given a frozen welcome by the official presiding, who did not believe that marriages were made either in heaven or the Caxton Hall Registry Office.

Rushing through the proceedings without any feeling, he made them sign the appropriate forms, collected the money due and pronounced them legally married. The young bride was obviously relieved, as their child was already three months of age.

As they were about to leave the Hall, Patrick noticed a sign pointing up the stairs to the floor above which read "Registry of Births." He turned to his bride. "Might as well register the little one while we're here, eh?" They then proceeded to mount the stairs, until stopped by the uniformed doorman. On learning their requirement he informed them that due to the manpower shortage in wartime, this department had been closed and was being handled in another office. With this he led them back to the room where they had just been married to receive a welcome even chillier than the first from the boot-faced official.

Twenty

It was during these early days in the hospital that a small group of us started a club that is now world famous. With the original idea of forming it as a drinking club, it was soon to change its nature, although the basic premise has always been to the fore.

The Guinea Pig Club held its first meeting in a small hut between the wooden wartime wards, over glasses of beer and sherry. Why the name "Guinea Pig?" It started as a joke by us on our brilliant surgical team of Archie McIndoe, Jill Mullins and John Hunter.

One of the founder members had a very attractive wife, who was also a superb artist. At our request she came into the ward one morning, and drew a beautiful sketch of a guinea pig on her husband's chest before he went off to the operating room. We knew that once on the table the surgical gown would be removed, revealing the drawing. As both the medicos and ourselves were fully aware that we were to an extent pioneers in the modern techniques of skin grafting, it was right and proper we should send our message of being "guinea pigs" to our medical partners.

At our first meeting we collected a modest entrance fee, and put these into the safekeeping of our elected Treasurer. He had been unanimously elected, as his burnt legs were in plaster, and he was therefore incapable of running away with the club funds.

At our second meeting I proposed that we should extend our activities beyond those of pouring large quantities of liquid down our throats. My suggestion was that those of us who could return to a useful normal life should insure that our less fortunate members should be looked after by us financially. I had no faith in the generosity of a grateful country when it came to handing out disability pensions. The motion was passed, and after some financial birth pangs the Royal Air Force Benevolent Fund took us under their wing, and have very generously donated funds to assist the needy. Archie McIndoe was naturally elected permanent Life President, and after his sad death, the Duke of Edinburgh graciously agreed to become his successor.

The Club now [1990s] has over six hundred members from all over the Commonwealth and many other countries, including even Russia.

Annually there is a "lost weekend" at East Grinstead (known as "the Sty") to which members come from all over the globe.

Once we had regained sufficient strength after a surgical bout, Archie McIndoe saw to it that we made sorties into the outside world, either individually or in groups. The welfare side of our lives was very capably dealt with by his younger anaesthetist, Dr. Russell Davies.

My first excursion to London was not a brilliant success. A welcome-out party had been arranged for me by my sister Daphne and her husband, to which they invited a pretty girl named Jill (not Jill Mullins, of whom I shall write later).

The dinner dance at Hatchetts in Piccadilly was a great success, despite my embarrassment at being stared at by the other diners, who considered I was some sort of freak masquerading in R.A.F. uniform. On reflection they were probably right.

Despite my injuries, Jill acted as if I were perfectly normal. How wrong her judgement was to prove. When the evening ended, I volunteered to see her home in a taxi, my sister and brother-in-law living in a different part of town.

When we arrived at Jill's apartment, she invited me up for a drink, and I saw the writing on the wall. This was confirmed when the lift operator asked her at what time he should bring the early morning tea. Before answering him she turned to me and asked me, "do you take sugar?"

"No thanks," I replied.

The preliminaries didn't take long, and soon we were jumping into bed the way God made us. God, however, had not designed anti-aircraft guns, and the first one to open the defence barrage appeared to be in an adjoining room, such was the noise of the explosion.

Such was my fright that I could not even raise an eyebrow, let alone any other part of my anatomy. Jill tried her best to elevate my morale, but each time the gun went off my enthusiasm waned. She was not amused.

Early next morning I gulped down my tea (which contained sugar), and made a hurried departure!

I returned to the hospital to have a new pair of eyelids grafted on. The searing heat of the fire had caused a general skin contracture about my eyes, with the result that top and bottom eyelids could not meet together when closed for sleep or other purposes.

Some re-organization had taken place during my absence, and on returning I found that a long wooden hut with greater bed accommodation was now the ward for burned aircrew and other casualties from the Army and Navy. Rank did not exist.

Common suffering in blazing airplanes reduces us all to the same denominator. The only person scorned was the type who wheedled his way in to have plastic surgery in order to satisfy his own vanity. Not many attempted this, and those who did rued the day the idea entered their heads. Ward three set its own standards.

A hasty wartime erection, the interior decor of the hut started with a dark chocolate colouring from the floor to chest height. Above this the paintwork consisted of a dirty cream, the overall effect being that of a dimly lit Victorian public lavatory. In the centre of the hut stood a battered upright piano much in need of tuning. McIndoe and Kathleen Dewar were later to be instrumental in having the ward tastefully redecorated and comfortably furnished. However, the earlier days were primitive.

Then another Jill entered my life, and we had two years of great happiness together until I departed to fly in North Africa after leaving the hospital.

Jill Mullins was an attractive tall woman with corn-coloured hair. Her hair, combined with large green eyes and an infectious laugh, made her a great favourite with the aircrew patients.

Besides being a very attractive woman, she was Archie McIndoe's Surgery Sister, and in the operating room their combined skill and teamwork were thrilling to watch. It was their sense of humour, combined with that of John Hunter, the anaesthetist, that kept us sane.

This was best shown when one day a Royal Navy Captain was admitted to the ward.

Poor sod!

The fact that he was not in the R.A.F. made no difference to us, but his pomposity, combined with an air of condescension to those of us in the Junior Service, led to his undoing. Added to this, he was in the Accounts Branch, and had probably never been further out to sea than the end of Brighton Pier. His medical complaint didn't help either. He was suffering from a contracture of two fingers caused, as one Sergeant Pilot would have it, "by wanking too often in his youth!"

With disdain he watched our activities in the ward, and with shock when the evening beer sessions started, but his complaints to Sister Mealy, the ward sister, were of no avail.

He was number four on the operating list the next day, which meant he would be dealt with in the afternoon. First on the list was Group Captain Tom Gleave, who had undergone several previous operations to graft a new nose onto his face. Tomorrow's operation was to be a minor one, merely to allow him to breathe more freely.

The next day dawned, and I decided that with three other aircrew, we would trundle Tom Gleave to the operating room and watch his operation. At the appointed time, suitably gowned and masked, we arrived with the trolley. Tom was lying drowsily in his bed which was alongside that of the Naval Captain. Tom slid himself onto the trolley and we covered him up with blankets in the prescribed manner. Out of the corner of my eye, I could see that not only was the R.N. Captain following our movements carefully, but that a nervous strain was now showing on his face in anticipation of his own operation in the afternoon.

Rapidly we wheeled Tom along the corridors and into the operating room and lifted him on to the operating table or "slab," as we cheerfully termed it. We chatted away with John Hunter and Jill, until Archie came in from scrubbing up in the adjoining room. We exchanged warm greetings before he turned his attention to the sleepy-looking prostrate body. Jill deftly removed the bandage and swabs covering Tom's sterile nose.

Archie grunted and prodded the nose with a rubber-gloved finger.

"How difficult is it to breathe now, since I last examined you, Tom?"

"Not too bad, Archie. Seems to have improved recently."

Archie was thoughtful for a moment. Finally, "We'll get the dental branch to make you a plastic mould to insert in your bad nostril, and that should help to enlarge the air passage. No need for me to operate."

Tom naturally looked relieved, as none of us looked forward to being cut up, however minor the operation.

Then inspiration struck me, and I explained my plan to the others. The medical team went into gales of laughter, and even Tom, our primary victim, produced a sleepy grin. Quickly Jill produced a bottle of mecurochrome, a disinfectant the colour of blood. Pouring a generous amount onto a swab, she covered all of Tom's face until he looked as if he were bleeding to death. She then placed the gory swab on his nose, and proceeded to bandage it on in a way that would have been a disgrace to a Boy Scout having his first first-aid lesson. A surgical towel was placed on his chest, and this too was saturated with "blood." Leaving our surgeon and his team writhing with laughter, we left the room and headed back for the ward. Sister Mealy was surprised not only to see us back so soon, but at the sight of a blood-stained apparition. Quickly we briefed her, and she immediately joined us in the joke. Accompanying us into the ward, as was her duty, we pushed the trolley alongside Tom's empty bed. A pair of very horrified naval eyes took in the evident state of the patient's face.

"O.K., chaps," I called from underneath my mask. "Usual procedure to get the bastard into bed, but try and not drop him on the floor again." I could both feel and hear the gasp from the next bed.

The normal routine for getting an unconscious body from a trolley into bed is for the four attendants each to take a corner of the thick rubber sheet under it, and to lift it up carefully and deposit it on the bed.

This time however, we took the four corners and proceeded to swing Tom's body as if he were in a hammock. Having swung him from side to side several times, at my order, we let go. Tom sailed through the air over and past his bed, as if on a magic carpet, and landed on the floor on the far side and finally stopping under the Captain's bed, from which his voice emerged.

"Bloody hospital! The treatment gets worse each week!" Last seen was the figure of a Royal Navy Captain heading rapidly for the lavatories.

The weeks passed by, and despite the pain and misery that followed each operation, the rest periods between bouts of surgery were enjoyable. Much of the time was spent with Jill and Archie, either having happy evenings at his cozy little cottage, or she and I would seek the bright lights of London to dine and dance alone.

The worst period for me was the summer of 1941. On beautiful sunny days, if bedridden, the orderlies would push us out on the lawn alongside the ward. These days were hell. Lying in the sunshine, I would look up and watch the squadrons of Spitfires, as they passed overhead to carry out fighter sweeps over northern France.

How my heart yearned to be one of them, and not just a burnt cripple lying in a hospital bed. However, it hardened my determination even more to get back in the air as soon as possible. Then I made a bitter vow to myself that, for each operation I underwent, I would destroy one enemy aircraft when I returned to flying.

The task was getting big, as I had already undergone eleven operations, and there were obviously many more to come. Shortly afterwards I received my first serious setback to my plans for revenge. One day, between operations, I was driving to London to stay for a few days with Archie in his flat in Chelsea.

Finally I broke the light conversation we had been indulging in, and spoke what was uppermost in my mind.

"How long do you think it will be before I can return to flying, Archie?" When he replied I knew I had touched a sore spot, as there was anger in his voice.

"You can forget about going back flying."

"But – "

"There are no 'buts.' You've done your stuff, and now the other silly sods can get on with it."

For the first time I realized how deeply he was affected by the useless death and injuries sustained by all the young men. The journey continued in silence.

McIndoe's words were still ringing in my ears when Hillary came and sat on the edge of the bed. "One more operation," the surgeon had said, before he discharged me from the hospital. Not that this would mean the end of the surgical treatment, but he felt that after fifteen operations and two years in the hospital the patient had earned some respite.

"How are you enjoying it?" The words interrupted my train of thought and with difficulty I brought myself back from the incredible thoughts that discharge from the hospital brought to mind. "Oh, the book!" I glanced at his copy of "The Last Enemy," lying on the blankets. Hillary had an unconcerned air about him but I knew that my criticism was awaited eagerly. "I think it's beautifully written, Richard. In fact I'm surprised a supercilious bastard like you could produce something like this." Hillary grinned. "However, there's just one thing I don't quite understand." The author was now alert and tense.

"You write," I continued, "of your being an irresponsible, conceited young undergraduate before the war, then, as a result of your wounds you change, and presto, here you are, a different person." I shook my head before continuing. "In my opinion, you're still as bloody conceited as ever." The grin returned to Hillary's face. "Perhaps you're right. Anyway that's the way I felt when I wrote it." I changed the subject. "I'm being discharged from here after my next op."

"Lucky man, any plans?"

"Yes, I have plans. I'm going back on flying duties." My companion whistled softly in surprise. "You too, eh?" It was my turn to be surprised.

"Don't tell me you're going back flying as well, Richard?"

"Certainly, but no more of this bloody day fighter nonsense." I raised my only remaining eyebrow questioningly.

"Night fighters – that's the answer, my boy."

Richard leaned forward confidingly.

"If you get in a dog-fight by day, one's hands might not be able to cope with the lightning speed of the situation.

"Whereas at night, you creep up behind the target, take your time and shoot the bastard down."

I was silent for a while, digesting his words. Finally I worked my shoulders around as if to shift a load on my back.

"I don't think I agree," I stated thoughtfully.

"You see, Richard, we know the day fighting game and we know how to fly Spitfires. With a night fighter aircraft you've got a much heavier machine to handle and in the darkness – " Hillary broke in.

"Don't agree!!" I did not reply at once and when I did it was on a different tack.

"Funny you should want to fly again as well. I'm scared stiff at the idea, but I'm even more frightened of what people will say if I don't go back." Hillary nodded in agreement.

"I think that sums up my feelings as well."

He rose from the bed and pushed back a straggle of long hair from over his ear.

"There is of course," he added with a twinkle in his eye, "the small business of getting passed as fit for flying duties by the R.A.F. Medical Board."

A week later Richard and I held a private conference and agreed on our course of action. Although we differed in viewpoint between the merits of day and night fighters, we were of one accord that Archie McIndoe should be badgered until he gave his support to our ambitions. After weeks of propaganda and nagging, the surgeon finally threw up his hands in mock disgust.

"If you're determined to kill yourselves, go ahead, only don't blame me."

Like a couple of happy schoolboys we went off to celebrate.

Central Medical Establishment occupied two floors of a dingy building lying in the shadows of one of London's largest hospitals, the Middlesex. A large waiting room filled rapidly early each morning as a horde of young men, almost all with aircrew brevets, invaded the cloistered atmosphere. Magazines that had been thumbed through a thousand times littered the large table in the centre of the room. A huge, unattractive clock on the whitewashed walls loudly ticked away the minutes of bored waiting. As wild animals in a cage, so these men looked out of place and confined in this atmosphere. Theirs was a world of white clouds and blue sky, of green grassy airfields and wooden dispersal huts.

"Flying Officer Page, please!"

The medical orderly's voice rang out and temporarily silenced the tick-tock of the clock. A few heads looked up from their magazines as I rose to my feet and left the room. Following my guide I was led into an office marked "Adjutant." Behind the desk sat a sallow faced administrative officer. Picking up a file he glanced up, "Page?" I nodded. The eyes returned to the open file. Quickly the adjutant read through the case history.

" – third degree burns, hands, face and legs; gun-shot wound, left leg." He put down the file and looked up again. "You should get your bowler hat without any trouble."

I felt my heart sinking.

"I've come here to get a flying category, not to be invalided out."

The adjutant snorted deprecatingly.

"Forget about it, you haven't a chance." He indicated the door. "You still have to undergo a full medical examination for us to discharge you. They'll call you from the waiting room."

With a sick feeling in the pit of my stomach, I returned to my seat.

An hour passed before I was called again, and then only to provide a urine specimen for analysis. Another dragging hour passed, during which time a steady stream passed in and out of the room as their names were called. My gloom deepened as the memory of the adjutant's words bored cruelly deeper and deeper into my mind. The administrative officer was relegated to a position of hatred alongside the Germans in my thoughts. Finally my name was called again and this time the medical examination began in earnest.

Blood pressures were taken, columns of mercury blown up and held by lung pressure, reflex muscles tapped, and blindfolded one-legged tests carried out. Examinations by the ear, nose and throat specialist followed. With one ear blocked whispered words floated across the room for me to repeat. Tuning forks hummed, tonsils and nasal passages were looked at. Then to the eye doctor. A darkened room – flashing red lights and diagonal bars. A pencil of light played into each eye. After that came the colour blindness tests and the inevitable reading of the letter chart with one eye closed.

Another long, interminable wait until I was told to come back after lunch.

Sick with worry and anticipation, I left the sandwich I had ordered in a nearby pub untouched. How had I fared with the various doctors, I wondered? And if they invalided me from the service, what then? I felt fit enough to fly, so why not let me? All this red tape when I was obviously one hundred percent fit. I caught sight of the pitying expressions of the two bar-maids as they discussed my injuries. Obviously they did not think I looked one hundred percent fit. I fled from the pub.

Again my name was called. This was it, the final summing up by the President of the medical board, and then the verdict. Respectfully the medical orderly tapped on the glass door of the Air Commodore's office. He opened it on hearing the muffled summons.

"Flying Officer Page, sir."

The grey-haired man nodded from behind his desk without looking up.

"Have a seat, Page. I won't keep you a moment." The door closed behind the departing orderly, and I sat tensely on the edge of the chair as the President continued to record his findings on paper of the previous examinee. With a flourish he signed his name and placed the file aside before reaching for my documents. Carefully he read through the findings of the various specialists.

"Hmm – " He looked up thoughtfully. "Apart from your injuries you seem fit enough, Page. What would you like us to do, invalid you out or give you a limited category?"

"Limited in what way, sir?"

"Oh, fit for ground duties in the United Kingdom only."

I swallowed hard. I disliked the use of falsehoods, but I knew that this was a critical moment in my life.

"Well, actually sir, what I'm after is a flying category. You see," I added hastily as I saw a frown appear on the doctor's face. "I managed to get some unofficial flying recently through a friend of mine in one of the squadrons."

Both of us knew I was lying.

"Grip my hands."

I stood and leaned across the desk grasping the President's hands in my own. Every ounce of physical and nervous energy I possessed was concentrated into my two maimed hands as I forced them to tighten their grip. Months of hard work with the rubber ball stood me in good stead. The Air Commodore raised his eyebrows again, this time in surprise.

"More strength in those than I imagined possible, Page," he picked up his pen and commenced to write.

"I am passing you fit for non-operational single-engine aircraft only. At the end of three months you will be boarded again, and if you've coped all right, we'll give you an operational category." I passed to the door in a dream.

"Oh, and Page."

"Yes, sir?"

"Good luck, and don't let me down."

* * *

The two elderly women stopped and stared after the figure of the young R.A.F. pilot as he half ran down the street, tears of joy pouring down his cheeks.

"Poor boy," said the skinny one. "He must have heard some bad news – so young too!"

A week's leave was granted to me following the successful medical board. Archie invited me to stay in his cottage. Despite his sincere belief that I should not return to flying, he put a good face on it, and we had several riotous evenings with Jill, John Hunter and dear old Bill Gardner.

Bill was the manager of our local restaurant cum bar in East Grinstead, and many was the Guinea Pig who had returned horizontal but safe to the hospital, due to Bill's protection.

Jill and I went up to London for a night on the town, and found Archie still laughing at his experience the previous evening. Returning from a hard day in the hospital, tired and hungry, he had cooked himself a modest supper when there was a knock on the back door. On opening it he found a youth dressed in the garb that bicyclists wear. The young man explained he was on a long cycling trip, was desperately thirsty and could he please have a glass of water.

Archie invited him into the kitchen, and three pints of water later gaspingly asked if he could ask his pals outside in for a drink as well. Naturally Archie agreed, and a moment later five more tired and thirsty young men trooped into the small kitchen. Then Archie did a typical "Archie."

"When did you lads last eat?" he asked them. Lunchtime was the answer, and by now it was after nine in the evening. Half an hour later the six cyclists were sitting down to a hot meal washed down with beer.

"Been working in this place long?" inquired the original youth.

"Oh, about two years," came the answer.

"Your boss treat you well?" asked another youth.

Because they had found him washing up his own supper things, the young men had mistaken him for a household servant. Despite their offer, Archie refused to let them help with the washing up, explaining that he had plenty of time as his employers were out for the evening.

The young men departed in fine fettle, and Archie commenced clearing the kitchen table. Lifting a plate, he discovered a two shilling piece which had been left as a tip for the manservant.

The most eminent plastic surgeon in England collapsed with laughter.

Twenty-One

At last the situation had to be faced, and I headed my car westward into Wales to take up my new posting. Number 3 anti-aircraft Cooperation Unit was based at Cardiff Municipal Airport. The name Municipal Airport suggested modern buildings, a fine control tower, and paved runways. It turned out to be a small grass airfield on the outskirts of coal-grimed Cardiff with its south side edging on to the Bristol Channel. It was a hutted camp. Arriving late I found a sleepy steward in the deserted mess and retired to my room. At nine o'clock the following morning I reported at the station commander's office, but it was not until an hour later that the C.O. put in an appearance.

He proved to be a man in his forties with little interest in flying, but a sense of importance at being in charge of the station. He was disliked by his junior officers. I had no quarrel to pick with him. I intended to get what I could from a flying point of view, and after three months return for another medical board, and then ....

The work of the unit was dull to an extreme. The aircraft, Lysanders and Masters, had to be flown back and forth along pre-arranged routes and at set altitudes, to allow the anti-aircraft units to train their gun crews. The monotony of the job reflected itself in the boredom and discontent of the aircrews. Pilots and observers alike were fed up with their lot and resorted to perpetual grousing and an antipathy toward the station commander. My spirits were still too high to be dampened by the general atmosphere. On the second day it was arranged I should have my first flight. I slept fitfully the night before, conjuring up thoughts of burning airplanes and all that went with it.

Tired and feeling washed-out I could not face breakfast in the Mess, but counted the minutes left before reporting to the flight offices. Flying Officer Constant was a tall, jovial character, and nothing but the mention of the station commander's name would dampen his spirits. He was ordered to give me some dual control in a Master before allowing me to go solo. Almost all of Constant's conversation hinged itself on two expressions – "Good show," or "Bad show." He arrived in the crew room to find his pupil already there and checking over his parachute for the tenth time.

"Good show, Page," he hailed jovially. "Never know when you might need it, eh?"

He received a sickly smile in answer.

* * *

I found my hands were shaking as I struggled into specially made gloves; long zippers down the sides allowed my bent and cripped fingers to work into place. Constant moved about the hut signing the authorization book and the Daily Inspection Form 700, whistling merrily away.

"Did the C.O. give you any special orders concerning me?" I asked. The whistling ceased abruptly.

"That bastard couldn't order a one-course lunch! No, my lad, he didn't but I suggest we do a few circuits and bumps until you're happy, and then away you go on your own."

As we walked out to the waiting machine Constant sang merrily away. I felt that the song, an R.A.F. ditty on flying over the Northwest Frontier, was somewhat ill chosen. The words ran –"when your engine cuts out you'll have no balls at all."

"Same old kestrel engine that you're familiar with," came Constant's voice over the intercom.

"About nine primes starting from cold – good show – rudder trim neutral, elevator about – there. Good show."

The patter from the rear cockpit went on and suddenly I realized I just could not absorb the words. Sweat covered my face beneath the tight-fitting oxygen mask. With difficulty and a certain amount of pain I had been able to unscrew the primer and administer the nine strokes of the pump. After that my instructor's words failed to register.

"Can you hear me, old man?" The traces of anxiety were noticeable in Constant's voice.

My mind was searching wildly for an excuse to postpone the flight. Could I say that I was ill or that my hands hurt? It was then that I caught sight of the ground crew standing by the starter battery and looking up at me expectantly.

"Ye-yes, I can hear you."

"Good show, I'll start her up, taxi out, and you can do the take-off, O.K?"

I nodded, aware that the man in the back seat could see my head. The little yellow gull-winged airplane taxied swiftly across to the east side of the airfield and turned into wind, the engine throttled.

"Usual score on take-off, bit of a swing if you open up too rapidly. Otherwise a piece of cake. Watch out in front of you when we get airborne – have to fly through the Cardiff barrage balloons – bad show."

My mind now was too numb to be worried about mere barrage balloons. It was up to me to cope with the situation or confess to my mortal terror and abandon the whole project.

Almost in surprise I looked down and saw my left hand pushing the throttle firmly but steadily open. The airplane surged forward under the power from the Rolls-Royce Kestrel engine. Automatically my hands and feet moved to keep the spritely little aircraft under control, and my thoughts had no time to stray from the immediate situation. A final rumble from the undercarriage and the ground slipped away. The wheels retracted neatly and I set the engine and propeller controls to climbing boost and revolutions.

No sooner had I time to relax for a second than a blind gripping fear took possession of me again: What if the engine failed now over these houses? We were too low to bale out. In a matter of seconds we would be charred and smelly corpses burning amongst the rubble of what once had been a Cardiff house.

My imagination remained fixed on that one thought until Constant's cheerful voice broke through.

"Balloon ahead – turn a wee bit to starboard – good show."

The very act of banking and turning the aircraft brought me back into the right perspective, and although the fear returned it was less violent.

After two more take-offs and landings Constant climbed out.

"All you're doing is wasting my time acting as a wet-nurse sitting in the back."

Half an hour later I was walking towards the hangar with my parachute slung over my shoulder and singing merrily away. "When your engine cuts out you'll have no balls at all." Blood smeared my wrist from a knocked hand, but the enemy had suddenly became a great deal nearer.

After three months with the anti-aircraft co-operation I applied for another medical board. Out of this I emerged with an AI.B flying category, the highest obtainable, and immediately asked for posting to a fighter squadron.

Permission was granted and soon I found myself on my way to Martlesham Heath to fly Spitfires again. The posting was that of supernumery flight lieutenant, a job that carried the rank becoming a flight commander, but without the attendant responsibilities. Not that I cared. I was getting back to my beloved Spitfires, and only the Channel and the North Sea stood between me and eleven attacks that I wanted to make. Apart from the thrill of flying the beautiful little fighters again, my first month in the squadron proved disappointing. The days consisted of interminable boring convoy patrols, as we kept watch over the shipping plying back and forth along the east coast. A vital job, but deadly dull. No enemy aircraft showed up to attack the merchant ships, and to add fuel to my discontent, I daily read combat reports from squadrons based further south, recounting train-busting exploits and brushes with enemy aircraft.

I could stand it no longer. Now I must prove to myself that I did in fact possess enough courage to fight again. Flying itself was not enough.

The squadron commander was agreeable to my idea of attacking a German army encampment lying between Dunkirk and Nieuport. The plan was to attack the camp at breakfast-time when most of the troops would be moving back and forth from the canteens. As first light paled the dismal grey sky on a November morning, three Spitfires shattered the silence with the roar of their engines as they took off in tight formation. Wheeling round at a low altitude, we came streaking back over the airfield and settled on course for our destination.

Two minutes later the English coast slipped by beneath us as we hugged the white-crested wave tops. Startled seagulls squawked out of our way with flapping wings protesting at being disturbed from their rocking watery beds. The aircraft were now spread out waiting for the enemy coast ahead to show up. I leaned forward slightly in my cockpit. The bleak North Sea offered no landmarks by which I could check my position, and unless my landfall was deadly accurate, the chances of finding the camp would be small.

The plan was to slip in over the coast five miles south of the target, fly inland a short way, turn about and attack from the direction from which we would be least expected. The three Spitfires roared on through the gradually lightening sky.

I glanced at my wristwatch. We should reach the French coast in two minutes.

Two minutes. – What awaited us at the end of that pitifully short space of time? The German flak batteries were notorious for their accuracy and number, and an airplane hit at this low altitude would stand little chance of survival; if it were set on fire there wouldn't be much chance of climbing up to bail out.

I was wet with sweat.

Then I saw them. The low-lying dunes began to take shape as the distance between aircraft and land dwindled rapidly.

Almost in a panic I glanced down at the map on my knee again and again. None of the contours or landmarks tarried with the map or the special photographs I had studied day after day.

In a flash the sea disappeared and sandy soil appeared beneath our wings as we roared inland.

I knew at once that I had missed my landfall. By now it was broad daylight and I could see the barge puffing serenely along the canal ahead of us. Quickly my thumb flicked the gun switch from "safe" to "fire."

Barges came under the heading of approved targets. The 20mm cannon shells sprayed up fountains of water as they played on the surface before ricocheting into the wooden hull of the barge.

Behind me the other two aircraft closed into the attack. Following the course of the canal northwards, I found a group of barges being loaded direct from a grainery standing on the banks. The three graceful airplanes wheeled twice, each time leaving rending gaps in the sides of the heavily laden barges. We continued northward.

The fireman and the engine driver were walking along the track to their locomotive when the first shells ripped the boiler open, sending clouds of steam issuing upwards. The last I saw of the two men was their fat figures running down the track as fast as their pudgy legs would carry them. Leaving the locomotive with the appearance of a giant colander, our Spitfires followed the railway line, still heading northwards. Soon houses began to appear and I realized we were approaching a large town. Suddenly my eye caught sight of the tell-tale smoke of another locomotive. Banking rapidly in its direction, I found it to be a lengthy passenger train standing at the platform of a large railway station. Passengers thronged about the doors.

Taking an accurate sight on the engine, I poured rounds of cannon and machine gun ammunition into the hissing machine. People fled in all directions.

As my aircraft climbed away I saw the harbour lying alongside the town and beyond the grey waters of the North Sea that led back to England and safety. But with the sight of the harbour wall came a sudden knowledge of our whereabouts. We were flying over the centre of Dunkirk, a town infamous for the amount of anti-aircraft batteries that ringed its perimeter and particularly the sea wall. My Spitfire leapt forward as I gave the engine its maximum power and uttering a fervent, silent prayer, I dived my aircraft low over the harbour wall.

In an instant the sky was full of dancing lights that flashed around, above and below my weaving plane. Spread out on either side I could see my two companions receiving similar treatment from the blazing shore guns. The firing ceased as abruptly as it had started; we were now out of range and skimming back safely over the wave tops.

I found my knees trembling uncontrollably but my heart was singing. I had not killed any Germans but I had made a light dent in their transportation system.

Two weeks later I discovered by accident that the long stiletto knife carried inside a flying boot had high magnetic qualities. This had affected the compass in the airplane, causing the large navigational error when we crossed the enemy coast south of Dunkirk instead of north.

Soon after the epic flight to Dunkirk, volunteers had been asked to fly and fight in North Africa. Bored with the monotony of convoy patrols, I put my name forward and departed for a week in London.

This leave turned out to be another milestone in my life. Just before this time Jill Mullins and I admitted to each other that the spark had gone out of our romance, and we agreed to remain firm friends, which we did until the last time I saw her. She died of a brain haemorrhage while en route to South Africa with her newly-wedded husband. She was buried at sea.

The breaking-up of a love affair is not the happiest of things, and I was shy of starting anything new because of the state of my hands and face. Instead, I decided to leave for North African shores on a sea of alcohol.

The troop train ambled its way to the north from London, and seemingly weeks later passed into Scotland, and deposited its load finally alongside the dreary grey Clyde river at Greenock. Crowding the broad river were ships of all shapes and sizes, from rusty tired merchantmen to sleek killing destroyers.

I didn't have too much trouble finding the troopship "Letitia," as she was moored along the dock. She was no ocean-going giant, but a medium-sized passenger liner pressed into wartime service.

My embarkation papers were quickly checked, and a peace-time steward led me below to my cabin. This would normally have been comfortable for two people, but to my dismay I found it had six bunks, and all were to be occupied by R.A.F. pilots, which meant that apart from our baggage, there were also six parachutes to be stowed in this confined space.

Stumbling over each other, we finally managed to sort some sort of order out of the chaos. Then there was a rap on the cabin door and a steward entered.

"Dinner in half an hour, gentlemen."

"What time does the bar open, steward?"

A grin spread over the man's face.

"Sorry, sir, there ain't no bar, but you can get soft drinks in the main lounge before and after lunch and dinner."

He quietly closed the door amid the stunned silence.

That evening six dispirited (in every sense of the word) pilots clambered into their bunks. At least two weeks at sea in submarine-infested water and only bloody coca-cola and lemonade to calm our nerves.

I was awakened at about 4 a.m. in the morning by the sound of a tremendous crash. In a flash of light, all six of us were tearing up the companionway to the lifeboat deck, struggling into our Mae Wests (lifesaving jackets) as we went out. Convinced we had been torpedoed, we rushed on deck to find that probably because of our training we were the first. Despite the darkness of the night we could make out the silhouettes of the cranes and warehouses of Greenock. We were not even out to sea.

The officer commanding the troops in the ship, Colonel "Droopy-Drawers," as he became known, came on the public address system a little later.

"No need for concern, just a minor collision between us and another ship as the convoy was forming up in the dark. Return to your quarters, and you'll be advised further in the morning." The cold light of day showed that several plates in our hull had been badly buckled, and that we could not possibly sail with this convoy. Soon travel warrants were issued, and we were on our way to London for a further week's leave. During the journey to London the six of us worked out a campaign plan. The week in London passed quickly enough, and after another dreary train journey we were back at Greenock, where the scene appeared to have changed little, except that six R.A.F. pilots seemed to be heavily burdened as they climbed the gangway. Down in the confines of our cabin, bottles of whisky appeared from our suitcases, and these were stored away in our wine cellar which was an empty parachute bag. What better place in case of a surprise check by the Commanding Officer, Droopy-Drawers?

Six ginger ales were ordered in the lounge before dinner, and our "Duty Officer" disappeared below with one of the bottles. Quickly he emptied its contents down the wash basin in our cabin and promptly filled it with neat Scotch from our stocks.

Dinner that evening was a hilarious affair, although we received contemptuous looks from our brother officers, who obviously wondered how we could get "high" on a few ginger ales.

We proceeded to sea.

To escape some of the monotony, we started a bridge school, and the first cards were dealt immediately after breakfast. The two left out passed the time interestingly enough promenading the decks. The view of the grey Atlantic held little for the viewer, but the sight into the well deck below ours was far more rewarding. The "Letitia" had thirty very attractive Wren ratings on board, and these girls were on their way to Gibraltar with us. Then our peaceful life was almost shattered. One afternoon Droopy-Drawers announced that, as from the following morning, physical training would be carried out on deck every morning before breakfast.

We held a conference of war, and afterwards sent out our representative to see the Colonel.

That evening Droopy-Drawers made a further announcement.

"I am told," he said, "on good authority, that physical training is bad for the lungs of R.A.F. pilots, when it is considered the altitudes at which they have to fly. They are therefore excused from morning P.T. parades."

We were not very popular with our travelling companions, especially when we waved to them at breakfast time through the portholes of the dining room, as they pranced up and down the deck.

Despite a hurricane force gale which we hit in the Atlantic for three days, the voyage was one long laugh, and our whisky supplies just lasted. We were just thankful that our journey was relatively short, and that we did not have to do it year in and year out as did the courageous sailors who were conducting us there.

Eventually we sailed into sunlit Algeciras Bay, dominated by the magnificent Rock of Gibraltar.

But I had not reckoned with the heat of the African sun. After three months I was forced to admit that the heat on my newly grafted skin and on the scarred parts of my face was too uncomfortable. Reluctantly I applied for posting back to England. Disliking the thought of another two weeks in a slow convoy I hitched a ride in an American Air Force plane and was soon enjoying the sight of the lush green countryside of England. On arrival I was posted to Air Fighting Development Unit, a non-operational organization indulging in the assessment of all types of fighter aircraft, both allied and captured enemy machines.

It was here that I met Squadron Leader James MacLachlan for the first time.

The one-armed pilot was supposedly resting from a long tour of night intruder operations. These had consisted of sitting over enemy airports in the darkness waiting for the German bombers to return from their night's work over the British Isles. Blazing pyres of twisted metal and high-octane fuel confirmed the successes of this exceptional pilot.

The rest cure soon began to pall and he began to plot new mischief against the Luftwaffe.

Among the aircraft supplied to the fighter assessment unit were two Mustangs, each with the latest type of Allison engine. They were believed to be the fastest low-level fighters in existence at that time.

Somewhat reluctantly, Fighter Command granted him permission to carry out a lone raid into enemy territory.

Mac's theory was to penetrate the German fighter defence belt and get into those areas where Allied airplanes had not been seen before in broad daylight and at low altitude. He went to great pains to have the Mustang painted a dark green to blend with the French countryside, and to perfect low-level navigation by hours of practice flying around England at treetop height.

I watched all these preparations, but was afraid to suggest we should form a team.

However, one day Mac announced his immediate departure and shortly afterwards the sleek green Mustang roared away southwards. Several hours later, I watched him climbing stiffly out of the little cockpit, a disappointed man.

After crossing over the French coast he had been seen by enemy fighters. Owing to the construction of the aircraft his rearward visibility was limited, and reluctantly he had to turn for home. To have continued with Focke Wulf 190's able to approach without being seen from behind would have courted disaster. I listened to the tale being recounted to a group of eager listeners in the Mess. Getting Mac on his own later, I put forward my proposition.

It was simply that if Mac were to abandon the scheme, I would like to take over the machine for a similar attempt. The one-armed pilot slapped his knee with characteristic enthusiasm and delight.

"So you think it's a good idea too, eh? Thank God someone else thinks so. Nothing but opposition from everyone ever since I started." The words came tumbling out like water from an open sluice gate.

"Two Mustangs! That's the answer to it. Must get another aircraft, but come and look at the maps first."

With that I was hustled up to his room, and a few minutes later we were pouring over maps spread all over the bedroom floor. Mac's enthusiasm was overwhelming and soon I was caught up in the gay whirling bubbling stream of his fanaticism. Suddenly we came back to earth with a bump. We had taken the second aircraft for granted, but the commanding officer of the unit was a hard nut to crack. Although an efficient officer and able pilot, the C.O. lacked a spark of adventure in his soul and worse still, poor man, he had been deprived of a sense of humour since birth. He would without a doubt view the latest project as a crackpot idea dreamed up by two mentally deficient cripples. I underestimated my newly found partner. With a wave of his hand he dismissed the commanding officer.

"To hell with him. I'll get permission from Fighter Command, and then he'll have to lend us the second plane."

Within three days exactly that happened and I found myself working hard to prepare my machine for the fray. Guns had to be synchronized, sights harmonized and fuel consumption tests undertaken. Green paint was applied and finally it was ready to take its place beside the first Mustang.

Then came the most important task of all.

Hours of practice flying had to be devoted to split second teamwork at zero feet. A standard had to be reached that each of us knew automatically how the other would react under different circumstances. The lack of any form of radio made it more difficult. Mac found that his one arm was fully occupied flying the airplane and navigating without adding the push buttons and transmitting switch of a V.H.F. radio set.

After weeks of training and planning we at last felt we were ready to undertake our unique task. It now remained for the right weather conditions to prevail over the route. Flying as we would be, just skimming over the rippling corn in the French fields, any prey that might be around would be flying above us. To assist in spotting the quarry, a complete cloud layer at about three thousand feet was desirable; this helped to silhouette the enemy aircraft even at great distances. The visibility must be good for obvious reasons and little or no wind blowing. A strong wind would add navigational difficulties and probably produce bumpy conditions, causing added fatigue on what was already a tiring enough flight. Putting a tooth brush, razor and a stout pair of walking shoes (it was a long walk home from where we were going) into our aircraft, we took off from our inland base at Wittering for Lympne airfield on the south coast. There we would remain until news came through that our weather requirements were fulfilled.

It was also necessary to arrange for the Typhoon fighter-bombers to carry out their diversionary procedures.

"How about some shut-eye? Might be the last for some time."

I nodded in agreement and rose from the grass.

The two of us walked back to the officers quarters in silence, each preoccupied with his own thoughts.

For several hours I lay awake in an over-excited condition, my mind churning over the past weeks and trying to imagine what the next day would bring. The thrill of possibly shooting at an enemy aircraft was tempered by the sober thought of the distance that would lie between conflict and safety. Perhaps somewhere along those hundreds of miles a burning plane might plunge earthwards roasting the pilot inside. Would I be the one?

I looked at my watch for the hundredth time that morning.

Following my night of fitful sleep, I now had all the symptoms of a condemned man waiting for the last call. Nervously I kept on wiping my sweaty palms on my battledress uniform. From the edge of the grass airfield, I watched the unhurried actions of the ground crews as they prepared our aircraft for flight. My racing thoughts chased each other nervously like autumn leaves eddying in a whirlpool of wind. Why had I got myself into this awkward situation from which there was now no turning back?

Fear.

Each time my mind started off on a logical train of thought, a freshly remembered incident would destroy the sequence, and once again my thoughts would whirl off on a tangent. Fear, or was it fear of fear?

How did I come to find myself in this predicament on an overcast June day in 1943? To find oneself sweating with fear in the middle of a world war, and to know that bullets will be flying in one's direction within the next hour, is not a very enviable position. How I cursed the day I was posted to the Air Fighting Development Unit at Wittering. The hands of my watch pointed at 08.55. "Your aircraft is ready, sir." The flight sergeant's face betrayed nothing of his thoughts. I wondered how mine looked to him.

A voice behind me suddenly called, "All set?" My tense nerves jumped in surprise. Turning, I found Mac grinning at me. His warm personality had a cheering effect on my depressed spirits, and temporarily I cheered up.

"Let's get cracking." Saying this he juggled with the claw-like mechanism that was attached to the end of his artificial left arm.

"Fine bloody pair we are," I thought. "Going off to tackle the enemy with only one good hand between the two of us."

The operation itself was simple enough. Escorted by a squadron of Typhoon fighters, our two Mustangs would fly across the channel skimming the waves, until we were just off the enemy coast. The Typhoons would then climb up, firing their guns, and simulate a dog fight. Unnoticed, we hoped, our two green-painted Mustangs would slip in over the French coast, and proceed at treetop height to the Luftwaffe night-fighter airfields south of Paris.

Having destroyed some of the enemy air force, all we had to do was fly back two hundred miles, assuming German day fighters or anti-aircraft fire didn't interfere with our plans.

The time had arrived to put our plan into action, but fear was eating its way into my nervous system. It was almost three years since I had been in combat with enemy aircraft in the Battle of Britain. In my last fight I had been shot down in flames and spent two painful years in the hospital.

Yes, fear was my other companion on this flight.

In pairs the Typhoons taxied out over the grass of Lympne airfield, turned into the wind and took off. Soon they were joining up in squadron formation overhead, circling the airfield and awaiting our two Mustangs. The moments passed as taffy-stuck seconds as I sat strapped in my cockpit watching Mac's immobile aircraft. Then his propeller began to turn, followed by a bursting roar as the Allison engine took life. I didn't register the temporary abatement of my nervousness as my mind concentrated on the job in hand of starting my own engine. The next five minutes were fully occupied with positioning and taking off my heavily laden aircraft from the small airfield. As soon as the wheels retracted I levelled off at a hundred feet, and went into a tight turn to catch up with the other Mustang also turning about a mile ahead. The Typhoons were not our problem; their task was to position themselves on us. The English coastline flashed past beneath as I caught up with MacLachlan. Gently we dived down to about twenty feet above the wave tops. Out of the corner of my eye I could see the Typhoons settling into position slightly above and to either side of us.

So far so good.

Or was it?

No sooner had we comfortably settled on course than all the old fears came flooding back. Would a barrage of light enemy flack, with its horrid orange tracer balls, come out to meet us as we crossed the French coast? If my aircraft got hit, would it burst into flames the same way my Hurricane had exploded on that previous occasion?

Fire!

This time I would not be at fifteen thousand feet and with the opportunity to bale out. I would be roasted alive at this low altitude before I could ever crash land the burning plane. My imagination even recalled the smell of my own burning flesh after such a long passage of time. Perhaps it was the seagulls that kept me from completely losing my nerve and turning for home. Aware of the approaching formation, they arose from their undulating watery couch right in the path of our flight. Unable to alter course I watched fascinated as their flapping white wings were poised ahead of us then suddenly slipped past, only to be replaced by others. One bird striking the propeller blades would cause damage to ensure a watery grave.

Miraculously time passed without collision, and behind us we must have left a trail of squawking feathered aviators ruffled by our lightning passage.

Suddenly I could see it. Dead ahead it appeared as a murky grey outline on the overcast horizon.

Enemy coast!

I could feel the sweat hot and sticky inside my shirt, in contrast to the dryness of my mouth. "Fine sort of person you are," I thought. "Scared stiff even before the first shot has been fired." Mercifully the coastline rapidly grew bigger as we increased speed for the crossing in, and my mind became occupied with other thoughts.

Suddenly the Typhoons began to climb away, leaving a sense of unutterable loneliness around our two green Mustangs.

In a flash the coastline had come and gone without any enemy action.

MacLachlan's low-level navigation at treetop height was a masterly achievement in itself, when you considered he had only one hand to fly his aircraft and hold a map in, which needed constant turning as the miles raced by. Soon we were skimming over the rooftops of Beauvais and heading ever south towards Rambouillet. The broad waters of the Seine passed quickly beneath, and apart from the momentary thrill of flying under some high tension electric cables, the French countryside remained peaceful and serene.

All of a sudden there they were! Three enemy aircraft flying in close formation fifteen hundred feet above and ten miles ahead. Apart from the initial involuntary gasp of astonishment and delight at seeing the culmination of weeks of hard work and planning, there was little time to appreciate the beauties and the grimness of the moment. Important vital little tasks filled the flying seconds that passed as we rapidly closed the gap between ourselves and our slow-moving prey. "Camera gun to be switched on – ah, yes, gunsight and gun button to 'fire'; fine pitch and. . . ."

A crackle of gunfire ripped out over the peaceful woods beneath and the port aircraft burst into flames from Mac's withering blast. Fascinated, I watched our dying enemy fly along in a flaming mass of steel, wood and fabric, and dive in a seemingly slow and dignified manner into a house on the edge of the ageless forest.

Then the game of fox and geese was on with a vengeance as we endeavoured to destroy the remaining two aircraft before the enemy fighters took off to intercept our raid. Soon we were able to send them on the same journey that their companion had taken a few minutes previously, and we continued on our way southward and further away from home. Literally moments later we sighted another aircraft and Mac's unleashed Mustang leaped into the attack with his four cannons spitting fire. Strikes appeared over the unfortunate victim and he dived steeply to earth. It was my privilege to finish him off on the way down and the wreckage was strewn over a large field.

Onwards we flew to Bretigny where greater satisfaction awaited our blood lust. German night-fighters were carrying out their final checks before preparing for their nocturnal harassing of the R.A.F. bomber force. Two of them were preparing to land on their base as we closed in behind. Mac attacked the one furthest away from the airfield and pieces flew in all directions from the Junkers 88. Once again it was my task to finish off a job that needed little completion. The aircraft disintegrated on striking the ground.

For some incredible reason the observer in the second Junkers 88 had failed to notice the ignominious end of his friend, and his pilot continued to carry out his pre-arranged landing. As he held off a few feet above the runway the end came swiftly and mercifully. In a blazing sheet of flame, he struck the concrete and skated drunkenly down its length. Mac had struck again.

Needless to say, every flak gun around the airfield had witnessed the fate of their countrymen and all hell was let loose as we weaved our way across the centre of the airfield. But it was our day and we slipped through the stream of innocent looking orange balls that rose lazily from the ground in our direction.

Joining up together we set course northwards for England.

Then a new danger made itself felt, but it came not in the form of lethal bullets. It came from inside myself. I felt my blood boiling with the exultation of our recent killings. I gloated in my mind over the scenes of hideous violent death we had so recently meted out. Vengeance was mine, and I was enjoying every moment of it. I felt my years in the hospital had not been in vain.

This lust for killing was to grow and grow within me until the end of the war, causing me to inflict hurt on others than the official enemy. Youthful innocence had died alongside the Luftwaffe aircrews that eventful morning over northern France.

Delighted with the success of our first sortie, Mac and I waited impatiently for ideal weather conditions to permit a second attempt.

It was to end tragically.

Once again we set out with a Typhoon escort, but crossing in over the French coast Mac must have collected some machine gun fire. His aircraft climbed steeply from our treetop height, and at one thousand feet his canopy opened. He presumably changed his mind about bailing out, for the aircraft proceeded in a glide towards a small field. His approach speed was too fast, and the Mustang first touched the ground three quarters of the way across the field, with retracted wheels. Still moving rapidly, it ploughed into an orchard shedding its wings before it came to rest as a battered, dust-clouded wreck. I orbited the crash several times at a low height, but no sign of life emerged from the wreckage. For an instant I contemplated trying to land in the field to come to Mac's aid, but judgement ruled out the possibility of landing wheels down in such a confined area. Reluctantly I dived at the scene of the crash to register some camera gun photographs, and heart-brokenly headed for home. Years later I learned that Mac had survived the actual crash, but died three weeks later in the hospital. His body lies buried in a small French graveyard.

It was the passing of a very brave man.

After Mac's crash I returned to East Grinstead for a further operation on one of my hands. The bed rest did me good, and feeling refreshed I returned to operational flying, all the more determined to get my own back, not only for myself but for Mac now as well.

This time I was posted as a flight commander to 122 Squadron. My time there was brief. Count Coloredo Mansfield, the officer commanding 132 Squadron, was killed while returning from a sortie over France. I was posted to take over his squadron. Almost immediately the squadron was sent to Scotland for a rest, and I was posted to a special course at Milfield airfield. Milfield had an attractive setting a few miles inland from the coast of Northumberland. The uninhabited beaches and off-shore water lent themselves as excellent bombing and gunnery ranges.

On the airfield itself Spitfires occupied all the available dispersed parking areas, standing out against the snowy January background.

In contrast to the winter setting of the landscape was the cosy warmth of the officers' Mess. A milling throng of cheerful young men occupied the anterooms and bar, and despite their apparent youth sported the ranks of squadron leaders and wing commanders combined with decorations for gallantry. Together they represented the spearhead of leadership in the air for the coming invasion of Europe.

Despite his youthful appearance each man had proved himself as an outstanding member of the fraternity of fighter pilots. Immediately following breakfast on the morning after their arrival the pilots were summoned to the main anteroom. A young air commodore addressed them. His manner was businesslike and precise.

"Good morning, gentlemen. As many of you may have guessed, the invasion of Europe is not far away. The Army and Navy will do their jobs and we will do ours. That is why you are here." He paused to let the words sink in.

"For the next three weeks you will fire your guns and practice dive-bombing until it is second nature. On the beaches near here are convoys of brand new lorries of different sizes and shapes. There are also tanks. These you will attack with cannons and rockets followed by an inspection on foot of the damage caused." Again he paused for effect.

"You will learn through trial and error the best angle of attack for thin and thick-skinned vehicles. On the bombing ranges you will obtain a proficiency previously thought impossible. You will set a standard for the pilots in your squadron, a standard that you must demand that they in turn attain. You will keep up the highest traditions of the Royal Air Force." The air commodore sat down.

The peaceful silence of the Northumberland countryside was rudely shattered during the following weeks. The rattle of cannon and machine gun fire combined with the whooshing roar of rockets, and for a change in the lethal symphony, five hundred pound bombs burst out to sea after leaving the diving Spitfires. The tragedy of a pilot blowing up in mid-air drew comments in the Mess one night. All minds were tuned into the wave-length of a distant foreign beach where death would be reckoned in thousands as the soldiers waded ashore.

As the days passed so the pilots became more proficient in handling their deadly weapons. Fire was held until it was certain that the range and angle of dive were correct. Bombs were not released until height, wind direction and steadiness in the screaming dive were all taken into account. Evening discussions brought out useful hints and wisdom gained through error. When the time came to disperse, these young leaders left in the confident knowledge that when the moment came they could hit and hit hard.

While at Milfield I had one experience that was not without its thrills.

One crisp, cold morning we were ordered to carry out a routine dive-bombing exercise. This particular day I was to fly as number two to another pilot. This meant he was my leader for the sortie and I was to follow him at all times. We turned into the wind at the end of the runway which stretched ahead of us with three-foot snowbanks on either side. The ice on the runway itself gleamed in the early morning light.

My leader raised his hand and commenced the take-off. Tucking my left wing close behind his right one I opened my throttle firmly to keep station. Our tails came up as we roared down the runway.

Then I realized that a cross-wind was causing the other aircraft to veer in my direction as its wheels slipped on the icy surface. Naturally I had to ease over to the right as well to avoid collision. I could see the snow bank already under my right wing.

Just as we got airborne I was almost into the bank and the thought of hitting it with a five-hundred-pound bomb under my aircraft was not an encouraging thought. Swiftly I moved the "wheels up" lever, but too late. There was a thud beneath me and the aircraft gave a slight lurch. Knowing I was in trouble I turned away from my leader, but continued to climb. I then tried to figure out the situation. Firstly the two green lights on the instrument panel were not shining. As I thought, probably the right wheel had struck the snow bank and either the wheel and oleo leg had snapped off, or were hanging down in some distorted fashion.

My eyes swiftly took in the engine instrument readings, and were immediately arrested by the glycol coolant temperature. It was rising alarmingly, and soon the engine would stop through overheating. A dead engine meant a "wheels-up" landing in a field with a deadly bomb attached to soften the impact! A quick look at the altimeter showed I was too low to bail out. Even if I could, perhaps the abandoned Spitfire and its lethal load might dive into one of the farms or houses scattered below.

I had no choice but to turn my crippled aircraft seawards, and there jettison the bomb, provided the engine did not pack up beforehand. I throttled back to try and keep the temperature under control, but this meant eliminating the possibility of gaining more height. Painfully, slowly the coastline came towards me, and the temperature needle reached the danger mark. Thankfully, I limped over the beach and immediately afterwards pressed the bomb release button. Lightened of the load, the engine bore less weight, and with a singing heart I returned to the airfield, there to execute a belly landing on the snow-covered grass. My first introduction to skiing!

Twenty-Two

At the completion of the Milfield course I rejoined my unit.

The time spent in Scotland passed quickly and soon the squadron was winging its way southward, there to take up its role when the curtain went up on the Second Front.

At our new airfield at Ford on the south coast of England, the pilots were allowed no respite. Dive-bombing training now took a more practical shape, and every day a load of bombs was dropped on targets in France. These usually took the form of Hitler's secret V.1 launching sites hidden away in various corners of the French countryside. The objectives consisted of two or three small concrete buildings no larger than cottages, and a hundred-yard-long launching ramp.

The problem of navigating his way from England to a pinpoint reference on the map held in his hand was only one of the squadron commander's tasks. The target had to be identified while still many miles away, the aircraft in the squadron ordered into echelon formation for the attack, the best direction of approach obtained, so that the final dive was made without a difficult cross-wind component, and finally the accurate judgment of the moment at which to peel off from eight thousand feet so that all twelve aircraft could apply themselves to the task of screaming down in a steady dive, to release their bombs at just the right second.

From the instant the leader dropped his wing the vicious 40mm anti-aircraft guns surrounding the target would put up a fountain of orange-tracered flack through which the aircraft must dive.

Pulling his Spitfire up in an almost vertical climbing turn, the squadron commander must both assess the degree of success of the attack, watch out for enemy fighters, and ensure that his squadron re-formed as a single complete unit as soon as possible. Often he would land and wait for a pilot who had failed to rejoin the rest until common sense forced him to send off the hated letter to the missing man's next of kin.

I sat at my desk in the wooden hut. A thin partition divided my office from the larger portion of the small wooden building. Only slightly muffled, the voices of my pilots reached my ear as they indulged in a lively game of poker. From outside came the distant roar of a powerful engine as a Spitfire underwent its ground tests. Following a firm knock, the office door opened and two youthful flight lieutenants entered and saluted. They were my two flight commanders. The shorter of the two wore a forage cap under which showed his mass of blond hair. To emphasize the point, the flag of Norway stood out proudly on the upper part of his sleeve. "Skipper" Vinden, so named because of his likeness to the figure in oilskins depicted on every tin of Skipper Norwegian bristlings, commanded "B" Flight. A humourist by nature, he endeared himself to those under his command by his determination to get at the enemy on every possible occasion. His favourite English expression sounded like, "What the bloody hail!"

"Have a pew," I said, as I waved my hand in the direction of some wooden cases that served as furniture. Skipper sat down with a sigh of relief. He had been to bed very early the previous night, but not for sleeping purposes. Michael Graham leaned his broad figure against the door. "I'm O.K., Boss." Although quick to use a formal "Sir" when the occasion demanded, Michael used the term "Boss" to indicate his friendly subservience to his squadron commander's higher rank. I looked at them both in turn, but my eyes settled on Skipper as I spoke. I knew how much more it would mean to the fearless little Norwegian.

"You will inform your pilots that all passes out of camp are cancelled until further notice, and that they are to report to the briefing room at nineteen hundred hours sharp – you will not tell them yet that tomorrow is D-Day – "

The blond pilot's mouth opened as if to speak and then closed slowly. Graham's low whistle of astonishment was accentuated as the roaring engine outside was throttled back. "Raise you three," came the muffled voice through the partition.

The engine crackled and stopped.

There was complete silence.

Group Captain Jamie Rankin, the airfield commander, tapped the wall map with a wooden pointer.

"There are five main beaches. Three British – Sword, Juno and Gold, and two American – Omaha and Utah." He turned to face the ninety fighter pilots seated in the briefing room. "The task of our three squadrons is to provide close cover over the two American beaches from first light tomorrow morning." The group captain lowered his voice slightly as he spoke to the three squadron commanders seated in the front row.

"You will find details of times of patrol in there." The pointer tapped at the manual on my lap bearing the imposing title of "Operation Overlord."

For the next hour the airfield commander explained the broad outlines of the intended landing. Sentence by sentence he built up a picture of the vast sea and aerial armadas that would be approaching the Normandy beaches in but a few hours' time.

The palms of my hands were wet with sweat.

At last I abandoned the idea of ever getting to sleep, and stood outside the tent listening to the never-ending drone of the night-bomber force winging overhead. The last phase of the softening-up period was being completed, and after the bombers would come the fleets of paratroopers and gliders; arranging their time of arrival precisely at the beaches were the hundreds of landing craft now bobbing a determined way across the English Channel.

The greatest armada the world has ever known was underway.

Asleep in their beds the people of England slumbered peacefully on, unaware that their fighting sons no longer inhabited the same loved island. Unaware that many of these sons would find their rest beneath the rich soil of Normandy.

I envied the contented snores rising out from the tent I was passing. Inside slept four sergeant pilots. Passing on I caught sight of the glow of a cigarette burning in the darkness. "Who's that? Skipper?" The two flight commanders shared the same tent. "No, boss, it's Mike." I seated myself beside Graham on the grass. "Wart the blordy hail is going on," Skipper's blond hair hung down over his eyes as he poked a sleepy face out from between the canvas flaps.

"Come and join the happy throng, you oversexed Scandinavian."
Mike was in good form despite the early hour of the morning and
the vital implications that it held.

I suddenly felt old and alone. Despite my twenty-four years it
seemed to me that a chasm of time divided me from my two flight
commanders. I knew that I had lost the boyish spirits.

Mike was now expressing. Was it on account of my responsibilities, or was I getting war weary? I did not want to think of the answer,
but only to get on with the task that lay a few hours ahead. Idly I wondered if either Skipper or Mike would still be alive at the end of the
day. The Norwegian, I felt, stood the lesser chance of survival. His fa-
natical desire to kill anything German could easily lead to his own
undoing. As for myself, I did not really care. Death would at least allow
me to shed my mantle of tiredness. No more would there be that tight
knot of fear and anxiety gripping my insides every time a new operation was signalled through from group headquarters.

I was giving my pilots their final briefing. It was still forty-seven
minutes before H-Hour, our rendezvous over Omaha Beach. Four
minutes of this time would be utilized starting up and taxiing out to
the end of the runway, three minutes would go in a circuit of the airfield as the squadron of twelve formed up, and thirty minutes would
be spent in getting to our patrol area along the prescribed routes.

Ten minutes left before the engines roared into life.

"On no account whatsoever is anyone to leave the beach area during our patrol period – I don't care if there's a big fat juicy Hun a couple of miles inland asking to be shot down – our job is to give cover
to the troops below." I looked about me at the pale faces just discernible in the dark. "The odds are that a lone Jerry is bait to get us
out of the way while a big formation has a crack at the landing barges."

One of the pilots interrupted. "What happens if we get engine
trouble, sir?" "A forced-landing strip is being prepared here," I tapped
the map. "It may not be ready for a day or two, so you'll just have to
use common sense – any more questions? – All right, better get out
to your machines."

Silently the little group of twelve fanned out towards the dispersed
Spitfires.

I felt cold and lonely as I went through the routine cockpit check; by now, practice had made it almost automatic. By the glow of the dim cockpit lighting I followed the steady movement of the second hand as it crept round the dial of my watch. Fifteen seconds to go – ten – five – four – three – two – one. Giving a rapid thumbs-up to the ground crew, I leaned forward in my seat and firmly pressed the two black starter buttons. Immediately the powerful Merlin engine roared into life. Within seconds the mobile starter battery was pulled clear of the aircraft and the chocks taken from the wheels. All around in the darkness spots of purple flame flashed as the remainder of the squadron started up their engines.

Swiftly the graceful Spitfires taxied out to the end of the runway, there to form up in six pairs for the take-off. Restraining myself for ten seconds to keep to the exact time schedule, I opened up my engine slowly but firmly. Giving a flicking side glance to make sure that the second Spitfire was close alongside, I settled down to concentrating on the take-off itself. Gracefully the little fighter rose from the ground, tucking up its wheels neatly into the wing wells. Doing a gradual turn around the airfield circuit I watched the five following pairs closing up rapidly as they cut across my turning circle. Satisfied that we were together as a unit, I set course for the Isle of Wight, there to pick up the pre-determined route to the beachhead. The sky was beginning to lighten in the east. The land below began to take solid shape, and soon I could see the distinctive shape of the Needles.

Our Spitfires turned southward and opened out into battle formation as the shores of England receded behind.

My concentration relaxed for a moment as my gaze took in the roughness of the sea. It needed little imagination to conjure up a miserable picture of the thousands of troops cooped up in their landing barges, many of them prey to sea sickness despite their wonder pills. The greyness receded from the early morning, and soon I was able to pick out the shape of the Cherbourg Peninsular ahead on the starboard. My keen sight soon spotted the low cloud formation lying inland and covering the beach area.

Almost immediately afterwards I saw a sight that brought a flood of feeling into mind and body, both of which had felt little emotion, except resentment for so long.

Hundreds of ships of all sizes and shapes, from vast battleships to small barges, littered the surface of the sea. Some were still completing their rough passage across the Channel, others lay at anchor while the big grey men o'war belched forth sixteen inch shells from their gun turrets in the direction of the French countryside; two Seafire fighters buzzed above the battleships like flies around a cart horse, spotting the accuracy of the gunners below and supplying them with corrections.

Sleek destroyers guarded the flanks of the shipping armada, while overhead patrolled the ever-watchful fighter cover.

Minesweepers plied their steady patrol back and forth, and an occasional column of water rose to prove the value of their efforts.

Superimposed on this fantastic picture were the ghostly outlines, in my mind, of the pathetic little fleet that I had watched standing off the beaches of Dunkirk. The pendulum had gone full swing. A feeling of savage delight passed through me. "Right, you bastards," I thought, "you've asked for it and now you're going to get it." There was no mercy in my heart. Our Spitfires swept past the moored fleet and commenced the vigil over the two American beaches of Omaha and Utah.

Figures hurried about like busy ants, and tracks left by passing vehicles stood out sharply as indentations on the beach. Inland the high hedged Bocage countryside absorbed all signs of movement. Masses of coloured parachutes lay clustered together in fields, and troop-carrying gliders lay about in contorted positions like dead men, their task done. Time passed with seemingly no action taking place on the battlefields below, until suddenly a gush of flame from a barn or farmhouse would tell us that a grim struggle was indeed taking place.

The expected reaction from the enemy air force never materialized that morning, and after an hour's patrol I reluctantly led my formation back to England.

Only his service training stopped the irate Skipper from flying inland to shoot up the first German target he could find. The war held a very personal meaning to this homeless young Norwegian, and to return to base without firing his guns was tantamount to sacrilege.

Landing back at Ford, we were quickly surrounded by the eager ground crews, crowding around to get details of the landing and to know if a beachhead was being established. With my two flight commanders I strode off to the operations room to give a detailed report to the intelligence officer. As we came out into the sunshine half an hour later, we were attracted by groups of people staring up into the sky. Following their gaze we quickly spotted the big four-engined Stirling bomber towing a troop-filled Horsa glider. The port outer engine of the Stirling had stopped and it was obvious that it was in trouble due to the heavy load dragging along behind.

The watchers below saw the tow rope release and the glider turn towards our airfield below. It was apparent to all that the bomber would never have hauled its load across to the Normandy beaches.

Completing a half-circuit of the airfield, the Horsa pilot made a neat touchdown on the grass between the concrete runways. Within seconds troops poured out from the hull and rushed towards the nearby buildings, their Sten guns held ready for immediate action. Only after their pilot had shouted frantically at them did the moment of truth arrive. Sheepishly they lowered their guns on realizing they were on English and not French soil.

The N.A.A.F.I. tea wagon rolled up to complete their embarrassment!

The days passed in uneventful beach patrols, and still the Luftwaffe was not to be seen. The anticlimax was almost worse than the pre-invasion tension.

Tired but content, Michael Graham and I dropped our girlfriends off, the nightclub closed and we headed south for our airfield. First light was just breaking as we reached the airfield. Approaching the dispersal area, we were surprised to see the activity taking place around the aircraft.

"What on earth is going on?" asked Mike.

"God knows," I replied. "Our first show isn't until ten."

Skipper came out of the dispersal hut to greet us.

"Orf to blordy France, ve are and nort coming back."

The next hour was a wild scramble to pack our belongings and be ready for the imminent departure. I had foreseen the day when my personal belongings, few as they were, would not fit into the cramped cockpit of a Spitfire. I had obtained an old cigar-shaped long-range tank which the engineers had fitted with a detachable nose. It was only a matter of moments to put articles such as blankets, sleeping bag and an extra uniform into the tank. I just hoped that on the way over to France we would not have to go into action as this meant the tank would have to be jettisoned, and with it all my possessions. The flight proved uneventful, and later in the morning eighteen Spitfires curved in to land on a prepared strip of ground in the centre of a Normandy wheatfield.

The method of preparing the single strip runway was for a bulldozer to clear a path through the waving wheat, taking the top layer of earth with it. Pilots and ground crews soon became acquainted with the fine soil that was to be blown in all directions off the strip, to find its way into everything from our clothes to our food. Later it was to create vital problems by getting into the delicate operating mechanisms of our machine guns and cannons, resulting in stoppages that meant the difference between life and death. Dispersed away from the strip among the apple orchards were the tents of the air and ground crews. Ingenuity was soon at work, and hot showers were erected to combat the fine dust. The airplanes were also dispersed as much as possible to avoid widespread damage in case of surprise attack.

The days that followed were ones of intense activity. From dawn to dusk allied fighters ranged far behind the enemy lines, attacking any legitimate targets that moved along the roads. Seldom did my squadron and I return to our airstrip with our guns unfired. Rising columns of smoke bespoke of the funeral pyres of lorries and armoured cars. Only heavily armour-plated tanks could withstand the attacks of the Spitfires but these soon fell prey to the deadly rocket-firing Typhoons. Those vehicles that dared to move in daylight did so with an aircraft spotter gazing skywards, only too often to pick out the dreaded shape of the oncoming fighter when it was too late. Skipper and I each in our own way revelled in the daily bloodbath, and time on the ground to us was a necessary evil. Mike Graham treated it with his customary boyish enthusiasm and the fact that he was killing hardly penetrated his mind. Although I exulted in the sight of my cannon shells ripping into the lurching vehicles as they careened about the narrow Normandy lanes like stricken animals, my lust lay in the desire to destroy aircraft.

The fine dust from the airfield gave me the excuse I needed. Time and again the guns in the aircraft jammed after short bursts of firing, and although my own guns seemed less prevalent than most to the stoppages, I used them as an excuse to make special flights in order to test them.

I asked Flying Officer Hawkins to join me on the first of these "cannon tests," and an hour later our two Spitfires roared into the partially clouded sky. Heading south-westwards over the front lines, I pointed the nose of my aircraft in the direction of Lisieux. Theoretically the guns were to be fired into the sea, but I hoped to put the ammunition to better use.

Thirty miles behind the enemy lines my desires were fulfilled. Below us, flying in an easterly direction, was a formation of thirty Me. 109 fighters. Quickly informing Hawkins of their position, I half-rolled and dived down to the attack. As our two Spitfires streaked earthwards we were spotted by our prey, and immediately the grey mottled German fighters broke formation and climbed to meet the oncoming attack. Within a matter of seconds Hawk and I became separated in the general melee. The position of attackers and attacked was reversed immediately, and we found ourselves fighting for our lives. The vastly superior odds of enemy aircraft helped to a certain extent, as in the confusion of the dog fight the Luftwaffe repeatedly mistook their own countrymen for the insolent Englishmen. I kept my machine in a tight turn, relying on its manoeuvrability to save me. However, any attempt to straighten out to fire at one of the enemy instantly brought an Me. 109 to settle on my tail, and once again I would have to turn as steeply as possible. Soon the pressure of the imposed loads on my body began to tell and I knew that I must escape quickly – or die. Still turning, I climbed my powerful airplane towards the safety of the clouds several thousand feet above. Me. 109s swarmed around the spiralling Spitfire attempting to destroy it with difficult deflection shots.

An enemy fighter tore past and I straightened out for an instant to fire at the beautiful target presented. My guns chattered and white flashes appeared on the grey starboard wing of the German; pieces of metal flew off, but before I could notice more my own peril became obvious. Glancing back over my right shoulder, I could see the twinkling lights on the leading edge of the Messerschmitt as its pilot began firing at me. A violent explosion filled the cockpit with smoke and noise, but I was already turning steeply before the terror of the situation entered my soul. For a moment the deadly fear of fire gripped me in its clutch. The smoke cleared and with it my mind took control again as I realized the aircraft was not on fire. Instead, the sticky feeling of blood running down my left leg told a story of where part of the exploding shell had gone. I also knew at that moment that the protecting clouds would never be reached. I decided to gamble on one last chance for my life. Turning the machine on its back.

I pulled the stick hard back into my stomach, and with the engine and propeller turning at maximum boost, screamed downwards in the hope of shaking off my pursuers. Even before I commenced the manoeuvre I knew that the Messerschmitts could outpace me in the dive. My only chance of survival lay in getting down to treetop level and jinking around woods and other obstacles in the effort to throw them off the trail.

By now my left leg was numb and useless.

For the first few seconds of the dive I was elated to see that no telltale streaks of tracer were whipping past. Could I have thrown them off, I wondered, or was some swine of a Hun sitting fifty yards behind my tail and settling down to take comfortable aim? The tracer commenced as I got down to an altitude of two thousand feet.

Kicking desperately at the rudder bar with my one good leg, at the same time climbing and diving for fractional intervals, I tried to take as much evasive action as my condition would permit.

The actions were effective and although the tracer continued to flash past in bursts, no strikes registered. Getting to within a few feet of the ground, I once again pulled my aircraft into a tight turn. Looking back, I was relieved to see that only a solitary Messerschmitt appeared to be dogging me. Hatred brought with it new strength. "I'll get you if it kills me, you bastard," I thought.

Pulling harder on the stick I kept the Spitfire juddering on the edge of a stalled condition in my attempt to get around onto the 109's tail.

The German pilot sensed that it was becoming a duel to the death and knew that his own airplane was no match for the Spitfire in trying to out-turn it. Still having me ahead of him, he pulled his nose back sharply to get enough deflection on his target, fired his guns, and killed himself.

The Messerschmitt was just on the edge of a stall when its pilot fired the guns: the recoil slowed the airplane sufficiently to flick over and strike the trees twenty feet below. Circling the funeral pyre I watched the black column of smoke rising with morbid fascination.

It might easily have been the wreckage of a Spitfire burning in the wood below.

On returning to my airfield I was happy to find an ambulance waiting, but happier still to find that Hawk had survived safely. It took two weeks of boredom after leaving the field hospital, before I could take to the air again.

News came through one afternoon that the squadron was released until dawn the following morning. With a whoop of delight the pilots rushed off to collect money from the field cashier before descending on the town of Bayeux. For most of them, it was the first time they had been allowed outside the airfield perimeter since the squadron landed in France.

Led by my jeep full to overflowing, the remainder of the pilots followed in a large covered van. It was agreed unanimously that we would all foregather in an estaminet for a champagne party.

Two hours later small groups of threes and fours began converging on a small cafe in the main street. Each individual was well-supplied with boxes of Camembert cheese, but one young sergeant pilot had outdone the others in a big way his chin just managed to tuck over the column of boxes supported in front of his body with arms at full length. Carefully depositing his load in a corner of the bar, Jeff proceeded to pour quantities of bubbling champagne down his nineteen-year-old throat. With the flowing of the bubbling wine youthful spirits effervesced in unison, and soon the landlord and his wife and friends were shaking their heads sadly at the sight of the mad English and their method of enjoying themselves.

After a while the taste of champagne palled on our palates, and someone's suggestion that we returned to the airfield for English beer was greeted with approval. Picking up their parcels, my pilots poured out of the cafe onto the cobblestoned street. Staggering more from the effects of the wine than his mountain of cheese, Jeff tottered down the street saying "I may be pissed, but I've got an awful lot of fromage!"

The jeep, led by the lorry, swung out of the main street and into the open country. Normandy peasants stopped to gape open-mouthed as the vehicles loaded with lustily singing pilots tore by. Chickens ran for their lives as the big van rushed along close behind. Then it started.

Jeff at his station against the tailboard of the van was still keeping up his monotonous chant of being the possessor of vast quantities of cheese, despite his inebriated condition. The next thing he knew was that the top box had been whipped away, its contents hurled playfully at the jeep, where it found its target in the shape of Esky's broad face. Flying Officer Eskell was American by birth, and a volunteer in the Royal Canadian Air Force. He had the broad flat face of a lumberjack which was not enhanced by the soggy mass of Camembert cheese spread over it. Giving a sticky roar of anger, he whipped his .38 revolver from its holster and fired at one of the van's tyres. This was the signal for the rest of Jeff's load to be dispatched with haste and a duel between rounds of stinky cheese and bullets ensued.

Another pilot put his arm consolingly about Jeff's shoulders after each side had expended its ammunition.

"Never mind, Jeff, you haven't got any fromage but you're still pissed!"

"Twelve plus 190's two o'clock below, Red One."

Immediately my eyes searched the area just ahead and beneath my right wing. Quickly and methodically I examined the area where my Number Two had reported the enemy aircraft. Then I saw them.

The formation of enemy fighters were on an opposite course to our own and a thousand feet below. Between us lay a whispy cloud.

"Red one turning starboard and attacking," I called into the microphone and wheeled about to dive on the German formation.

Quickly the twelve Spitfires gathered speed as the unsuspecting Focke Wulfs flew steadily on their course. Coming in on a quarter attack, I followed the curve of pursuit as I closed range with the rear aircraft. Just like a copy book method of attack taught at gunnery school, I thought. Unfortunately I knew we would be spotted long before the time was ripe to open fire.

Quickly the range closed and I gave a gasp of astonishment as I realized that we were still unobserved. Taking a steady deflection at an estimated three hundred yards' range, I pressed the firing button for two seconds. The chug of the cannons and the chatter of the machine guns filled the cockpit with distant noise. Ahead a column of brown smoke appeared from the German as he peeled gently away from his formation which flew on still ignorant of the presence of R.A.F. fighters. Perplexed at the behaviour of my target, I closed to within a hundred yards and fired again. Pieces of metal flew off the FW 190 but it still continued in its steady gentle dive towards the battlefields below. The pilot must be dead, I thought, and pulled my Spitfire away to one side to watch events. In a loose formation, the German and two British airplanes dived earthwards. I shivered slightly; the whole thing seemed uncanny to me. Taking my eyes off the 190 for an instant, I registered the ground below and ahead. A violent tank battle was in progress on a large area of open land on the east side of the River Orne. Tracer shells and smoke from burning tanks filled the air with grotesque patterns as the three aircraft approached. I levelled out and circled about waiting for the moment of impact between the doomed 190 and the solid earth. To my great surprise, the German straightened out near the ground and skimmed over the fields as he lost speed, then in a cloud of dust effected a neat landing in the midst of the tank battle.

Our Spitfires dived twice and raked the grey-green Swastika-covered fighter with cannon fire. Nothing emerged from the cockpit.

"Right you are, sir," the intelligence officer said. "I'll put you down for one enemy destroyed. Pity there weren't more of you, you could have given that Hun formation quite a pasting."

I laughed harshly. I didn't mind. I'd paid off one more personal score with the enemy. Vividly I recalled the long watches of the night in the hospital ward, where I had vowed that for every painful operation I had to undergo, so would I one day destroy one German.

The score was getting settled.

"Can't understand it, sir," the intelligence officer said. "Group refuse to allow that last Focke Wulf 190 to be classified as destroyed. Seems a bit unfair to – ." I strode out from the operations caravan without replying. Bastards, I thought – how much more proof did they need than I'd already given. It had belly landed in the middle of a tank battle and been shot up by myself and Sergeant Ford until it resembled a sieve. Next thing they'd want would be the pilot's head on a platter before they believed you'd shot down a Hun. Distrustful bunch of sods!

I was finding it painful to walk along the deep ruts by the tank tracks. The recent wound in my leg made the muscles ache, and I longed to sit down and rest. However pride and the fact that the two men behind might mistake the action of stopping for one of fear, kept me going. The three of us were proceeding carefully towards the riddled wreckage of a FW 190 fighter that lay in the centre of a large field. It was the same field on which my victim had belly landed during the heat of the tank battle. Infuriated that my claim for destroying the German fighter had been disallowed, I was now threading my way through the mine-strewn field to bring back part of the aircraft as proof. This airplane would make the fourteenth to my credit. One more after this and the slate would be wiped clean. Fifteen surgical operations – fifteen enemy aircraft destroyed. They weren't going to rob me of this one.

Two days later Group altered their decision from one FW 190 "damaged" to the "destroyed" category. The swastika-covered fin and rudder presented to them with my compliments were too much to argue against.

The flight sergeant replaced the telephone on its receiver. "Operations have okayed your cannon test, sir." I jumped up from the grass.

"O.K., let's go," I said curtly.

Shortly before this I had been promoted to be Wing Commander Flying. This meant that in the air I now had four squadrons under my command. This gave a total of eighty aircraft and one hundred and twenty pilots to draw from. Full strength in wing formation consisted of forty-eight aircraft and their pilots, the remaining aircraft and pilots being held in reserve.

Squadron Leader Kenneth Charney took over command of my squadron.

Ken and Skipper had both volunteered to go with me on the cannon test in the hope that they might find some enemy aircraft. The Luftwaffe was putting in rare appearances near the beachhead during daylight hours.

Five minutes later our three Spitfires were climbing swiftly in the direction of Lisieux. In my cockpit I leaned forward to search the sky in all directions. I was convinced that today I would find my fifteenth victim. There was no elation in my mind, only the desire to find and destroy.

Soon after crossing the lines a carpet of cloud covered the land from sight except where it showed occasionally through gaps. For the hundredth time my eyes swept in regular search, to move on and then suddenly to return. A multitude of dark specks dotted the cloud layer many miles ahead and below on the starboard side. Rocking the aircraft to attract the attention of the other two, I opened up my engine to maximum cruising power and settled it into a shallow dive. Slowly the distance and height between the large and small formations narrowed. Still however it was too far from us to identify our quarry as friend or foe. I gulped hard as I quickly calculated the size of the formation, at least sixty or seventy machines and three Spitfires. Odds of twenty to one. Probably they would be American; they used large formations like these. Thunderbolts on an armed reconnaissance. What if they were German? I found myself sweating.

Even before I identified the aircraft, I realized that the large gaggle were also losing height and seemingly intent on descending through a large break in the clouds ahead of them. Rocking my aircraft once more, I opened the throttle wider and increased the angle of dive. The sound of air rushing past the cockpit changed the pitch to a higher note, keeping the mood of the race being run.

As the leader reached the edge of the cloud gap, so did I recognize them for what they were. There was no mistaking the businesslike outlines of the Focke Wulf 190s. I clicked the gun button over to the "fire" position. Closing the distance between us rapidly I noticed that the German formation was altering course as it descended below cloud. Gone for the moment were my thoughts of revenge. Instead I applied my brain vigorously to planning the best method of attack. I must lead my small formation swiftly into battle, strike hard, and climb away before the enemy was aware of what had happened. Diving and turning through the same gap, I found myself close behind the rearguard and gaining rapidly. Withholding my fire I made a snap decision and dived beneath them. It would be an added risk, but if I could reach the front of the formation and destroy the leader, a far better job would be done.

Sitting tensed in my cockpit, I knew how Drake and his men must have felt as they sailed through the might of the Spanish Armada – scared stiff! The enemy aircraft flew steadily on their course, oblivious that their ranks were increased by three in number.

Halfway through the group of vicious looking 190s I knew that my luck couldn't hold any longer. Satisfying myself with one of the deputy leaders as a target, I climbed to the same level as the Luftwaffe fighters and settled myself to shoot. As my thumb stabbed at the firing button so I noticed that the alarm had been given. Aircraft began turning in all directions and I only had time to notice a flash of white as one of my shells struck home.

The surprise was over and once again I was fighting to preserve my life. Skipper was sticking close beside me as I flung the nimble Spitfire into a tight turn. Glancing back I saw a flash and knew that the Norwegian had been hit. Looking ahead again I found a 190 straight ahead and a sitting target at a hundred yards. Firing quickly I saw pieces flying off the Focke Wulf in all directions. Realizing the German was doomed I was determined to see its end regardless of the risk. This was number fifteen and the climax to a long, long wait. The 190 rolled slowly onto its back and dived vertically towards the earth, two thousand feet below. Turning tightly over my victim's death dive I watched it fascinated as it exploded on impact with the ground.

I shook my head violently as if clearing it of a dream and climbed away into the protection of the clouds above, leaving the milling aircraft to sort themselves out.

Ten minutes after I landed Ken and Skipper appeared much to my relief. Skipper's aircraft had been hit, but not too badly. Inquiring if he had seen the FW 190 that had shot at him, he replied, "See him! The blordy borger was so close I could hear him!"

Chatting happily my two companions disappeared in search of liquid refreshment.

Suddenly I felt drained of energy. What had happened to the elation I should have felt now that my own private score was settled? Although only twenty-four years old, I felt like an old, old man. It all seemed so purposeless now. I tried hard to figure out this new feeling of emptiness. I had left hospital with a seething desire to destroy; this ambition now in reflection seemed shallow and puerile. Nevertheless the deed was now done and where did I go from here? I was tired, dead tired, both physically and mentally, and with nothing to look forward to. The girlfriends I'd had since leaving East Grinstead hospital I'd treated as doormats. There had been no room in my heart for love. Hate had filled it to capacity. Now hate was spent, leaving a void.

Breakthrough! Finally the beachhead burst at its seams, and the Americans broke through to the west, followed later by the British and Polish forces who were up against the main German armoured divisions at Caen.

What are one's remembered impressions of this history-making breakout? Hundreds of burning vehicles that we had strafed and set on fire in the famous Falaise Gap?

Red Crosses tied across lifeless German tanks?

The group of arrogant German soldiers sitting outside on the farmhouse steps, playing cards as their trucks burnt? I stopped their game with a few hundred rounds of bullets, and their arrogance disappeared rapidly.

Wildly waving peasant children welcoming the conquerors little knowing what it was all about?

Probably as pilots we saw more than most, but what we did see wasn't very attractive.

Then I met the man who will haunt me until my dying day.

Including ground-strafing, dive-bombing and air-to-air fights, I had probably by now killed several hundred people, but from the air it was completely impersonal, and made no mental impact.

This man was different.

I was out alone on another "cannon test," which was the usual thinly veiled excuse to look for trouble. None of the aircraft in the air had the slightest smell of the Luftwaffe, so I confined my searchings to objects on the ground many miles behind the enemy front. Suddenly I saw him!

His motorbike had caused a small cloud of dust to arise, giving away his position. Like a kestrel hawk pouncing, I wheeled my Spitfire and streaked towards the ground.

By now my man had stopped on the corner of a hairpin bend, and as the range closed rapidly, I guessed he was studying a map. His military camouflaged bike and his grey-green uniform spelt him out as a despatch rider, and therefore a legitimate military target. As I placed the orange reflected dot of my gunsight on the centre of his body, he looked up straight at me, and knew the moment of truth had arrived.

As I stabbed the gun button he threw up his left arm as if to shield his face from the impact. I cursed him with all my soul for making such a simple pathetic human gesture, and loathed myself as I saw man and bike disappear in a torrent of bullets.

I returned straight to base, and found it difficult to talk to anyone for several days.

I can still see his face and the raised arm.

On the lighter side, the B.B.C. made fools of themselves and us too. Listening to the radio one morning, I heard the suave B.B.C. announcer advise us that Paris had been liberated.

Immediately I asked and obtained permission to lead two squadrons over the city as a morale booster for its citizens. My plan was that one squadron should fly tightly together, forming a "V" for Victory formation, and that the other squadron form up as a Cross of Lorraine, the symbol of the Free French Forces.

We took off from the Normandy beachhead, climbing rapidly in open battle formation. We were to perform a routine sweep south and east of Paris before giving our pep demonstration. No enemy aircraft appeared, and an hour and a half after take-off I ordered the two squadrons into tight formation, and led them in a long steady dive towards the centre of Paris. Levelling out at ten thousand feet (a dangerous altitude for anti-aircraft fire), we flew above the Place de la Concorde, along the Champs Elysées towards the Arc de Triomphe. Then all hell broke loose.

Anti-aircraft shells burst all around our neat formations. I yelled "Break" and pulled my aircraft up in a steep climb to throw the German gunners off their range. For the next few seconds twenty-four Spitfires were climbing, diving, turning in all directions. By a miracle, not one aircraft was hit, and we returned somewhat shamefacedly to base.

It was most inconsiderate of the German flak gunners not to advise the B.B.C. that they were still very much in Paris!

Finally Paris fell, and with a few of my pilots I descended on the liberated city. Impossible to describe the reception my jeep, marked with R.A.F. roundels, and its occupants received. For two fatiguing days it was a constant whirl of alcohol, pretty girls and more alcohol. Taken into one beautiful home for yet another celebration party, I asked my host how he had managed to obtain so much wine and of such good quality. "Come with me," he instructed. Obediently I followed him down to the empty cellar. He led me to the far end, and in the bad light I could make out a break in the wall just big enough to pass through.

Lighting the way with a torch he led me through the aperture into a secondary cellar. There, from floor to curved ceiling were hundreds of bottles of wine.

"These," he explained proudly, "have been bricked up since 1940, and although the Bosche occupied my house for many years, they never suspected." It was a good party.

My experiences with the opposite sex turned out to be disappointing. Whenever opportunity seemed to be knocking a surfeit of alcohol blurred the scene. However, one evening I was sure I was on the right track. At the party I was attending were two very pretty girls who were also friends. Mentioning that I had nowhere to sleep that night,

I was promptly invited to stay at their place. "Their place" was a beautiful house in one of the chic Paris residential areas, and had been given to one of the girls as a divorce settlement from her artist husband. He was very famous for painting beautiful young nudes with elongated swan-type necks.

Hoping the party would break up early, I looked forward to an early night. On the arrival at the house I was shown to my bedroom, and that was that.

The two girls were lesbians and very much in love!

The Allied advance northwards was akin to the progress of a bolting horse. The problem became not one of beating the enemy, but of getting supplies up to our rapidly advancing forces from the Normandy beachhead. Hardly had we moved into a new airfield than we were on the move again to keep close behind our troops. Thousands of German soldiers were overrun, and they roamed the countryside behind our fluid lines.

At Douai I had a nasty example of what this might mean. One evening half a dozen of us decided to see the bright lights of Douai town, and so we piled into a "commandeered" German Opel car complete with its original camouflage, and set off for the town. Our choice of an auberge was almost perfect. The patron had been a poilu in the first world war fighting alongside the British. Excitedly he greeted us, and the wine began to flow.

The next pleasant surprise arrived in the shape of his daughter who served us with our drinks. She was one of the prettiest girls I had ever seen. Despite the beady-eyed glint that came from his wife behind the cash register, the patron sat and drank with us and ignored his other customers.

Between the wine and the beautiful daughter, the time slipped by and our voices and laughter rose in proportion.

Suddenly the landlord slipped away, to return in a few minutes with his arms loaded with liqueur bottles. The figure behind the till stiffened in horror. Her husband had obviously raided the cellar so long unused to produce for his new found and loving friends the valuable bottles that had been hidden from the Germans for so many years. Drinks were now on the house!

With each glass we re-fought the battles of Mons, the Somme, Marne and any other French river we could think of. The war ended with our host passing gently out, and we left him snoring the sleep deserved by a happy veteran poilu. With much fond embracing we took leave of the gorgeous daughter.

Mother did not dain to say adieu.

Pouring ourselves into the Opel, we pointed its nose in the general direction of our airfield and set off into the dark night. After a few kilometres, we entered a small blacked-out village, to find our route barred by a closed railway level crossing. At first we laughed because after several minutes the barrier raised and naturally we got under way to traverse the crossing. However, just as we were about to cross the railway lines an unlit engine and two empty coaches crossed our route and we were forced to stop.

So did the train.

Minutes passed by without movement as the engine and coaches remained stationary across the road. Wondering if I could find the cause of the trouble, I left the car and walked towards the level crossing. Then I began to notice the shadowy figures moving down both sides of the street in my direction.

The next thing I knew was that a sub-machine gun had been stuck in my stomach, and this was followed by a flow of incomprehensible French. Then the penny dropped and I realized the situation. Dressed in light grey-blue R.A.F. uniform and flying boots, and having just emerged from a German car, the itchy fingered young Frenchmen opposite me mistook my appearance for that of a jack-booted German soldier. Realizing my peril I tried to explain in schoolboy French that I was a "pilote Anglaise," but the only effect it had was to have the gun pushed harder into my stomach. By now my companions were tumbling out of the car, looking to my frightened eyes more Germanic than the real thing.

Quickly I called to them to keep their distance and explained briefly the problem. One of my Australian pilots tried to explain to the night in general.

"He's a bleedin' Pommy-understand? Pommy – like a bloody

apple." It didn't really help.

Other sinister and heavily armed Frenchmen had by now joined our throng, and happily one of them had a rough working knowledge of English. However, they were not completely convinced of our authenticity and we were marched off to the local police station to prove our identity. This was satisfactorily done two hours and two bottles of brandy later, but I can still feel the pressure of that gun sticking in my guts.

We left behind us some rather dazed gendarmes muttering, "C'est Pommies de l'air pas pommies de terre."

Our sojourn at the Douai airfield was minimal, and soon we were winging our way northwards to keep up with the advancing armies. Next stop was Antwerp and after that into the Arnhem area, but of this we were yet unaware.

Antwerp had its good and its bad points. On the bad side, only a canal divided our airfield against strongly entrenched German units on the north bank. They developed the singularly unattractive habit of lobbing shells onto the runway as we came into land. Miraculously during our relatively long stay, no aircraft were hit, but it was still unpleasant to see the shell bursts as you held off to land. Shelling also continued at night, and a canvas tent isn't much protection against an 88-millimetre projectile fired in anger. For myself and David Scott-Malden, the airfield commander, help was on the way. This arrived in the shape of the Mayor of Antwerp, who to show his appreciation of being liberated, offered us a beautiful suite of rooms at the Century Hotel in the centre of the city. His offer was accepted with alacrity, and we moved in that evening.

Following the luxury of a hot bath and a relatively good meal, we set out to see what Antwerp had to offer in the way of entertainment for two lonely pilots.

Our first efforts were disappointing. Unknown to us a curfew had been imposed, so we wandered down deserted streets lined by the sombre shapes of blacked-out buildings. Returning disgruntled and thirsty in the direction of our hotel, we passed a doorway emitting sounds of music and feminine laughter. We didn't bother to consult each other and promptly knocked on the door. This was shortly answered by a fat middle-aged woman, who instead of inquiring what we wanted, invited us in. So far so good, but better was still to come. Guiding us into a tastefully furnished room, I noticed with pleasure a well-stocked bar at one end. Also sitting around the room were ten young people. Nine of them were pretty girls, and the tenth was perhaps the most beautiful woman I have ever seen. Even the very attractive landlord's daughter would not stand comparison.

David had a fairly good command of the French language, and soon we were sitting at the bar with well-filled glasses. At the same time four of the girls rose from their places in the room and joined us at the bar. "Entwined" would probably be more apt than "joined." Lovely cool sweet smelling feminine arms embraced our necks and ran loving fingers through our hair. I was glad we'd bathed before setting out.

I then realized that for the first and only time in my life I was in a brothel, albeit of obviously very high class.

My only disappointment was that neither of the girls draped round my neck was the classically beautiful brunette, who still remained seated at the far end of the room. With David acting as interpreter, I inquired of Madame behind the bar the name and fee for her personal attentions. The price for Maria was high but she looked worth every centime. The trouble was that since arriving in Antwerp I had not had time to draw any money from the field cashier. I explained to David that although I had money, it was not enough to obtain the beautiful Maria.

We examined the amount our pooled resources added up to. It would pay for Maria plus a little more for drinks. I decided I needed another drink to bolster up courage, and meanwhile Madame sent for Maria as she could sense business in the offing.

Sadly Maria's fantastic looks were somewhat offset by a seeming lack of interest in anything, together with a zero sense of humour. Her English was sufficient for us to communicate, and over further drinks I discovered her mother was Spanish and her father German. I plied her with further drinks to try and get her warmed up, but the goddess relaxed not one iota.

Eventually David leant across to me, "Time to go, old boy. We've spent all our money on booze." Ah, well, it had been a nice thought lying in Maria's arms.

Although we flew every day on fighter sweeps, we were much more relaxed by day, and the nights were a long series of parties. I shot down another two Me. 109s, but recorded little satisfaction from the victories. Such is battle fatigue. Despite the length of our stay in Antwerp, I was sad to lose the squadrons that had fought with me since before the Normandy invasions. The powers that be decreed that they were due for a rest, and new squadrons were posted out to replace them.

With strange faces in the Mess I felt lonely and lost. Soon however, the fiasco of the Arnhem airborne attack began.

History is beginning to record this campaign as the brainchild of an egomaniac, who ignored intelligence information, skilled advice and anything else that didn't fit into his personal pattern of thinking. As soon as the advancing troops from the south had taken the Grave bridge, an airstrip was bulldozed for us nearby, and ourselves and another wing of Spitfires (Canadians commanded by my friend Johnnie Johnson) flew in.

Poor bloody sods, I thought. For a moment pity filled my heart as I surveyed the murderous battlefield thousands of feet below. Incongruously the flat surface of the River Waal lent a peaceful air to the countryside surrounding the Arnhem and Nijmegen bridges. For days now the Red Devils had been fighting their losing battle against the onslaught of the Wehrmacht. Tragically the foul flying conditions had prevented close air support during the critical days, and the massacre of the paratroopers had proceeded uninterrupted. I picked out a flash of sunlight reflected from the shiny cockpit canopy of an aircraft below and to the west of the bridges. Quickly my trained eye spotted the formation of the twelve Spitfires as it climbed away from the small airstrip on the southern bank of the river.

I glanced at my watch. Dead on time. Within a few minutes 602 Squadron would be relieving me of the standing patrol over the two vital bridges, around which every moment of our lives was centred. We had reached the eastern end of the patrol run, and so I wheeled the formation about and started the run to the west. The climbing Spitfires below were clearly visible as they continued their ascent. Perhaps it was the nearness of friendly aircraft that caused me to slip into reverie.

Somewhere, somehow I had lost my burning desire to attack the enemy and destroy him. It was not however, that I had become less efficient or that I flew less. It showed up more on the ground than in the air; now I was interested in people's personal problems and I tried to help in every way to make life easier for the rank and file of the ground crews. "Must be getting soft," I thought.

"Two aircraft, ten o'clock, below, Moleskin Leader." The crisp warning came clearly to me from the leader of my starboard flight. Craning forward I spotted the two machines and identified them as the latest German Me. 262 jet fighters. Much faster than our Spitfires, they lacked the manoeuvrability of our slower aircraft and were limited to hit and run tactics on account of their very limited duration in the air.

… "Break right, Moleskin aircraft." An urgent voice ripped through the sunlit atmosphere, and instantly twelve Spitfires spun round on their wing tips to avoid the onslaught of the attacking formation of Me. 109 fighters. The presence of the jets had attracted our attention, and the Luftwaffe had almost achieved a tactical surprise with an attack from out of the sun with the 109s.

The dog-fight wheeled and raged above the minute bridges fifteen thousand feet below. A blazing comet would streak earthwards leaving a black smoke plume to mark its passage, and a floating white mushroom of a parachute granted a fortunate pilot a reprieve from death.

Experience stopped me from hurling myself straight into the fray. Instead I climbed for a height advantage. As the swirling aircraft receded below, I sighted a German fighter spinning out of the melee apparently out of control. Knowing this to be a favourite evasive trick I kept watch, and expectedly the 109 straightened out and dived away from the battle. In a flash, I peeled over, and accompanied by my Number Two set off in pursuit. With the advantage of height and the 109's slower speed after recovering from its spin, I soon closed the gap between us. The Luftwaffe pilot dived his machine earthwards blissfully unaware of the two Spitfires close behind him. I placed myself directly behind and slightly below the 109 on its blind spot. As my thumb rested on the firing button I realized that my usual boiling fury was lacking and that the man sitting in the trim little fighter ahead produced neither positive nor negative feelings in me.

Mechanically my gloved thumb pressed hard on the firing button.

It was the ghostliness of their faces as they arrived dripping and shivering out of the night that filled us pilots with pity for our brothers on the ground. Horrific tales were brought across the river by the few paratroopers capable of swimming its broad width. With these stories fresh in our minds, we would take off the next day, only too anxious to strafe the enemy troops annihilating our fellow countrymen. Casualties ran high on both sides, and of the twelve aircraft in a squadron taking off to attack ground targets there would often be depleted numbers on their return, bearing testimony to the effectiveness of the light anti-aircraft opposition.

Danger lay on the ground as well as in the air for the pilots. Without warning a loud report would rent the sky above the airfield, and the bursting cannister released from the disappearing jet fighter would shower them with deadly anti-personnel bombs.

Ground crews alike shared the same dangers. One such attack killed our adjutant and the head cook. While superficially joking about the death of the cook, he did a good job under difficult conditions. It was ironic that the metal fragment that killed him hit him in the stomach. One had to laugh at or ignore death; any other course led to a breakdown in morale.

The Battle of Arnhem raged on and the massacre of the paratroopers continued. General Bernard Montgomery will probably not be kindly judged by objective historians.

We did what we could to assist the poor Red Devils on the ground, but despite our efforts the battle had already been lost before the weather cleared to allow air support. Also my own battle flying days were coming to a close. My last sortie was attacking enemy ground positions close to the bridgehead. The sun was setting in a golden hazy glow as I lowered my wheels and flaps prior to landing on our airfield strip. All I remember is a dazed recollection of diving into the ground in the middle of the airstrip. The aircraft broke in

pieces and the engine began a torturous scream as, bereft of its propeller, it increased its revolutions far beyond the designers' intentions.
Instinctively I groped for the ignition switches as I became semi-conscious, and the nightmare noise died away.

Within seconds the breathless ground crews came running to my
aid, and helping hands lifted and carried me from the tiny cockpit.
With blood pouring from my face (I learned later I had broken a quarter inch steel plate supporting the gun sight with my left cheek) and
a fractured back, I was carried on a stretcher to the ambulance which
had arrived. I heard murmurs around me saying that my ailerons had
been hit by anti-aircraft fire, but unconsciousness prevailed at that
point. My active part in the war was finally over and the grim struggle
taking place about the Arnhem bridge a few miles away was now of
only academic interest to me.

After spending a pain-ridden night in a Dutch farmhouse an ambulance arrived to take me away to the nearest R.A.F. casualty clearing
station.

That was in a convent!

I learned later that no male had crossed the threshold of this sanc-
tified place since the fourteenth century, and now to be carried in on
a stretcher, temporarily incapable of offensive action, seemed to add
insult to injury.

A small wing of the convent had been handed over to our medical
services, and apart from the airfield doctor, I was alone under the attention of R.A.F. male nursing orderlies. My accommodation consisted of a small room whose only furniture was a bed, an upright,
unpainted chair and a crucifix on the whitewashed wall. Years of
scrubbing had turned the floorboards a colour almost matching the
spotless walls. It was fascinating to conjecture on the lives of the
countless nuns who had occupied this cell during the course of cen-
turies, and to wonder how they would feel if they knew that a young
man with a bandage over one eye, looking like a poor man's Horatio
Nelson, now occupied their former sanctuary. I liked to think of all
the nuns as very pretty.

The rattle of china and cutlery outside my door brought my irre-
ligious thoughts back to the present, and to the breakfast that was still

to come. The door opened.

"Porridge, sir?" Before I could answer there was a startled squeal and the rustling of heavily starched skirts as two figures scuttled down the corridor in full retreat. The orderly grinned, "Mother Superior and her deputy, ain't never seen a man in bed before – must have given them a fright." This piece of information was then followed by one of the best-cooked meals it had been my pleasure to eat. The food was prepared by the nuns, and the Mother Superior's presence outside my room was due to her care and attention for my welfare. The wonderful meal topped off with an injection of morphia caused the morning to pass in deep sleep, and I awoke again to the sounds that accompanied the arrival of lunch. This time when the door opened the Mother Superior stood her ground and inquired after my health.

"Are you feeling better now, Wing Commander?" Her English was excellent. We passed a couple of minutes in polite conversation, and she excused herself as the distant peals of a chapel bell came floating down the cool corridor. Behind her, her shadow in the shape of the deputy bobbed a nervous curtsey and rustled away. The afternoon passed in fitful sleep punctured by the swelling and receding chants and hymns of a distant female choir, and then it was supper time.

As a bird of the air gradually overcomes its timidity of human beings, so after the evening meal did the Mother Superior enter my cell and sit beside my bed. For an hour she told me fascinating stories of her youth, and how she had travelled the world and not until early middle age had she dedicated her life to God. She neither volunteered nor did I ask what caused her to make this vital decision. I suspected a tragic love affair but it was only conjecture on my part. During our long talk together she never mentioned the subject of religion yet her very presence at my bedside made me intensely conscious of the goodness and the air of grace around her.

Later that evening the Church of England padre visited me. After a few inane remarks he knelt at the foot of my bed and intoned the Almighty in that stupid chanting fashion that is seemingly necessary to penetrate to Heaven. By and by, I confess that I find the Clergy living in a No-man's land, neither in touch with man nor God. Anyhow the contrast between this individual and the Mother Superior was most marked. The medical officer thought I was a good excuse to get him back to England for forty-eight hours leave, so the following day under his care and after a rather sad farewell with my kind benefactress, I was flown home in a transport aircraft.

As my taxi turned into the sloping green lawns of the Queen Victoria Hospital I felt I was almost indeed returning home. So many memories came crowding back as we drove up to the entrance around the circular flower bed. Memories of friendly faces bearing the searing marks of fire, memories of gay parties and laughter drowning its constant companion, pain, for the thousandth time in a sea of comradeship. Laughter and pain. Yes, they summed up two happy, bittersweet years. "My goodness, not you again!" Did I suspect a groan of despair in Sister Hall's voice as they wheeled me into the small casualty room. Archie McIndoe commented, "The trouble with you is you're just plain clumsy." Between leaving hospital after finishing my surgery and my present arrival I had collected a bullet wound in the air over the Normandy beachhead, and it was to these previous wounds that he was referring.

After a series of searching x-rays I found myself comfortably tucked up in bed again in ward three. When I had first viewed ward three in 1940 I had been noticeably struck by the similarity of its interior to that of a public lavatory. Now as I lay here the soft pastel shades of curtains, walls and bedspreads blended soothingly to my one visible aching eye. Archie McIndoe, ably assisted by the wives of some of the rich local landed gentry, had put paid to the dark browns and dreary deep creams which ward three had started life with.

I blinked my unbandaged eye at the wall opposite. Was it imagination, or could I still make out the stains beneath the coat of paint? Three years had passed since that night, and yet it seemed like only yesterday. However, the occupant of the bed opposite was now dead. No one would ever throw eggs at Richard Hillary again as he lay in bed. Much has been written about Hillary in the press and in books to attempt to create a legend around his name. Ignoring for an instant his superb command of the written word, I for my part like to remember him as a basically pleasant young man hiding behind a barrier of cynicism, a defence mechanism perhaps evolved from an over-doting maternal influence. We had argued over the merits of flying day or night fighters often or when we returned to flying duties. We never did agree over this one, although our arguments were of a very amicable nature. Alas, he was killed while training and the world of literature lost a valuable asset. It has been said by irresponsible persons that Richard deliberately crashed his aircraft as an act of suicide, but knowing him I refuse to believe that his nature would allow him to carry his observer to a violent death.

I am quite sure that I know what caused him to crash.

Again I blinked my eye to see more clearly the stains of the wall opposite, but the paint showed clean. The past had disappeared.

Twenty-Three

A few weeks later I left the hospital to return to duty. Although passed fit by a medical board to continue flying, they informed me that a three months spell on the ground would do no harm. With a twinge of sadness I said my goodbyes to staff and patients and walked away from ward three. Pain had been the common denominator here and agony had held no respect for rank and persons, be he flight sergeant or flight lieutenant.

Archie McIndoe waved his magic wand, and with the help of Viscount Willoughby de Broke at the Air Ministry, I found myself in the *Queen Elizabeth* crossing over to America.

In order to bring home the British war effort and to improve Anglo-American relations, a system was evolved whereby relays of R.A.F. pilots toured the United States on goodwill lecture missions. Never having spoken to any group other than the pilots under my command, the idea of addressing thousands of strangers over the forthcoming weeks sounded a formidable task.

With the war and blackout restrictions still on in Europe, the impact of the bright lights and remoteness from fear in New York was very great.

One taxi ride, and fear returned!

A few days of briefing followed from various British officials, and armed with letters of introduction to film celebrities in California I set forward on my journey alone.

My first port of call was to the famous Twin Cities of Saint Paul and Minneapolis where I was duly met by the British Consul, Mr. Lion. The month was January, the snow feet deep, and the temperature unfit for brass monkeys. Lion and his charming wife took me under their wing, and I remained as their house guest during my three days in the Twin Cities. The morning after my arrival I was driven off to the slaughter.

"Your first lecture," explained Lion as we drove along in his car, "will be to talk to about five hundred students at the Minnesota University of Agriculture." Thoughts rushed through my mind. How much would these young men understand of warfare and airplanes?

"Do these chaps receive any military training whilst up at the University?" I inquired hastily.

"Oh no," Lion replied. "Nothing like that. They're all young women."

Suddenly January in Minnesota became extremely hot!

The Dean of the University accompanied me onto the stage of the modern campus theatre, and having effected an introduction, left me nervously facing the steady gaze of an audience of attractive women between the ages of eighteen and twenty-one. Sensing that their knowledge of aviation was about on a par with my knowledge of agriculture, I decided to keep my conversation at ground level, and tell them how we lived on the Normandy beachhead and during our subsequent push up through France. All went fairly well until I came to describe one particular incident.

"It was late at night," I told them, "when myself and three other pilots were returning to our airfield after visiting a sister unit a few miles away. We were hungry and thirsty, and decided that we would get some refreshment in the village that lay just ahead. On entering it," I explained, "we found the only cafe shut so we picked out the most imposing looking house in the village and knocked-up its inhabitants."

The gasp that arose from my audience was rapidly followed by smothered laughter. As we walked from the theatre to the cafeteria for lunch, the Dean took me quietly to one side. "I suggest, Commander, that you don't use that expression 'knock-up' over here in the States."

"Why not?" I inquired innocently,

"Over here," she replied. "It means to make someone pregnant."

I found the experience of receiving whistles and catcalls embarrassing to say the least!

Soon I was on the move again heading over the desolate, flat snow-covered Dakota plains for Spokane, Washington. Shortly after the train pulled out of Minneapolis I found myself in the drinking company of three Americans. All that I can recall of the two men is that one was young and fat and the other lean and short. The girl I remember as being one of the prettiest I had seen for a long time. The train stopped at a wayside station shortly after leaving Minneapolis just long enough for us to purchase six bottles of whisky for the long journey ahead. The afternoon passed in liquid minutes as the four of us tackled the contents on the table that stood between our opposite facing seats. I do not quite know how it started, but sometime during the afternoon I felt my knee rubbing against another shapely nylon-covered one under the table, and a pair of beautiful blue eyes levelled at my own.

The next drink went down in one gulp.

Night rapidly followed evening, and soon the black attendant was disturbing our party as he converted the seats into sleeping compartments. My pretty young companion excused herself, but not before squeezing my hand and quietly suggesting that I come and say goodnight to her later on. All of this had apparently been registered by a pair of watchful eyes. As I prepared to disappear through the curtain entrance to my bunk the attendant approached with white teeth flashing in a broad grin. "Say, boss," he inquired, "are you going to lay that dame?"

I relaxed on my bunk fully clothed, waiting for the moment when all was quiet and the last of my travelling companions had settled down for the night.

I closed my eyes and reflected with a chuckle on the passing events of the last few hours.

I awoke with a hand shaking my shoulder.

"Breakfast in ten minutes, sir." I was still fully clothed and with the mother and father of a headache.

At breakfast I received a very dirty look from a pair of beautiful blue eyes!

The lecture tour continued, and from Spokane a brief sortie was made up into the beautiful Rocky Mountain country on the Canadian side of the border. Accompanying me was Jock Ridland, a Scot by birth, who filled the role of British consul in Spokane. Although quite a few years my senior, his boyish spirits and excellent sense of humour made him a delightful travelling companion.

We saw the beauties of Nelson, and inspected the vast mines at Kimberly. However, it is the Mayor of Trail that I remember best. One afternoon he arrived up by road at Kimberly to take us down to Trail, there to attend a dinner given in our honour. Our charming hosts in Kimberly saw to it that all of us except the Mayor's chauffeur were sent on our way with a healthy filling of liquid nourishment. After a few miles I was forced to wind down the window of the comfortable heated car and let some of the bitterly cold Canadian air inside, so strong was the aroma of aniseed from the Mayor. Jock saw my action and sensed the cause.

"His wife's head of the local temperance league, and he gets hell from her if she thinks he's had a couple."

I wound the window up and suffered silently out of sympathy for His Worship. Dinner that evening was for an all-male group, and Union Jacks were in profusion. Canadians are more pro-British than the British when they choose to be.

It was a very patriotic evening and finally came the moment for the Mayor to introduce me as the guest speaker for the evening. Looking uncomfortable in his dinner jacket, the civic leader of Trail personified life in that part of the world; rough and tough by nature, he made no pretence to be familiar with the social graces, and one liked him all the more for it. Before dinner began Jock had obviously briefed him on one or two points in my career, and it was apparently with reference to my efforts that his Worship was now talking.

"You may recall those famous words, gentlemen, said by someone – I forget who it was that said, 'Never in the field of something or other had so much been owed by somebody or other to these guys.'" Apart from that he was word perfect!

Once again I was on my travels as the Canadian Pacific Railway carried me westwards to Vancouver. A few days here and I turned south and re-entered the United States. San Francisco, to me the most attractive of all American cities, followed Seattle, and it was with some reluctance that I headed further south to Los Angeles. Little did I realize then what a big part the City of the Angels was to play in my life. On reflection, I'm sure that any self-respecting Angel would disown the place.

The usual courtesies of being met at the station by the local consulate were not forthcoming here, and I found my own way to the hotel.

The Hollywood-Roosevelt Hotel is situated in Hollywood itself and stands across the street from Graumans Chinese theatre, famous for its film premieres and for the concrete impressions of famous stars' hands and feet. Hollywood itself I found to be dreary beyond belief, and the fabulous scene conjured up by its famous name just no longer existed. Instead it offered the same picture as Hammersmith Broadway on a busy Saturday morning. However, my stay at the Hollywood-Roosevelt was to be short-lived, for immediately after unpacking I began to make contact with the film celebrities to whom I carried letters of introduction.

I spoke to Mrs. Nigel Bruce on the telephone, and promptly received an invitation to lunch at their home the following day. Destiny was beginning to take an interest in my affairs. Joan Fontaine asked me round for cocktails on the following day, and so the Los Angeles scene began to improve rapidly. The Bruces and Joan Fontaine lived near each other in Beverly Hills. By way of an explanation, Los Angeles is a big sprawling city larger in area than London and although they claim independence, places like Hollywood and Beverly Hills are suburban areas of Los Angeles, and a visitor would never know where one section began and another ended but for signs marking the boundaries. The most noticeable feature of Beverly Hills was the grandeur of the homes, but today the lovely houses are being surpassed by those in other areas such as Bel Air and Pacific Palisades.

North Alpine Drive in Beverly Hills is a cool tree-lined avenue in the residential district bounded by Santa Monica Boulevard in the south, and Sunset Boulevard in the north. Nigel Bruce occupied No. 701 near the Sunset end of Alpine Drive. An imposing white Spanish-style house topped with orangy-red pantiles, it stood on slightly raised ground from the road. As I approached I noticed that the house number was inset into a wooden model of a dachshund standing on the lawn. The reason was soon apparent. No sooner had I pressed the bell than a yapping and scampering of feet followed. A booming voice reached me through the thick front door. "Be quiet Monty! Shut up, Franke, you little bastards!"

Nigel Bruce opened the door. The big burly figure dressed in cool white slacks and an open neck shirt stood framed in the doorway while four excited dachshunds barked and sniffed my feet. A large hand extended in greeting and the gruff voice kept up its friendly commentary. "Ah, my dear fellow – glad you could come – shut up you bloody dogs

– sorry I'm not wearing a tie – too damned hot – come on in – Bunny will be down in a minute but we can have a drink – what would you like – plenty of beer, whisky or gin – Can't touch beer myself – border line diabetic – " Slightly dazed, I allowed myself to be led through the large hall to the intimate little bar at the back of the house, passing a well-stocked library and a beautifully appointed drawing room on the way. My host's flow of conversation only ceased for an instant when his wife entered the room so that she could say a few words of welcome. "Ah, there you are darling – This is Geoffrey Page – my wife, Bunny – his first visit to California –" Bunny Bruce was a handsome woman in early middle life. Beneath a head of beautiful hair shone a pair of twinkling eyes. The face had the effect of calm waters. One had the feeling that while he bubbled and blustered his way through the seas of life, she stood in the background with a steady hand on the helm.

Lunch was an amusing affair with Bunny pretending to be shocked whenever her husband produced one of his many vulgar phrases. The three of us hit it off extremely well, and before the meal was over they were insisting that I leave my hotel and be their house guest. Despite my protests they were adamant that I occupy one of the three spare bedrooms. One of their daughters, Jennifer, was married and the other, Pauline, was up in Canada serving with the Royal Canadian Air Force. Apart from the two Bruces there was a German manservant and his partly mental wife, but they occupied their own flat at the bottom of the garden. Karl had served as a stretcher bearer in the Kaiser's forces during the first World War, and on the strength of this insisted on the formal address of "doctor." He was only tolerated by "Willie" Bruce for the merit of his wife's cooking and the general shortage of available domestic help in Beverly Hills. Apart from some of his many uncouth Teutonic habits, Karl had a happy little way of joining in the conversation at a formal dinner party while serving the vegetables, much to the consternation of the guests.

The next day I was comfortably ensconced in my own room at 701 North Alpine Drive. They handed me the key of the door and told me I was free to come and go as I chose, and they meant it. Soon after my arrival it was time to present myself for drinks, and five minutes' walk from the Bruces, I found myself at Joan Fontaine's house on North Rodeo Drive. There were two other guests, both men, invited along for cocktails. The older of the two was a charming old gentleman. Sir Charles Mendl was married to the internationally famous Elsie de Wulf, and their lives revolved around the great names of movieland. Sir Charles was extremely popular with the young actresses and could be found escorting some beauty to a party or chic restaurant most nights of the week. I envied his success.

The third guest was a tall good-looking Englishman of the suave cafe society breed. Counterpoints of Bill Burnside are to be found in all the fashionable corners of the world. For some reason he took a liking to me and invited me out to dinner a few days later with amusing repercussions. Joan Fontaine is my idea of English feminine beauty personified. A strange mixed-up person within herself, she showed me the kindest side of her nature and went out of her way to make my time pleasurable. I left her house that evening with a date to meet her at a broadcasting studio to watch a programme in which she was featured, and then on to dinner afterwards. She stressed the fact that her earnings were considerably larger than my air force pay, and the evening was to be on her. I tried to argue the point even if only for the sake of my manly pride, but Joan was a strong-minded woman.

I arrived by taxi at the studio and as the star's personal guest was shown into a private little viewing box. For half an hour I watched with pleasure the polished performance of those on the stage below me, and then it was time to join my hostess in her dressing room. Already half a dozen well-wishers crammed the little room and I felt justifiably proud as her escort for the evening. Soon we were on our own and ducking out of a side door to avoid the horde of autograph seekers lined up outside the main studio entrance. She asked me if I would drive her Packard convertible, and two minutes later we were sliding smoothly out of the car park – Joan emitted a horrified shriek and sank to the floor of the car. "Drive on quickly," she commanded in an excited voice. Obediently I accelerated the powerful car and we were moving swiftly down Sunset Boulevard. I asked what the cause of the trouble was as she rose to the seat again. "Autograph hunters," she informed me. I refrained from comment as I had only seen a couple of uninterested pedestrians as we left the parking lot. Obviously the famous had more experience in this sort of thing, I thought, and left it at that.

We drew up in front of Ciro's night club on the famous Sunset Strip and were ushered by a bowing and scraping headwaiter to our table. Joan had changed her attitude to the adoring public and was now sweeping between the tables bestowing regal smiles in all directions. Finally the stir her arrival had caused died down and we selected our dinner from the menu. Then for the second time that evening she gave vent to another mild shriek, this one more genuine than the first. "I've been robbed," she gasped. "My money's been stolen from my bag – it must have happened when I was doing the show as I left it in my dressing room."

Rather unkindly I laughed at this, and explained to her that she now could not argue over which one of us paid the bill!

Bill Burnside phoned me up on the following morning and asked if I had any objections to his dinner partner for the evening bringing along a girlfriend whom I'd never met. At the very worst I knew the dinner would be excellent, and if my dinner date turned out to be a frump, I could bury myself in La Rue's superb cuisine. We arranged to meet at La Rue's bar and arriving a few minutes early I settled down with a drink to inspect some of the renowned clientele. A bearded figure I recognized as Monty Wooley stood at the bar with an open book before him at which he never glanced. I learned later that he had been carting the same book about for years, but that nobody had ever seen him read a word of it. In another corner Dorothy Lamour draped her slightly overweight body over a small chair. At this point Bill walked in with his two companions. Before I had time to register their faces, the beauty and perfection of the mink coats adorning the two women struck me forcibly. Bill introduced me to his friend Liz Whitney and in turn her friend Barbara Sears. Most dinner parties consist of those who give and those who receive. By that I mean that one or more people make the conversation while the others sit back and listen without contributing anything towards the self-made entertainment. This latter type of person I deplore. However, on this occasion all three of them were bubbling enthusiastic conversationalists and the dinner passed merrily. After the meal we felt in gay spirits and someone knew of a party in progress, so off we went. Wine and laughter flowed in someone's fabulous home up in the hills and the hours slipped by.

Liz Whitney suggested a nightcap at her ranchhouse near the polo ground, and off we went again. By this time Barbara and I had decided we would feel cosier if we held hands. All in all, the evening was turning out to be a great success.

It was broad daylight by the time I left the Whitney home, but without difficulty I managed to get a lift from a passing motorist. Quietly I let myself into the Bruce house, and with my shoes under one arm and two large photographs of Barbara under the other, I crept up the stairs. Halfway up, to my horror, I was met by four scampering, squealing dogs followed by Bunny. She took one look at me and with an impish smile said, "You can tell me about it at lunch, Geoffrey!" In my room I glanced in the mirror to discover my face covered with lipstick.

My engagements in Los Angeles were now coming to an end, and in theory I had now to return to New York and then to England. However, the Bruces insisted that a cable be sent to the R.A.F. headquarters in Washington requesting two week's leave. To my delight this was granted, and I continued my mad whirl around the town, now mostly in the company of Barbara.

It was during this time that the Bruces introduced me to many of the better-known names of the English people in the movie world. Of them all, Aubrey Smith and Herbert Marshall took my fancy the most. In real life, Aubrey Smith played the part he usually acted on the screen, that of the fine upstanding honest old English squire. Apart from his passion for cricket, he had no vices and found it difficult to understand dishonesty in others. A very fine old gentleman.

I was taken to tea at his house perched on the top of Coldwater Canyon and amused to see the weather vane consisted of a cricket bat and stumps. Bushy eyebrowed Aubrey came out of the house to greet us, resplendent in a Hawks Club striped blazer, Hawks Club tie, and Hawks Club cricket cap. I had to smother a laugh when a few minutes later he produced a Hawks Club tobacco pouch. I have often wondered about his pyjamas.

Freddy Lonsdale, also English, had established himself in the front ranks of the world's playwrights. Sharp tongued at the expense of friend and enemy alike, he brightened any gathering with his caustic wit and white socks. Willie and Bunny gave a dinner party one evening to which Freddy Lonsdale was invited. He arrived after several stops en route in a belligerent frame of mind. The first bottle of champagne was opened and poured. Then to Willie's consternation and the other guests' embarrassment he sipped at his glass and declared loudly, "corked, my dear fellow, CORKED." A new bottle was hastily opened and a fresh glass poured for Freddy. Again the performance was repeated with his cry of "CORKED" louder than ever. The pouring ceremony from the third bottle was watched by a hushed and apprehensive audience. Freddy was enjoying himself. As his cry rang out for the third time, Willie disappeared through the swing door into the kitchen, to reappear a moment later. "Try this, old man," he suggested. "New bottle from a different case."

Freddy sipped. Condescendingly he put his glass down. "Not bad, not bad at all."

"You stupid bastard," thundered Willie. "That's the original bottle." Willie Bruce knew the tricks of his pal Freddy.

A few days before my leave expired the Bruces took me along to a party at Ronald Colman's house on Benedict Canyon. As we stepped from the car Freddy Lonsdale drove up, and the four of us walked up the pathway together. He handed me a white envelope.

"Open that when you get home, my lad." Before I had time to question him we were being greeted by Ronald and Benita Colman. Ronald Colman struck me as a somewhat pathetic figure. So engrossed in himself and his own opinion of everything, he gave the appearance of going through life with his eyes shut, and thereby missing much.

The Colman house and grounds might have been moved straight out of England. Beautifully appointed, it had an air of luxurious living slightly spoiled by the owner being a member of the Table Wipers Union. They are those who rush round and make clucking sounds if a damp glass is inadvertently placed on a table top. Richard Greene is another of those. I am all for looking after good furniture, but it should not be ulcer-forming material.

Benita was an attractive woman, later Mrs. George Saunders, who always knew who was doing what and with whom.

On my return to my room that night, I opened the white envelope. Inside a note tersely said, "Have an evening out with some young lady – Freddy Lonsdale." A cheque for a hundred dollars was enclosed.

Bunny and Willie came to see me off at Union Station. During the three weeks I had been their guest we had become very attached to one another, and now the sorrow of parting was upon us. We chatted about everything except my imminent departure until the car swept into the station area. Willie put his arm round my shoulder. "Only one thing for it," he growled. "You'll have to come back when the war's over and marry Pauline, our daughter up in Canada." Bunny told him to stop being a fool.

The black attendants called "All aboard," and I was on my way eastward. Los Angeles slipped out of sight.

Twenty-Four

The European war was all but over on my return to England, so it seemed pointless to get into flying again on the European front. The fighting in the Far East called to me, but first I had to return to the hospital. I was still carrying a lump of German cannon shell about in my left leg. It had been there since 1940, so it was high time to have it out. The operation was a minor one after the thirty or so I had already undergone. Nevertheless it confined me to bed for a few days. During this period I received a long letter from Willie Bruce containing an enclosure. His friendly chit-chat ended, "– thought you might like to have a photograph of the girl you're coming back to marry." Marriage was the last thing in my mind, but it was a very lovely face that gazed at me from the photograph. I chuckled to myself at the thought of Willie B. sending the letter off from his home in California. Pleasant memories flooded back. I looked about me in the Ward. Most of the faces were strange to me. They were new in more senses than one. There was nothing wrong with my health, only a painful leg that kept me tied to this bed.

I was bored stiff.

When you've spent long periods in bed over a period of years the novelty wears thin, and to this day I dislike staying between the sheets as soon as I'm awake. My thoughts returned to the Bruce family, and with another chuckle reached for a writing pad on the bedside table. "Dear Miss Bruce," I wrote. "I have received a letter from your father in which he states it would be a good thing if you and I were eventually married. Will you therefore please consider yourself engaged, and in future behave yourself with all those young Canadian officers on your airfield."

I offered a silent prayer that she had a sense of humour and sent the letter off to Pauline Bruce, care of her parents' address in Beverly Hills.

Two days later I was free.

* * *

Archie McIndoe, very sensibly, talked me out of volunteering for the war in the Far East. "By the time you get out there," he said, "it will all be over and then you'll be stuck while everybody back in England gets the plum jobs."

I decided to become a test pilot.

It was simple common sense that with only single engine and single seater experience, I would not have much to offer the post-war world. So through the old pals act, I got myself attached, still as a serving officer, to the firm of Vickers Armstrongs at Weybridge in Surrey. At the same time I applied to the Air Ministry for a permanent commission. The Royal Air Force would be my career.

I reported to Mutt Summers, the Vickers chief test pilot. "You're just in time," he said. "Your predecessor's just been killed, my brother's in the hospital with a fractured skull, I've just crashed one into a field and another type has crashed through some high tension cables." I gulped and he continued. "The rudder is locking on at low speeds but we're fitting a dorsal fin which we hope will cure it." So did I! Mutt Summers glanced at his watch. "How about a drink?" I needed it.

My time at Vickers was a thoroughly happy one. Apart from one or two exciting moments in the air, the work was fairly routine and I was more or less my own boss. We were a small little community of five pilots, two flight engineers and a girl who acted as flying control officer. A very attractive old gardener's cottage mildly converted did service as the control tower. When flying was not in progress the bunch of us could usually be found with Doris Wagstaff in her control room, drinking coffee and playing liar dice by the hour. Visitors would often be shocked to hear a respectable looking chief test pilot saying to a young lady, "You're a bloody liar!"

One day as I stepped out of a Warwick bomber following a test flight, the fitter said I was wanted on the phone. I walked over to the dispersal hut and picked up the receiver. It was Doris. "I've got Air Ministry on the other line," she explained, "and they want the details of exactly how you were killed. What shall I say?" Dear old Air Ministry! For once in their lives they were ahead of the game. "Tell them to phone the Talbot Hotel, my ghost's going round there now for a pint!"

A few days later I received a letter from Canada. It was from Pauline Bruce. She thanked me for my letter and said she was behaving impeccably with the male element of the R.C.A.F. The rest of her letter was in a pleasant light vein, for which I received a sigh of relief.

I had been with Vickers about six months when I was faced with a tempting offer.

At the wedding reception for Tony Bartley and Deborah Kerr, Mutt Summers approached me through the milling throng. Tony had also been attached to Vickers, hence Mutt's presence. He came straight to the point. "How about leaving the R.A.F., Geoffrey, and joining us? We're about to form a Flight Demonstration and Sales Department to promote our new airliner, the Viking, and we're looking for people." The salary he mentioned was reasonable and the work extremely interesting. However, I still wanted to have a permanent commission in the Air Force. Moreover, my application to attend the Empire Test Pilots School had just been sent in, and the thought of going on this much sought after course was uppermost in my mind.

The Air Ministry wrote to me and in their most pompous manner imparted the information that my request for a permanent commission had been granted. I was now a Regular.

Three days later I was attending the interview for the Empire Test Pilots School. There were over two hundred applicants for the course, but we knew that little over a dozen would be selected.

A friend of mine, Neville Duke, was among the many, nervously reading ancient magazines in the waiting room. Feeling let down and depressed, I left the building. "They'll let you know," said the granite-faced selection board. Why couldn't they let me know now, and end the suspense and misery?

Archie McIndoe called me up and suggested a week's shooting in Scotland. I accepted with alacrity. The thought of a week's holiday with such a stimulating companion was most appealing. I went off to my day's work with a light heart.

"Special job for you today," Doris informed me. "The Associated Press has sent down a photographer to get some air to air pictures of the Viking."

The Viking airliner was in the early stages of its flight testing and an object of news value. I contacted Bob Handasyde who would be flying the Viking, and together we worked out a brief programme. The photographer would ride with me in a Warwick bomber on its second test flight. On reaching the airplane I found my flight engineer recounting gruesome stories of test flying to an ashen-faced photographer. Jack Dunkley possessed a macabre sense of humour.

"Our friend here's never flown before," Jack said innocently. With that he disappeared down the fuselage to show the photographer his best vantage point.

I had finished my cockpit check and was about to start the first engine, when a scampering of feet announced the return of our friend from Associated Press. "W – what do I d – do if anything goes wrong? How do you bale out of this airplane?" Jack kept a completely straight poker face as he answered, "Don't worry, old lad. Just follow the pilot and myself. We'll lead the way out!"

I was surprised the photographs eventually turned out as well as they did.

The day we left for Scotland another missive arrived from Air Ministry stating I had been selected to attend the course commencing the following month for the Empire Test Pilots School.

My heart sang as Archie's car raced up the Great North Road.

I suppose in physical appearance one would have described Archie McIndoe as being on the short side of medium height, with broad shoulders and a solid body. His hair was parted in the middle and brushed back above a broad open face that was difficult to imagine without glasses. His walk which was usually rapid had the slight rolling gait of a sailor. His humorous, twinkling eyes and enormous workmanlike hands were perhaps the most striking features of this unique man. Unique inasmuch that apart from indefatigable skill as a surgeon, he had an insight into human nature and a willingness to help that is rare. Perhaps an unsuccessful marriage gave him an early insight into problems other than medical. After being recognized in his own right as a general surgeon at the Mayo Clinic in America and as an expert in tropical diseases in London, he joined his older cousin, as a junior partner. His personal skill and a contractual contretemps with Gillies brought an end to the partnership, but he was established on the road to success.

With the commencement of the war, he was appointed Senior Consultant Plastic Surgeon to the Royal Air Force, and placed in charge of one of the three dispersed Maxillo Facial units. Oddly enough the heads of the other two units, Sir Harold Gillies and Andrew Mowlem, were also New Zealanders. McIndoe selected East Grinstead for his unit as it had the merit of being close enough to London to collect air raid casualties, yet sufficiently far outside to avoid the main bombing.

As a social companion, he was with few equals. Brilliant on his own subject which he seldom discussed unless invited, he had a knowledge and interest in every mortal activity.

On returning from Scotland I found disappointing news awaiting me. My course at the Empire Test Pilots School had been postponed. The powers that be explained that now that I was a regular officer it was time I learned to do some paperwork. I really had little cause for complaint since I had been flying without a break, except for hospital, for nine years.

The Senior Officers Administration Course brought it home to me how little I knew about ground organization. The course over, Air Ministry offered one of three jobs. The first, a staff job in England. Second, a tour of duty with a military commission in Cairo, and lastly, to go as Personal Assistant to the senior R.A.F. officer on the Military Staff Commission to the newly formed United Nations in New York. New York I felt was half-way to California and the thought of seeing the Bruce family and Barbara Sears again was most attractive.

Air Chief Marshal Sir Guy Garrod was a long suffering man. He had to be to put up with me. He little realized at the time, that he was taking on as his P.A. someone least suited to such a task. Poor man! Soon after I joined Sir Guy's staff in London I realized I was a fish out of water. The other R.A.F. officers attached to him took their paper work seriously, and I envied the manner in which they forgot about airplanes as such. I resented strongly being on the ground and added to which I had no faith in the efficacy of the United Nations.

With the Royal Navy and Army contingents, we were soon on our way across the Atlantic in the *Queen Mary* heading for New York. New York, the city of expectant women and expectorant men, is one of the dirtiest in the world, and contrasts oddly with the cleanliness of the other major cities in the U.S.A. Provided you have enough money, I find it an excellent place to visit for about two weeks. The theatres are good and the night life is exciting, but as a steady diet it causes indigestion.

The weeks dragged by in a series of dreary days in an office, followed by even drearier dinners given by Sir Guy and Lady Garrod for senior officials of the other nations. Sir Guy also thought them dull but he was conscientious in all forms of work.

Apart from one romantic interlude with a very attractive redhead, life in New York palled, and my thoughts continually wandered towards California. As June approached I asked Sir Guy for permission to go on leave, and with his approval I was soon winging my way westward. The flight seemed never-ending, but at last we touched down at Burbank Airport. I was back in Los Angeles. With that strange feeling of elation that only three places in the world give me, I rushed to the nearest phone booth and dialled the Bruce number. A woman's voice answered, "Joe's Chop House, Joe speaking." I murmured apologies for dialling the wrong number and prepared to hang up. The voice at the other end let out a cry and confessed it was only a joke, and not, after all, Joe's Place. The prankster at the other end was Jennifer, the married Bruce daughter. I learned later she was living with her parents and going through the throes of a divorce.

She confirmed my welcome and promise of a bed, and ten minutes later a cab was driving me from the airport to Alpine Drive, Beverly Hills. Pleasant thoughts came rushing back into my mind as the familiar street scenes flashed by. This was the city of beautiful girls, fun, and laughter.

The cab stopped with a jerk and I felt as if I'd arrived home.

Savouring the seconds, I paid off the taxi driver and walked slowly up the winding garden path. Jennifer answered the ring of the bell. She was a tall, statuesque blonde, extremely attractive and with a beautiful figure. We had met on several occasions during my previous stay. She had appeared happy enough then, but now her marriage was on the rocks.

Everybody was out, she explained, but assured me that her parents would be delighted to know of my arrival. So far I had kept my presence in America a secret from them. Her sister, she added, was out playing tennis, but would soon be back. At the mention of this a trapped feeling came over me. Quickly I gulped my whisky, and cursed inwardly for ever having written to the girl in Canada. Despite her photograph, she would turn out to look like the back end of a bus, and as a result of our correspondence and my friendship with her parents, I'd be expected to escort her out with regularity.

My heart sank. Mentally I dialled Barbara Sears' telephone number and cried for help. Inspiration came to me in a flash. With Jennifer now living at home the house was obviously overcrowded, and the only decent thing for me to do was to stay at a hotel. I breathed a sigh of relief.

Firmly, I thought, I explained the position to Jenny, but even more firmly she turned down my suggestion. I was about to protest even more vigorously when Jenny cried out. "Ah, here's my sister."

I glimpsed a flash of white passing the library window and an instant later the front door opened. Never will I recall the words of introduction, or what Jenny said to me immediately after Pauline departed quickly for a shower and change. I was stunned by the looks of this tall, dark-haired beauty.

Suddenly life had taken on a new purpose and a new meaning.

POSTSCRIPT

The soothing female voice resounded loudly in my ear with a faint background echo. "It's all over – just try and breath deeply, that's good."

The sound of the words receded quickly, but in the distance I could still hear the intermingled male and female voices. The anaesthetic cleared temporarily just as a gentle breeze momentarily dispels a thick bank of fog. Recollection returned; I was in an operating theatre again. The distant voices came nearer and although they were subdued they sounded strangely loud in my ears. My mind formed the words I wanted to say clearly, but my tongue seemed to be glued to the roof of my mouth. Evidently some sound ensued through my parched lips because a pair of lovely eyes only inches away looked down at me.

My prepared words of "please give me something for the pain" disappeared, and only the thought of kissing that lovely girl entered my mind. "You'll soon be back in bed," she said and suddenly all was right with the world.

Blurred impressions followed – being lifted on to a trolley, rides down never ending corridors, being lifted again and placed between soothing cool sheets. A final gentle prick of a hypodermic needle and then the encroachment of temporary oblivion.

Emerging finally from the drug induced sleep I lay flat on my back with nothing to impinge on my thinking time. Thinking about what?

Whilst having the anaesthetic influence behind me, I was still under the happy releases from tension and pain from the heroin. This drug used under proper medical surveillance is bliss. Misused, it is probably the most degrading and unpleasant way to an early pauper's grave.

Heroin associated with suffering somehow does not become addictive. Of the many hundreds of badly burned aircrew with whom I shared my happy days and years, I cannot recall one who on leaving hospital became a drug addict.

So, as I wandered mentally in this flower strewn garden of memories shortly after this, my thirty-fifth operation, I had the time and the freedom to pause for a little reflective thought about what now felt like my "Alice in Wonderland" past.

Hackneyed, over-used and abused questions naturally hammered at my mind. "Was it worth it?' "What would I like to do if I had my life over again?" etc, etc.

Simpler questions and answers immediately sprang to mind, such as "How long is a piece of string?" Easy reply, "Twice the distance from one end to the middle!"

Not quite so easy to answer are multitudes of posers regarding one's own life. I sometimes wonder if a computer could come up with the answers to simple little queries such as "If I took the left fork in a street and met a stranger or friend, which in turn led to being invited to a party, where in turn I met other people, then more fork roads – or what would have happened if I had taken the right fork in the first instance? Is the answer simply 'fate', or is it all predestined?"

To follow these trains of thought can lead to madness, or in its mildest form, mental confusion. Omar Khayyam was probably right when the old Persian tent maker wrote: "The Moving Finger writes, and, having Writ, moves on: nor all thy Piety, nor wit shall lure it back to cancel half a line, nor all thy Tears wash out a word of it."

That being said, and for my part, accepted, there is much to be questioned and reflected upon concerning one's own personal life.

What did the war mean to one?

Seen in its total context, it can only add up to loss for all the participants. Medicine is perhaps one of the few fields that develop rapidly, but is the price worth it?

From the individual's point of view it is an entirely different matter. One person will suffer tragic loss such as the death of parents, brothers, sisters and others near and dear.

To others like myself it was an exciting, dangerous game. To be young, to be paid to fly a beautiful fast aeroplane, to combat one's wits and skills against an equivalent young man was to live (or die) with every fibre of one's being. Despite being badly burned, sustaining bullet wounds and a fractured back, I would not want to change one moment of those wonderful, youthful years. Unless you have personally experienced it, imagination cannot conjure up the joys – and fears – of hurling one's magnificent Pegasus through space. The beauty of it all is summed up in High Flight written by a Spitfire pilot, the deceased Pilot Officer J.G. Magee Jr. Although his lines are so often quoted, to me he sums it up exquisitely:

OH! I have slipped the surly bonds of earth

And danced the skies on laughter-silvered wings;
Sunward I've climbed, and joined the tumbling mirth
Of sun-split clouds – and done a hundred things
You have not dreamed of – wheeled and soared and swung
High in the sunlit silence. Hov'ring there
I've chased the shouting wind along, and flung
My eager craft through footless halls of air.
Up, up the long, delirious, burning blue
I've topped the wind-swept heights with easy grace
Where never lark, nor even eagle flew –
And, while with silent lifting mind. I've trod
The high untrespassed sanctity of space
Put out my hand and touched the face of God.

And what of today's youth? Simple comparisons between generations divided by several decades are difficult, if not impossible.
"Bunch of yobs and vandals," declares an older citizen with fury. Given
too much money, a decline in behaviour (usually the result of too
little discipline by parents of the older generation!) and boredom, it
is not surprising that manners, honesty and pride in work have almost
become archaic.

I do believe sincerely however that if and when these shores are
once again threatened, the majority of them would rush to defend
them against the invader. Provided, of course, the politicians had supplied sufficient weaponry for them to use in the defence of their
homeland. When will they ever learn?

Looking on my contemporary fellow pilots who survived, and
like me are now an aging band, I cannot but reflect a little sadly on
the professional war heroes, and publicity seekers that some of them
have become. Somehow it makes those awful, but wonderful memories into a sordid and self-glorifying circus which it certainly never
was, and hopefully will never be remembered as such.

Sleepily I reflect on my wordly possessions. Money in the bank?
Nothing much to boast about there. Yet I am rich beyond belief according to my own values. An attractive and wonderful wife, a beautiful daughter and two tall, handsome sons. Of earthly rewards for

one's efforts, a grateful King and Country bestow medals which are naturally proudly received.

My own awards give pride and pleasure to my family, for which I am grateful. It was the investiture at Buckingham Palace however that perhaps gave me the most satisfaction. Waiting in line to be received by King George VI, I remembered my first encounter with the monarch when I had stuttered and stammered with nervousness, despite being briefed that His Majesty had a nervous impediment of speech. My turn finally arrived and King George pinned my decorations on my uniform, shook hands and said something in a low voice. "I beg your pardon, Sir", I answered. "What did you say?" His badly stammered repetition made me feel I had evened the score with royalty.

These are my riches, and add to those flying experience and comradeships, then indeed my cup is full.

The pain is easier now and life continues.

INTERLUDE

In the preceding pages I've described my activities as a young fighter pilot in the Second World War, followed by my visits to the United States as a regular officer in the Royal Air Force.

I told of my meeting and friendship with the actor Nigel Bruce, how he had suggested that when the war was over, I should return to California and marry his daughter whom I had not met, due to her absence in Canada with the Royal Canadian Air Force.

Whilst serving on the British Military Staff in the United Nations, I revisited the Bruce family in Beverly Hills, California, and after four days became engaged to the beautiful Pauline Bruce, and we have been happily married ever since.

After serving an unhappy year in the U.N., I asked my chief if I could be relieved of my post and return to flying duties in England. He had probably spotted some of the dozens of paper aeroplanes I sailed out of our office windows on the sixty-fourth floor of the Empire State Building, and could understand my heart was not in my desk-bound job.

It was at this time that my young bride kept on at me to write an autobiography about my wartime experiences. In my usual way I procrastinated, excusing myself on the grounds that because of my burnt hands, the physical problems of writing in longhand excluded the arduous task of writing a book.

With true feminine logic, Pauline pointed out that modern science had produced dictating machines which could be rented. We duly set off for New York City from our charming little house in Old Westbury on Long Island.

Returning in the late afternoon with a rented dictaphone, we placed it on the packing case which served as a coffee table in the living room. Our finances limited our furniture to bare essentials.

Pauline and I looked at one another, which prompted her to say, "Well go on, start talking." An inert shyness prevented me from saying a word into the monstrous metallic machine, and I told her so. Immediately she departed for the kitchen and returned with a bottle of whisky which we obtained "duty free" through the United Nations. "Go into the bedroom with the machine, have a couple of good slugs of whisky, and start dictating. Tomorrow we'll play it back and I'll type out what you've done," she said kindly but firmly.

The next day, with somewhat of a hangover, I sat and listened to the shock of hearing my own words coming back to me. The first few sentences came over reasonably well, but after that disaster struck (in the shape of the whisky), and the remainder of the words were lost in an alcoholic slur!

The machine was promptly returned.

In spite of all this, thirty-four years later my book first appeared in print, which worked out at an average of six words per day. Perhaps something for the Guinness Book of Records?

This book, originally titled "Tale of a Guinea Pig" (because a Guinea Pig has no tail) did quite well and even made the *London Times* best-seller list. All credit to Pauline.

In this narrative I continue my life story in aviation. I do not call it my "profession", as flying is a "disease" and not a "profession."

So let us pick up the threads as Pauline and I set out on our return to England, where I am to take command of a fighter squadron.

The British Treasury decreed that personnel returning to the United Kingdom were to travel by sea, thereby saving the tax-payer a few pennies, whilst at the same time (and still doing so) squandering millions of pounds on the uselessness of the United Nations. We were given a sailing date from Nova Scotia in the old transatlantic liner, the S.S. *Aquilania*.

On arrival on board we learned to our horror that she was still fitted out as a troop transport, and sexes were segregated into male and female cabins. Having only been married a few months I didn't take to the idea of a semi-monastic journey for the next ten days. Presenting myself to the Chief Purser I pointed out the problems of being separated from my wife. "She helps me to get dressed, does up my shoelaces, and all those other things that make life difficult to cope with," I explained to him. Two hours later we were transferred to a private suite in the ship's hospital and crossed the Atlantic in supreme comfort. On our arrival in England I hadn't the heart to inform the Chief Purser that I was about to fly fighter aircraft again, and that they were a bit more complicated than tying a pair of shoelaces.

Despite a severe gale in the Atlantic, our cup of happiness was full.

Linton-on-Ouse (pronounced "ooze") is an R.A.F. airfield a few miles to the north of the ancient city of York. As its name implied, it was cold, wet and damp. Not the best place for a young wife who spent most of her life in sunny California, nor for myself who suffered from any form of cold as a result of the severe burns I had received flying during the war.

We arrived at the airfield or "Stations" in service parlance in July, so we were not aware of the rigours of winter that lay ahead. The adjutant advised me when I reported to the Station Headquarters, that as the second senior officer at Linton, I was allocated a married quarter commensurate with my rank.

Our marriage quarter or house was a large four-bedroomed place with a spacious living-room and separate dining room. Central heating, as I was to find out, was provided by an enormous coke-fired boiler. This boiler had enough fuel capacity to drive a small ocean-going ship. In the coming winter it proved that our monthly fuel allowance (coke and coal being still rationed) would keep the boiler fired for two days if a reasonable temperature were to be maintained in the house.

The morning after our arrival I reported to the officer commanding the Station. It would be fair to say that neither of us took a shine to the other. For his part, he looked down his nose at the fact I could not get enraptured by paper work and administration, and I could hardly conceal my contempt for his studied failure ever to fly our fast Hornet fighters.

Having spent all of the six wartime years, except for my enforced period in hospital, either being shot at by the enemy or shooting back in return, I found "paper pushing" dull in the extreme. Added to this was the fact that I was commanding a front-line long-range fighter unit with only half the number of aircraft specified, no long-range fuel tanks to enable us to carry out our bomber escort role, and finally no gunsights in our aircraft to shoot at whoever the enemy might be.

The chilling cold and damp did nothing to help the circulation in my burned hands, so after much discussion with Pauline and my dear friend, Archie McIndoe, I decided to resign my permanent commission in the Royal Air Force. Pauline by now was getting fairly close to the time for delivery of our first-born child, so we left R.A.F. Station, Linton-on-Ouse, and rented a little house in Sussex to await the arrival of the baby.

Pauline's parents, Nigel and Bunny Bruce had by now arrived in England from California to be near during her time of delivery, which thankfully went without problems. We were to be blessed with two more children.

Twenty-Five

"Eccentricities of genius, Sam" said Mr. Pickwick
Pickwick Papers

In the early 1950s I was employed by British Aircraft Corporation (B.A.C.) selling airliners. We got involved in talks with the legendary Howard Hughes and I was introduced to the eccentricities of genius. At the time of these negotiations with Howard Hughes, Jock Bryce had replaced "Mutt" Summers as chief test pilot at Weybridge. Jock was a highly experienced and qualified test pilot, and as his nickname implied, a true Scot. Brian Trubshaw, who later became well known for his testing of Concorde, was his deputy.

Hughes had requested of George Edwards that a Viscount be flown from England to Idlewild (later John F. Kennedy) Airport outside New York. Hughes wished to fly the aircraft personally. Jock, with Bill Cairns as co-pilot and Derek Jones as navigator, set off accompanied by three technical ground crew.

Arriving tired but safely at Idlewild, they taxied to an area owned by Trans World Airlines, and were duly met by Gordon Gilmore, Vice-President for Public Relations for T.W.A. In attendance also were two enormous Cadillac limousines with tinted glass windows ensuring privacy for the occupants. Gilmore explained that the crew were to be lodged in the Waldorf Astoria Hotel in New York which by any standards ranks amongst the best in the world. Whilst they were talking, Jock noticed out of the corner of his eye that the Viscount was being locked up and the passenger steps removed. He interrupted Gilmore. "Excuse me, Mr. Gilmore, but my crew and myself need to get our personal baggage out of the aircraft before we leave for New York."

Gilmore was adamant.

"It is Mr. Hughes's policy that no one, but no one, re-enter the aircraft once it is delivered. My instructions are, Mr. Bryce that tomorrow I take you and your crew to buy in New York replacement items such as suits, toilet articles and anything else you require."

Jock realised that he had no option, but was happy that in his hand he held his pilot's bag, containing not only the aircraft papers, but travellers cheques and other important documents.

The limousines set off for the Waldorf Astoria. On arrival they were quickly ushered up to adjoining suites of rooms on the ninth floor. Luxury was the keynote.

Gilmore advised them that by picking up the telephone room service would pander to their every need. After an excellent meal in their suites, Jock and his crew crashed out on their beds after the exhausting transatlantic crossing combined with the fatigue of time changes.

The next day, Gilmore reappeared and the party set off shopping to replace their personal possessions.

By this time Jock and Gordon Gilmore were beginning to get along very well together, and were to become firm friends. Soon after returning to their rooms Jock decided to go down to the lobby to buy some cigarettes. Arriving in front of the elevator doors, his path was barred by a powerful looking individual who apparently knew him.

"Sorry, Mr. Bryce, but you're not permitted to leave the suite. Mr. Hughes's instructions."

Jock was perplexed.

"But I only want to go down to the lobby and to buy cigarettes," he explained.

"Sorry, Mr. Bryce, but I have my orders that none of you British airmen are to leave your rooms. I'm so sorry, sir, but you can appreciate that it's more than my job's worth."

Jock couldn't argue with the man's evident embarrassment, so he retired to rejoin his fellow "British airmen."

A few minutes later there was a knock on the door, and a waiter entered with a tray loaded with cartons of cigarettes of every brand and variety.

They were prisoners in their rooms.

The telephone rang in the suite.

Jock answered it.

"Hughes here," a distant voice declared. "Is that Captain Bryce?"

Jock affirmed it. The voice continued.

"You're not to eat any pork."

Jock was astounded. "I beg your pardon," he said. "No pork – too much of it on the market – some of it is dangerous, so you and the other British airmen are not to eat it."

The phone went dead.

Gordon Gilmore was not in the least surprised when he heard of the telephone conversation. He dismissed it as just one of Hughes's quirks. Jock protested. "That's crazy," he commented. "He's not going to know if we ask room service for half a dozen steaks or six pork chops, sitting where he is in California."

"Don't you believe it," Gilmore replied. "He's got his spies everywhere, and he'd soon know if you disobeyed his instructions. And I'd lose my job!"

Jock shook his head slowly in wonderment.

After about ten days the British airmen were bored and exasperated at being cooped up in their rooms. Jock explained the problem to Gordon on one of his routine visits. "We need exercise, Gordon, and fresh air. Why can't we just go for a walk around the block?"

Gilmore said he would attend to the matter, having checked with Howard Hughes of course.

The following day the airmen were escorted into the lobby of the hotel, through the main doors, and into the two large limousines waiting outside. They were driven only a short way to the New York Athletic Club, one of the most elite clubs in New York.

For the next two hours they were put through their paces in the club gymnasium, followed by hot sauna baths, and finally they were pummelled almost to death on marble slabs by muscular Swedish masseurs.

They were returned to the hotel where they collapsed in a state of exhaustion. The need for exercise was not mentioned again!

Jock was anxious to continue the flight across America to California in order to demonstrate the aircraft's capabilities to Howard Hughes personally. Another telephone call from the great man destroyed that idea. "Captain Bryce," Hughes commented (he never explained), "There is talk of another experimental atomic explosion taking place in the Nevada Desert shortly, and I would not wish to expose you and the other British airmen to the dangers of flying through nuclear fall-out. I have decided therefore to fly a Trans Canada Airlines Viscount at Montreal. You will meet me there, meanwhile you will be sent tickets, etc., and you can meet me on the appointed day."

There was no mention of the aircraft that Jock and his team had brought across the North Atlantic being flown up to Montreal!

Duly the airmen arrived in Montreal, to be met in the normal "abnormal" Hughes style.

During one of Jock's conversations with Gordon Gilmore he raised the question of perhaps Jock and his crew appreciating some female company. Jock thanked him for the thoughtful offer, but pointed out that he was happily married. In view of the unusual nature of the circumstances, he felt that a little enforced celibacy would not harm his crew, and so declined on their half as well.

Instead of indulging in the earthly pleasure of the flesh, he enquired if they could attend a show in New York's famed theatreland. The answer was an immediate affirmative, and they opted for the smash musical "My Fair Lady," currently running on Broadway. A little research by Gilmore's office proved that the show was sold out for months ahead.

Such was the power and influence of Howard Hughes that the same evening they were sitting in six of the best seats in the theatre.

Eventually Hughes decreed that he would meet up with the British in Montreal. In his own quixotic way he had decided to fly a Viscount belonging to Trans Canada Airlines (later to be renamed Air Canada). Jock and his crew thankfully left New York, only to find themselves again installed on the ninth floor of a hotel in Montreal. Once more the accommodation was sumptuous in the shape of suites of rooms. Hughes's own suite was flanked by an empty one on either side to ensure top security and privacy.

He was a man unaffected by the time conventions of other mortals. Lunchtime or dinnertime were not milestones in his twenty-four hour day. He ate when his stomach dictated.

On one occasion he and Jock were talking in Hughes's suite, and suddenly he decided he wished to eat crêpes suzettes. Within minutes waiters arrived from room service, wheeling in trolleys bearing the suitable ingredients for preparing the food.

Each time the delicious flaming crêpes were served to him, Hughes would take a mouthful and then reject it on some small pretext. Finally, after several attempts by the nervous maître d'hotel, the great man was satisfied. He then ordered that the earlier attempts be delivered to the British airmen, as he saw no reason to waste the food!

In the early hours of one morning Jock was awoken to be told to get to the airport as Hughes wished to fly in a Viscount. A limousine was waiting and Jock was driven to a cross-roads on the outskirts of the city. Here three other cars waited patiently pointing in different directions of the compass. Jock was transferred to another vast car, and the convey set off for Dorval airport outside Montreal.

He was driven up to an awaiting Viscount, to find Hughes already sitting in the left hand (or Captain's) seat studying the aircraft Flight Manual. Without further ado, Hughes started the four Rolls-Royce Dart engines and they set off down the taxi track heading for the duty runway. Jock was immediately impressed with the competence with which the other man handled the controls for adjusting the various systems prior to take-off.

The aircraft whined its way down the runway and eased itself off into the night.

Up to this point Jock had no cause for criticism. However, after they had completed three quarters of the circuit of the airfield, he was surprised at the method adopted by Hughes on the final approach to the illuminated runway. Using a great deal of engine power and with the nose of the aircraft well up, Hughes was dragging the Viscount in at a relatively low altitude.

Again on the next practise circuit he adopted the same procedure. After the third take-off Jock politely suggested that he demonstrate the aircraft's capabilities and proceeded to take over control. Effecting a smooth normal procedure, he brought the Viscount in to land. Despite this, Hughes recommenced his take-offs and landings using his own particular style. Jock left it at that. He concluded that as Hughes flew so many different types of aircraft, he used the same precautionary type of approach. It was an acceptable method of landing, but a long way off from getting the best handling characteristics out of the aircraft.

This flying technique was to have its repercussions. A few days later Jock and his British airmen returned to England by scheduled airline, and the Chief Training Captain of Trans Canada Airlines took over from Jock to monitor the eccentric millionaire's conversation flying on to the Viscount. Very shortly afterwards he was removed from this post. Evidently he had criticised Howard Hughes's landing techniques when talking on the telephone to a senior executive in the airline. The telephone conversation had been tapped.

Long phone conversations between Hughes and Sir George Edwards ensued in the following weeks, and the American finally placed an order of one initial aircraft. Meanwhile the Viscount Jock had flown across the Atlantic continued to stand and rot at Idlewild airport outside New York. Shortly afterwards a team arrived in England to negotiate the purchase contract and to inspect the technical production facilities at Weybridge where Viscounts were being produced. The group was headed by Bruce Burk and a lawyer who will simply be referred to as "Bob" for the purpose of this story. Also with Bruce and Bob were technical experts.

Bruce was a quiet young man with a good balanced mind, and a friendship between us rapidly developed. He visited us in our little house in Wonersh in Surrey, and Pauline liked him equally. Meanwhile the American technicians were busy with their work at Weybridge and Bruce and Bob were having contractual meetings with our finance people in our London offices. All seemed to be going well until four o'clock one morning. The phone rang, and waking out of a deep sleep I staggered downstairs to answer it in the living room.

"Geoffrey?" enquired the distraught American voice at the other end of the line.

"Yes," I answered sleepily. The agitated voice continued.

"Geoffrey, this is Bruce. Sorry to wake you at this hour, but I've got big problems."

"What's happened?" I enquired.

"Bob's in hospital with a broken arm, and the police are asking a lot of questions."

By now I was wide awake and concentrating on our conversation.

"Bruce," I interjected, "will this keep for a few hours? If it will I'll get up to London and we can discuss the problems over breakfast at your hotel."

He agreed that he could probably pacify the police until the morning, and we agreed to meet at Claridge's Hotel where he was staying, for breakfast. I duly arrived, and over toast and coffee he explained the events of the previous night.

Following a good dinner (all expenses on Howard Hughes, of course), they had repaired to a night club in Bond Street. Bob, it appeared, was all set for a "Night on the town", and drank accordingly. Bruce, who was a moderate drinker, could not keep up the pace. Bob, by this time was getting belligerently drunk and commenced a vendetta with the waiters. After a while Bruce had had enough and decided to leave. Not so, Bob. As his partner was insistent on continuing his carousal, Bruce bade him farewell, having agreed to settle up the costs the following day. Having got back to Claridge's he retired to bed until awoken by a phone call from the Metropolitan Police.

The police explained that they had found Bruce unconscious in a doorway, not far from the night club. Apart from being robbed, he had been viciously beaten up, and his injuries included a broken arm. An ambulance transported him to St. George's Hospital at Hyde Park Corner where his injuries were immediately attended to. After medical attention, the police began asking questions. Bob's inebriated replies were not of great assistance. When asked where he was staying, he insisted that he was in London, Ontario, Canada and not London, England. This didn't help matters much but fortunately the police found on his person enough to identify him with Claridge's Hotel.

When Bob had sobered up, he remembered having had an enormous row with the staff in the night club. Departing in anger without leaving a gratuity on top of the horrendous bill, he had obviously been "worked over" after leaving the premises. Bruce decreed that he be sent back to America with his arm in a cast and sticking plaster over his face. His main concern seemed not to be Howard Hughes, but how he could explain matters to his wife. I suggested he said he had slipped getting out of the bathtub, and he departed reasonably happy but somewhat chastened.

This was just the beginning of a series of troubles in the Hughes saga. It must be remembered that an order from Howard Hughes, although for one aircraft only, could lead to a multi-million dollar order from Trans World Airlines, in which he had controlling financial interest.

The purchase contract for one aeroplane was duly signed and happiness exuded from the Weybridge factory. An industrial dream of achievement was to turn into a manufacturing nightmare.

Most airlines, when their aircraft were being built at Weybridge, would send two or maximum three resident engineers to oversee their orders which could be thirty or more aeroplanes.

Hughes sent four engineers for one aircraft.

His aircraft fuselage duly arrived at the commencing end of the production line. Normal procedures were carried out, consisting of riveting the metal skins to the ribs, and formers placed in the jigs. A thin plastic coating was then removed from the skin metal, and then lightly polished.

Without question the American team of engineers, headed by a pleasant character named John Bossiker, were in daily contact with the great man in California. On learning that the fuselage had been polished, Hughes ordered Bossiker to reject it on the grounds that the polishing would weaken the metal! This was just a series of frivolous rejections which played havoc with the production line, as each time a point was raised and conceded to, the aircraft had to be taken out of the line and dropped back in position. This is no easy matter once the wings are on in a none too broad manufacturing hangar.

Finally the great moment arrived, and the Viscount was wheeled out of the assembly line for the engine test-runs. Up to this point construction had taken more than double the time than for an ordinary standard airline Viscount. Then came another message from California. The engines were not to be tested in their usual way by the Rolls-Royce experts, but Mr. Hughes himself would come over to

England in the fullness of time and run them himself. He did not appear to have complete confidence in the engine manufacturers doing their own testing. Howard Hughes never did come over to run the engines.

Four interesting points arose out of this incredible story.

Firstly the Viscount that Jock had ferried over to New York rotted for about a year at Kennedy (Idlewild) Airport, and it cost thousands of dollars to put it back in flying trim after mice and rats had eaten away at the upholstery and other edible parts, not to mention corrosion and other factors.

Secondly, Hughes eventually sold the aircraft so strictly surveyed at Weybridge to a Central American airline. (Jock, when he eventually test flew it said it was no better than a normal production Viscount.)

Thirdly, Trans World Airlines never placed an order.

Finally, the Central American airline, on the first commercial flight, crashed and killed all passengers and crew aboard.

Twenty-Six

Eric Warburg has many assets to his credit. A stocky man with a good mind and fine athletic prowess, which is a rare combination. Add to this his ability to speak French and German fluently, and an excellent sense of humour, you then find yourself with a first-class travelling companion, when faced with the dull task of visiting some of the Eastern Europe communist countries. His company, International Aeradio, acted as our agent in certain Iron Curtain countries.

Using Vienna as our departure point for all stations East, we armed ourselves with two large bottles of Scotch whisky, and boarded the night train for Budapest. Finding an empty compartment, we uncorked the first bottle and settled back to enjoy the journey.

Our peace and quiet was short lived.

The train began to fill up rapidly with grey-looking passengers bound for Hungary, and soon our compartment was fully occupied. Blank grey eyes staring out of grey humourless faces that matched drab grey clothing, regarded our bottle of whisky as it passed between us. Realising that our bottle symbolised capitalism with fluid assets, we proffered our fellow travellers a drink. Shyly at first they accepted the paper cups we offered around, and soon sparks of life replaced the greyness in their eyes.

By the time we had opened the second bottle it was apparent that the capitalist system was beginning to make its mark. Conversation in German and Scotch flowed freely, and although I speak no German I soon knew that we had been accepted as brothers under the skin.

Sadly our happy little party came to a halt on arrival at the Hungarian border. Boot-footed and boot-faced officials worked their way down the corridor demanding passports, and the dull looks rapidly returned to our companions' eyes. From the arrogant officials we received dirty looks.

Budapest in its days of glory must have been magnificent. Although the shattered remains of buildings and bridges marred the view, it required little imagination to visualise it during its greatness. Despite the indignities that man had carried out, the broad silent Danube flowed sedately between the banks of Buda and Pest.

Eric, (or Bottle by Bottle, as I nicknamed him) had a friend in Budapest working as the Reuter news representative. Sandy and his wife were extremely kind to us, and the Reuter telex machines gave us a very useful business link with the outside world. However, friendship with the Reuter man meant that we were immediately under surveillance from the secret police. Everywhere we went we were tailed by at least two of these goons, dressed in copy-book Gestapo leather jackets and felt hats. Sandy was hardened and paid no attention to them, whereas Eric and I would constantly nudge each other and point out our shadows, be it in a bar, a restaurant or in the street.

The Sunday following our arrival, Eric announced he wanted to ski having heard that there were some slopes not far from the city. He loaned the necessary gear, and we set forth with Sandy and his wife in their car on a crisp, sunny morning. "Why can't the bastards leave us in peace on a Sunday?" muttered Sandy looking in his rear-view mirror. Turning in our seats, we saw the usual sinister-looking black car, with its leather-jacketed occupants, following about fifty yards behind. Arriving at the ski slopes we forgot about them until midday, when it was agreed a drink was called for. Sandy drove out of his parking spot, and we started off down the snow-covered road. I looked back, and sure enough, our faithful shadows were starting off in pursuit. However, another car came out of the parking area and positioned itself between us and our followers. Sandy had also observed this in his mirror, for shortly afterwards he said, "let's have some fun with these goons."

At this point we were travelling down a fairly steep icy gradient with a small side turning coming up on our right. At the last moment Sandy swung the wheel hard over and we slid more than turned down the side road. The car behind us continued straight on, and our shadows also continued after it, until they realised too late the direction we had taken. Looking back we had the wonderful view of the secret police car slewing madly down the hill as the driver braked violently in an endeavour to stop his car. Laughing merrily we continued along the country road until we reached our restaurant. "Don't worry," said Sandy, "they'll find us again soon enough. I'm just sorry the bastards didn't skid into the ditch and wreck their car!"

Over an hour later, warmed with large quantities of good Hungarian wine, we emerged into the clear air. Two pairs of sullen, angry eyes regarded us with hate as we happily walked to our car.

Our sojurn in Budapest was shortly after the Russians had violently quelled a political uprising, and the bullet-scarred buildings bore grave testimony to the ruthlessness that had been used. However, despite the morbid atmosphere, Eric and I had tremendous fun. One could not help but feel sorry for the Hungarians who were virtually prisoners in their own country. Perhaps the day we lunched with the British Air Attaché brought the truth home to us most of all.

As the Attaché explained to us as we had a pre-lunch drink in his sumptuous house, working in the Foreign Service in a communist country, was one of the best chances for gracious living. With diplomatic privileges, he pointed out, you lacked nothing and the cost of living was extremely cheap. Despite his enthusiasm, I had a creepy feeling in my bones always when inside the Soviet Communist bloc. However, one had to agree that to have a stately home such as the one we were lunching at, duty-free liquor and all the other perks was not to be belittled.

At this point an elderly little woman neatly dressed in a maid's uniform quietly entered the room and announced lunch. The Attaché courteously acknowledged her, "Sad figure, that old girl," he said. "She is the Countess of — — — —, and this was her home until the Commies confiscated it. The only concession they made was that she should remain on as a servant."

The sight of this frail, dignified old lady, handing around the food completely put me off my lunch.

At this point Eric and I parted for several days, he to pursue other business for his own company, whilst I stayed on in Budapest for technical talks with Malev, the national airline of Hungary. We agreed to rendezvous in Sofia, the dreary little capital of Bulgaria.

My work finished in Hungary, I booked a flight with the Bulgarian airline, and we took off from Budapest in a snowstorm. "Staggered-off", would be a more accurate term than "take-off" in the ancient twin engined IL-4, the Russian equivalent of the excellent Douglas DC-3. My fears were first aroused when getting into my seat, in a cabin that had the interior of a Victorian public lavatory. The seat belts had no buckles, and the stewardess merely shrugged when I pointed this out. Finally, I tied a knot in the straps, and that combined with the knot in my stomach would have to suffice.

I then noticed on the bulkhead at the forward end of the cabin, two instruments. One was a temperature gauge and the other an altimeter for registering the height of the aircraft when flying.

Reluctantly we left the ground.

For the next two hours my laundry bill hit new heights.

Fully aware that a high mountainous range ran east to west across Bulgaria, with Sofia in the centre, I watched with near panic as the altimeter needle rose to and remained at 3,000 feet. The mountains reached at least six thousand feet and we were still flying in the middle of a blinding snowstorm. In desperation I literally shouted for the stewardess as the call button naturally didn't work. My demand for whisky was answered by a shake of the head. Despite not being able to communicate verbally due to language problems I discovered it was Slivovitz, (plum brandy) or nothing. A quick glance at the altimeter and I quickly settled for two miniature bottles of Slivovitz, except, she would only take Bulgarian money in payment. Sadly I watched her retreat down the aisle with the two little bottles of liquid courage.

Suddenly, as if by divine compensation, we burst out of the snowstorm into cloudless blue sky with the ground clearly visible thousands of feet below.

Then I started to chuckle to myself now that the fear was gone. Of course! The altimeter was calibrated in metres and not in feet.

Eric was at the airport to meet me with the manager of the Sofia office of K.L.M., the Royal Dutch airline. When I tried to thank him, he brushed it off by saying he was only too happy to help. It transpired that K.L.M. had only one flight a week transitting through Sofia, and the poor man was bored to tears. He did, however have a very smart looking Volkswagen bus painted in the livery of the airline, and it caused crowds to gather round it when parked in the city centre.

Having collected my baggage we set off for the city centre. It was amusing to find ourselves halted from time to time at those cross-roads that boasted a traffic policeman. A solemnly raised hand would bring our progress to a halt. We would be kept waiting about thirty seconds before being waved on. Despite the fact that the only other traffic was an oxen drawn wagon plodding along about half a mile away, authority had to be exercised by the law!

After taking leave of our friendly Flying Dutchman, we registered and then set off to explore Sofia on foot. Our first stop was to call in at the British Legation, always a wise precaution in communist countries. After that we could see little of interest within walking distance. However, just across the road from our hotel was the newly opened multi-storey department shop.

The building was packed with excited Bulgarians.

Never in their lives before had they seen or experienced a moving staircase escalator system, and they were queuing up to take a ride on this fantastic modern technical achievement.

On the ground floor we examined the merchandise for sale. This consisted of counters packed with bottles of rose water and racks of shoes and boots of very poor quality. The second and top floors also offered more quantities of rose water and plastic footwear. We retired to our hotel in depression.

The talks we had with the national airline the next day proved to be frustrating. Apart from displaying a mild interest in the aircraft we were offering for sale, it became obvious that in no way would the airline be allowed to purchase aeroplanes manufactured outside of Russia. So once again we returned to our hotel, bored and dispirited. Awaiting us was an invitation to dine that night at the British Legation. Meanwhile we planned our departure for the following day for Yugoslavia where we would visit J.A.T., the national airline with headquarters in Belgrade.

Through our Dutch friend we learned that no connecting air

flights existed the next day, and he suggested we should take the famous Orient Express train which passes through Sofia and Belgrade.
We immediately arranged bookings through the hotel porter. That
evening we presented ourselves for dinner at the British Legation.
The diplomatic minister in charge (Legations do not rank for an am-
bassadorial post) greeted us warmly, and soon we were mingling with
the dozen or so other guests. It was soon obvious that in this Balkan
backwater, new faces recently out from England were very welcome,
bringing with them fresh news from home.

One of the guests turned out to be a Queen's Messenger on his
way back to London via Sofia and Paris from Istanbul. Queen's Mes-
sengers are a special corps of men, usually selected from retired officers of the armed services, who carry diplomatic baggage between
the Foreign Office in London and British Embassies and Legations
throughout the world.

Colonel Adrian Holt sat next to me at dinner and I learned that
he and his bodyguard were also travelling on the Orient Express to
Paris the following day with their load of diplomatic mail. On discovering that Eric and I were fellow passengers, he cordially invited us to
visit his compartment after the train started for what he termed, a
little light refreshment.

Next morning we arrived early at the station to find a scene rem-
iniscent of a Tolstoy novel. Snow was falling lightly as an old-fash-
ioned engine complete with snow plough shunted goods wagons to
the sound of metallic shrieks. Awaiting a local train were groups of
peasants, the women all wearing shawls about their heads and clutching shopping baskets.

Majestically the Orient Express pulled into the station exactly on
time.

As we were to disembark the same evening at Belgrade, our reserved seats were in a normal coach. Eric suggested we wait about a
half-hour before finding Adrian Holt's compartment. Again, precisely
to the minute the train got underway again.

After a decent interval of time we rose to our feet and set off along
the swaying train to locate the Colonel. The *wagon lits* section was not
difficult to find, and we duly knocked on the door of his sleeperette.

The sight that greeted us was astonishing. Not only was there a very impressive display of bottles of whisky, vodka and gin, but somehow Adrian Holt had conjured up plates of smoked salmon and caviar on bread. In contrast we saw through the open connecting door to the adjoining compartment, the figure of his burly bodyguard (an ex-Metropolitan police sergeant) down on his hands and knees lighting up a paraffin stove to brew his early morning tea!

The Colonel noticed our glances towards the interconnecting door. He grinned. "Prefers a cup of char to the better things in life."

Although it was still only about ten o'clock in the morning, we were soon tucking into the smoked salmon and caviar, washed down by large vodkas and tonic. The police sergeant discreetly closed the connecting door and left us to our banquet.

There was a tap on the door leading out on to the corridor. On opening it, the Colonel was faced with the figure of the train conductor politely speaking in Serbo-Croatian, the language of Yugoslavia. As none of us could understand a word, Eric came to the rescue by addressing him in German which had the desired effect. From that point on we were able to communicate with him with Eric acting as interpreter. His reason for knocking on the door was to make a routine examination of our tickets. We noticed his eyes had taken in the array of bottles.

Adrian Holt insisted that the conductor enter the compartment and join us in a drink whilst we found our tickets. He was duly handed a gin and tonic which seemed to me to contain a quadruple measure of gin. It disappeared in one gulp, and our visitor accepted the offer of a second one. Having given a cursory glance at the tickets, he accepted the next offer of a seat together with a third large drink.

He became chatty.

English, he explained through Eric, was the language he needed to learn for his profession. With so many American tourists it was vital that he had a working knowledge of the Anglo-Saxon language.

As he was passed his fifth extra large gin and tonic we decided that his education should commence immediately. He hiccuped agreement. "Go and examine the rest of the tickets on the train and come back here for your first lesson," suggested Eric, although by now the

three of us had formed an educational committee to further mission-
ary work in our mother tongue. Whilst not imbibing at quite the
same rate as the railroad official, we were nevertheless beginning to
take a very amicable view of life....

Quarter of an hour later our new found friend returned and the
party continued. How he had managed to inspect all the tickets on
the express train in that short space of time remained a mystery.

The gin and vodka bottles were getting lower in their contents as
the first English lesson began. The pupil sat on the edge of the settee
clutching a notepad in one hand and a minute stub of a pencil in the
other. He would lick the point of the pencil every few minutes to show
his determination to learn.

During his temporary absence inspecting tickets, the committee
had decided that in view of the short time available for this crash
course, not to forget the inebriated condition of the pupil, it would
be best if we taught him phonetic phrases connected with his profession.

His glazed eyes attempted to focus on the pad and pencil as he repeated and then wrote down in his own fashion the first phrase.

"Good morning, ladies and gentlemen."

Intermittent hiccuping didn't help very much, but we persisted
until his pronunciation was deemed reasonable.

Then came the next phrase.

"Where is your bloody ticket?"

That called for another round of drinks and more salmon and
caviar. Then back to work. It was assumed by now that the imaginary
unfortunate passenger had passed over his ticket.

"This is no fucking good."

And so it went on with other bon mots.

"You are on the wrong damn train."

"The Orient Express does not stop in Paris, you must change
trains at Clapham Junction."

Then disaster struck the classroom. We had eaten all the bread,
although large quantities of salmon and caviar remained. Our pupil
tapped the side of his nose cunningly, leered at us and then peered
out of the window. "Five minutes," he said knowingly, and kept his

gaze firmly fixed on the passing countryside. The train was passing through a mild depression with rising snow-covered slopes on either side. Some farm buildings came into sight on the right hand side and our protégé leapt to his feet and pulled the communication cord. Quite violently the long express pulled to a halt. Amazed at the happenings we watched our companion dash out into the corridor, open a door and jump to the ground. With hiss steam enveloping the engine, the Orient Express waited patiently.

We ourselves were now out in the corridor watching our pupil scrambling up the slithery hillside towards the farmhouses.

Windows all along the train opened, and enquiring heads peered out wondering what crisis could have occurred to stop this famous train.

The conductor disappeared among the buildings, to reappear moments later to begin his lurching sliding descent down the hillside. From time to time he would lose his footing and tumble like a snowball, only to rise again, firmly clutching his round loaf of peasant bread to his bosom.

A few minutes later the Orient Express continued on its way and we continued drinking and eating our fresh sandwiches. Never had bread tasted so good!

I have often wondered how passengers on the Orient Express reacted to their English speaking conductor on subsequent journeys!

Twenty-Seven

When it was announced by the Greek government that Aristotle Onassis, the shipping tanker tycoon, was to modernise the national airline under the title of Olympic Airways, we at British Aircraft Corporation immediately sensed an opportunity to market some more of our very successful Viscount airliners. Fortunately we had a good friend in Colin Simpson, who headed up the new offices of Olympic Airways in London and he was also a Director of the company and had the ear of Onassis.

Meetings were held with Colin, and it was agreed that the best way to further our sales efforts would be to get together with Onassis himself. Colin promised to arrange suitable discussions the next time the great man flew in to London. A few weeks later he phoned to say that Onassis was arriving the following week, and had agreed to meet us for talks. A date and time was arranged for a rendezvous in Claridge's Hotel in London.

Rolls-Royce, whose engines powered our aircraft, agreed to have three of their senior executives join Bob Handasyde (the British Aircraft Corporation's Sales Director) and myself at the meeting. Arriving a few minutes ahead of schedule, we were greeted by Colin Simpson. He explained that Onassis had flown up during the night from the south of France (his office was in Monte Carlo), and would be about half an hour late. As it was now midday, one of our party suggested a drink might be in order whilst we awaited our potential client.

We seated ourselves around a table in a sumptuous reception room in this elite of hotels. Immediately a waiter arrived and we duly ordered a round of gin and tonics. Colin had meanwhile gone up to see Onassis in his suite.

Very shortly afterwards the drinks arrived, and the Commercial Director of Rolls-Royce declared he would pay. After some fumbling in his pockets, he turned pink with embarrassment and told us he was short of the required amount.

The haughty look on the waiter's face turned to contempt when it transpired that for various reasons, none of us possessed the cash to pay for the drinks. Fortunately Colin reappeared at this moment and vouched for a cheque one of us was able to produce. "Fine start," I thought. "Here we are representing two of the wealthiest companies in England, about to meet one of the world's richest men, and we haven't the money to pay for a round of bloody drinks."

Perhaps it was an omen of things to come!

Duly Aristotle Onassis joined us and the discussions began. All seemed to go very well and it was agreed that our commercial department would shortly send him a quotation for six new aircraft. We departed in a spirit of optimism.

Several weeks passed without news from Monte Carlo. I checked with our commercial department in London, and they assured me they had written to Onassis but had not received a reply. A cunning thought passed through my mind. Never having seen the beauties of Monte Carlo, why not fly down there at my company's expense and get up to date on the situation?

Bob Handasyde agreed to my suggestion, so I immediately sent off a cable to ask if he, Onassis, would receive me. Promptly he replied and was agreeable to my visit. Innocently I set off and arrived at Nice airport where I rented a car and set off for Monte Carlo.

I was not kept waiting long when I arrived at the office building overlooking Monte Carlo harbour with the wealth of yachts lying at their moorings, overshadowed by the immense size of almost ocean liner dimensions of Onassis's ship "Christina".

Minutes later I was in the office of the great tycoon himself. After passing the usual pleasantries of the weather and other polite conversation introducteries, I ventured to ask him if he was still intent on buying our aeroplanes. Despite the barrier of the sun-tinted optical glasses, I could see the eyes behind contracting into flints of steel.

"I think you should know, Mr. Page, that in view of the way your company has treated me, I have decided to buy American aircraft for Olympic Airways."

A remark like that is akin to being hit below the belt when boxing. I was winded and stunned.

"I'm sorry," I mumbled, "but in what way have we offended you?"

"Ask your commercial people" was the curt reply. He then indicated politely but firmly that our meeting was terminated.

I departed with my tail between my legs and slunk away back to England the following morning.

Immediately on arrival I presented myself at our London office and demanded of the Contracts Manager the Onassis file.

I was aghast on reading the copy of the one letter that had been sent to our potential multi-millionaire client.

The letter stated that before quoting a price for the six aircraft we, British Aircraft Corporation, would require a Bankers Reference from Onassis to the effect that his credit was good. Asking that of a self-made man who was extraordinarily proud and arrogant of his wealth was waving the proverbial red rag to a bull. I could well understand his turning to the Americans for a source of supply for aircraft. He ordered Douglas DC-6B aeroplanes for Olympic Airways, and British Aircraft Corporation lost a multi-million pound order.

Just a simple draft of the letter copied to us in the Sales Department could have stopped this incredible blunder. More was to follow.

More than a year later we found ourselves with a big problem at British Aircraft Corporation. An American airline had ordered and received a quantity of aircraft from us. In a fit of over-enthusiasm they had placed another order for more planes, but had over extended themselves financially. We now had to accept the fact that we had built and were landed with a batch of these machines. This put heavy pressure on our Sales Department to dispose of them in a hurry. We naturally approached the forty-five or more operators of Viscounts around the world, and I even contacted Colin Simpson again although without much optimism. To my great surprise he replied that Onassis might be interested as our airlines were turbine powered, and a great advance on the piston-engined DC-6Bs Olympic were currently operating. I advised him that our surplus aircraft were in mothballs at Hurn airport on the south coast of England, and that we would require a few days notice to get one ready for Onassis to inspect. It could then be flown up to Wisley aerodrome not too far from London.

In due course Colin came back to me and gave me the state of affairs which I relayed to Sir George Edwards, Managing Director of our company. He suggested I offer Onassis an invitation to lunch in his name, followed by an inspection of the aircraft. He left the details to me, but gave me the assurance that he would ensure the arrival of the Viscount the day before the luncheon so that all would be well in order for the visit.

Liaising with Colin, we arranged a mutually convenient day for the luncheon at Weybridge where we had our administrative and design offices. The month was March.

Sir George Edwards personally issued the orders to the factory at Hurn to prepare an aeroplane and have it flown up to Wisley. Everything seemed to be under control.

The day before the luncheon Hurn advised Sir George that one of the aircraft's four engines was overheating on tests, and an engine change might be required. This would normally be a matter of a few hours, but it proved otherwise. The following morning the aircraft was still on the ground at Hurn being worked on by the engineers. Sir George himself was on the phone every half-hour demanding a situation report. Both of us were well aware that the time of arrival of our guests at eleven-thirty was rapidly approaching.

The weather did not help to dispel the gloom of the situation. It was a typical March day; strong gusty winds blew rainsqualls horizontally beneath low grey scudding clouds. Eleven-thirty arrived, and with it our guests, but not the aeroplane.

The opening words of Onassis did nothing to help the situation. He regretted he was pressed for time and that he and Colin Simpson would be unable to stay for lunch. In which case he would like to have some preliminary commercial talks before the aircraft inspection.

Sir George excused himself and left the conference to telephone to Hurn again. On his return a few minutes later he looked at me and merely said "take-off in about fifteen minutes."

I glanced at my watch. With a half-hour flight time between airfields and allowing time for taxiing both ends, it should arrive at Wisley about twelve-thirty. The discussions would have to be kept going. Fortunately I had fifteen minutes up my sleeve in reserve, as it would take us a quarter of an hour to drive over to the airfield.

At quarter past twelve Onassis showed signs of impatience and further stalling tactics would be useless. The door to the secretary's office opened and she announced to Sir George "She's just landed, Sir." Even his normal poker face showed a hint of relief.

"I won't be able to accompany you to the aircraft," apologised Sir George. "But Geoffrey will look after you and set you on the road to London after you've examined the Viscount." Having said their polite good-byes, the two men followed me down to the main entrance where their chauffeur driven car was awaiting. I instructed the driver to follow my car, and we set off in convoy in the miserable weather. Arriving at the main gates at Wisley I was happy to see outlines of the aircraft standing on the tarmac. My pleasure turned to icy horror as we drove towards the lone aircraft. Not only were there no ground crew in sight, but nor were there any passenger stairs to gain access to the cabin. Our cars came to a halt amidst the sheeting rain and howling wind.

I tried to pretend to be nonchalant. "The ground crew must be sheltering in the hangar" I explained.

"Jump in," said Colin. "We'll drive you over there."

Onassis stared out into the distance in cold silence.

Inside the hangar no sign of human life showed. It was lunchtime! Standing to one side was a set of very rickety wooden steps used by the ground crews to get into the aeroplanes.

What followed was a continuation of the nightmare.

"I'm sorry, Colin," I said. "I'm afraid we'll have to push these steps out to the aircraft ourselves. Mr. Onassis had better sit in your car until we've got things sorted out." Together we started to push the steps out of the hangar, and then to my surprise, without breaking his stony silence, Onassis began pushing this pile of wooden wreckage across the tarmac towards the silent and wet awaiting Viscount.

"What a way to sell a fleet of aircraft to this man," I thought as we soddenly pushed our load. The chauffeur of the rented limousine followed behind in the dryness of his car. Presumably his trade union forbade him to offer physical assistance.

At last we pushed the wind and rain buffeted steps to the side of the aircraft's fuselage. I mounted in a rush. In almost a state of panic I grabbed the door handle. It was locked. Without daring to look at the two drenched figures, I descended the stairs and muttered desperately, "the pilot must have the keys," and rushed off back to the hangar, the far side of which was the luncheon canteen. Finding the pilot in the middle of his meal I obtained the keys, without pointing out to him what an idiot he had been, as he had been briefed on the telephone about the importance of the occasion by Sir George himself. My reception on returning to the foot of the steps was coolness itself. Or was it dampness? At last we entered the passenger cabin. The interior was devoid of seats and contained only one object. This was a vast ugly metal fuel tank which filled almost half of the cabin. Onassis stomped towards the forward end of the aircraft, peered into the cockpit, retraced his steps to the open cabin door, and descended down the rickety steps into his waiting car. Colin shrugged his shoulders in understandable resignation and followed his master down the flight of stairs.

Shortly afterwards Olympic Airways announced their intention to buy a large fleet of jet aircraft from the American Boeing Aircraft Company.

I never saw Aristotle Onassis again!

"Et penitus toto divisos orbe Britannos." (Where the Briton dwells utterly estranged from all the world.)

Twenty-Eight

David Sykes, a colleague of mine, was responsible for aircraft sales in Mexico apart from other areas. One morning he arrived in my office.

He opened the conversation by saying, "I need a woman". My reply of "Who doesn't?" didn't really help, as we were both happily married men. He explained his problem.

The President and Vice-President of a Mexican airline were shortly about to arrive in London, and David was hopeful of achieving a sale to their airline. Having spent some time with these two in Mexico, he knew that their favourite pastime was taking exercise – horizontally!

"But you see," David continued. "It's no use just taking them to a night club and getting a couple of hostesses because there's no guarantee the night will end up the way they want it to."

I thought for a moment.

"Leave it with me," I said. "I may know someone who can lead you in the right direction."

I had in mind one of our sales agents in London whose knowledge of worldly affairs would undoubtedly encompass the answer to a problem such as this one.

I picked up the phone and within a few minutes I was supplied with a London number and the name of a lady to ask for. When about to dial the number I hesitated. Perhaps this wasn't the best type of call to make on the company telephone. I left the office building and walked down the road to a public phone box. A somewhat breathless young woman's voice answered. "Mavis is busy at the moment. Can I help you?"

Briefly I explained about the intended visit of the two Mexicans, and that there was a requirement for female companionship for them.

"That's no problem," came the reply. "As long as you can give us some advance notice."

"About how long in advance?"

"Twenty minutes be enough?" she enquired.

That appeared to me to be more than reasonable, but the next question shook me to the core.

"Would you like a special appointment for yourself, then?"

I hastily refused the kind invitation, and returned to my office hot under the collar, but contented in my achievement. I gave David Sykes all the pertinent information and left the next step up to him.

The final stages of the story came in two parts, as I heard it from David. The Mexicans arrived as expected, and an evening's entertainment was arranged with two young ladies provided by Mavis. David remained with the group during dinner, but excused himself from the proceedings when a night club was suggested. Discreetly he passed an envelope containing cash to one of the girls. David told me that they were, in fact, two very attractive females. The following day David received a phone call from one of the Mexicans expressing their delight at having enjoyed their evening and ultimate fulfilment.

Three weeks later David received a telephone call from an enraged Mavis. "Where is my money?" She demanded.

It transpired that the two ladies' Latin lovers requested an encore for the following night after their first satisfactory evening. When payment was asked for the Mexicans had said that our company would pay in due course and departed for the Continent by dawn's early light.

David was livid with anger. Not only was he now faced with explaining to the company accountant, but the Mexicans had since placed a firm order with a rival aircraft manufacturer!

Publisher's Note

In July 1993, after a monumental amount of hard work, fund raising and organization by Geoffrey Page, amongst others, the Battle of Britain Memorial was unveiled on the White Cliffs of Dover by the Queen Mother as a fitting and lasting tribute to the men with whom Geoffrey fought his finest battle.

Confirmed Combat Victories

56 SQUADRON 1940 – FLYING HURRICANE I

13th July	Messerschmitt 109E	
20th July	Junkers 88	Shared with two other pilots
25th July	Junkers 87	

AFDU 1943 – FLYING MUSTANG

29th June	Henschel 126	
29th June	Henschel 126	Shared with MacLachlan
29th June	Junkers 88	Shared with MacLachan

132 SQUADRON 1944 – FLYING SPITFIRE IX

26th April	Junkers W.34	Shared with three pilots
29th April	Messerschmitt 110	
23rd June	Focke Wulf 190	
1st July	Focke Wulf 190	Half share
7th July	Messerschmitt 109G	

WING LEADER NO. 125 FIGHTER WING – FLYING SPITFIRE IXB

12th July	Focke Wulf 190	Shared
14th July	Focke Wulf 190	Also damaged a FW 190
20th July	Messerschmitt 109G	
26th September		Messerschmitt 109G

AWARDS

Distinguished Flying Cross	30th July 1943
Bar to D.F.C.	18th July 1944
Distinguished Service Order	29th December 1944